WHERE WHALES SING

14 YEARS SAILING THE SOUTH PACIFIC

By Daniel H. Van Ginhoven

Vero Beach, Florida

2015

BOOK 2 of 2

Copyright © 2015 by Daniel H. Van Ginhoven

All rights reserved. This book or any portion thereof may not be reproduced or used in any manner whatsoever without the express written permission of the author except for the use of brief quotations in a book review.

Printed in the United States of America

First Printing, 2016

www.WhereWhalesSing.com

This book is dedicated to our son...

We have drunk long of the elixir of life, and have learned that the only thing that matters is just to love and be loved in return.

To have been privileged to see one's son as he rushes through the life of youth to then stand where he too is called father, is that most wondrous of all voyages in time.

Love well son, as you have always been loved.

His name is:
David Carlton Van Ginhoven

Acknowledgments

Overhearing my father's discussion regarding international monetary rates of exchange which in my very early youth had a ten to one advantage to the US in purchases from China, caused my consideration of what China may have that I might buy. Chinese sailing junks were the first entrants into my mind; and my sailing interest was born.

Emmett Early, a friend of early sailing days, flew me to Oxford, Maryland from Arlington, Virginia where the 41 foot sailing sloop *Osprey* was found and "who" soon welcomed my wife Peggy and me into her water world of the huge Chesapeake Bay.

Good Ed Cutts, owner of Cutts and Case Boatyard, is a naval architect who designed a full keel for this center-boarder, and transformed the *Osprey* into the proud and powerful ocean sailing yacht upon whose magic carpet we spent a 14 years sailing voyage, which included crossing the South Pacific from Panama to Australia via most of the tropic islands from East to West, and from Fiji in the North to New Zealand in the South.

Our wonderfully good friend Buddy Hart is recipient of our accolade for longest sustained duration of assistance to us for the length of time during our entire voyaging. Buddy maintained a perpetual watch over our financial matters, and enabled our peace of mind that our funds be available via our system of access at the far flung and often quite remote locations of our ventures. Buddy, we salute you, and we thank you!

And my very good wife Peggy, whose accompanying presence during this voyage brought beauty and elegance everywhere we went; is herewith presented with the epitome of all highest acknowledgement from this simple sailor and husband, that though not a sailor herself, I could not have done it without her.

Acknowledgements for the great professional assistance in preparing the book for publication was the work of the editors, Justine Goldberg of Write by Night, Austin, Texas; and formatting the book and designing both the interior of the book and its artistic cover; my grateful thanks and praise are warmly extended to Cynthia Noonan, renowned owner of Advanced Graphic FX, Inc. of Vero Beach, Florida, USA.

While these acknowledgements have voiced praise worthiness, there is one portion of the author's participation in which he hopes for your recognition that he is a sailor, not an aspiring photographer. Yet the photos in the book, though not all of artistic quality, still speak with a worthy voice regarding these events that will enhance your voyage with us.

Introduction

You have now sailed thousands of miles with us aboard the good ship Osprey. That 41 foot sloop has carried us half way across the mighty South Pacific Ocean; where we have been met by severe storms with giant seas of fifty feet, to peaceful waters where we have anchored in magnificent lagoons with tropic islands of rare isolation where seldom others have gazed.

It has been a magnificent voyage thus far, filled with marvel.

Book one has enjoyed bringing these adventures to you, and BOOK TWO impatiently awaits!

Sail on, fellow sailor! Sail on!

WHERE WHALES SING: BOOK 2 OF 2

Table of Contents

Chapter 1: Westward Bound Again 1

Chapter 2: Dining Out 13

Chapter 3: Or Not 27

Chapter 4: The Solomon Islands 55

Chapter 5: Toward Australia 85

Chapter 6: Down Under 97

Chapter 7: Lucy and New Guinea 115

Chapter 8: Peggy is Back!! 127

Chapter 9: New Guinea 149

Chapter 10: The Highlands 181

Chapter 11: And Then... 213

Chapter 12: Australia, The Third Time 233

Chapter 13: New Guinea Again 247

Chapter 14: A New Beginning 271

Appendix A: A Detailed Look at the Boat Handling Arrangement 293

Appendix B: Peggy's Log III: The Gove 301

Appendix C: In His Own Words 309

CHAPTER 1

 WESTWARD BOUND AGAIN

The *Osprey* smiled as we set sail again, though mindful of her reduced plumage. She was showing two headsails now, even though their square footage was less than her prior genoa. Even with her mainsail fully hoisted, she had the look of being reefed. The height of the new mast gave the appearance of being cheated with these old and battered original sails.

But her glare in the direction of all of her fellow yachts promptly dissuaded their temptation to laugh at her appearance; for she was known amongst her lesser peers as, "The Ocean Lady," and was worthy of the respect which her silent stare conveyed. With her royal demeanor, we were granted regal acceptance at the gentle hand of the tradewinds, as Fiji obediently fell into the increasing distance beyond our wake. We were westward bound, again!

Peggy had filled her larder with provision for a lengthy passage. She early discovered that my declared intent did not always also reside in the mind of the winds, much less the fickle fabric of her husband's mind which is subject to whim and wander. She has a firm grasp of reality, and instinctively knows that a small sailing yacht on vast seas may not take kindly to cruise line type schedules, and the *Osprey* is not embarrassed by concepts of shame in being found in uninhabited isolations while either having storm abuse tended or while she is obliged to turn her eye elsewhere, as her people cavort about in those intimate pleasures which seem perpetually to abound.

The weather continued its pleasantry, and the sky was blue and beautiful when called upon to be so, and magnificently black until the stars began to appear. The mast almost succeeded in its attempt to reach up to touch them.

What a spectacle is our life! Born by this vessel which is our world, cast upon a universe of sea and wind, amongst galaxies unglimpsed in far distance with peoples yet to discover, *this* is the universe we breathe! How magic are our days!

Perhaps only the few, the fortunate few, who have been granted the removal of everyday focused blindness by which we can see only the trees and none of the forest, can feel any kinship to this life. Yet, the door to this lifestyle has no lock by which to bar entry.

A man with his woman, as the only occupants of an entire world, to be without contact or diversion and yet be content without community assistance such as utilities, hospitals or neighbors near or far—to be sufficient unto one's self and stand against all harm and danger is a heady thing. It is a fruit, sweet beyond description. It is a taste fraught with addiction, but marvelous for the eye sight!

Never has any part of the complex fabric of life approached a kaleidoscope of reality such as this which vibrates our entire existence, such as being at sea aboard one's own vessel, and to be here with none other than one's mate.

It doesn't get any better than this.

The last couple of days, though great in many ways, have not been total perfection as some of the trade wind sailing has been. The food and frolic has been fun as always, but there have been times when we have wallowed about rolling more than we are accustomed due to the shortage in our sail inventory. But we are glad to have the ability to sail at all. The shortage of cash after the major hull repairs in New Zealand which followed our expenses due to the dismasting at sea, left us unable to acquire the new sails which we so badly need.

The idea that sailing as a cost free experience is not quite on the mark. In our case, given that in total we were fourteen years at sea, this also meant that we were fourteen years without either of our salaries, plus the maintenance of a wooden vessel's TLC, and finally her being destroyed by a typhoon a few years from now, might add toward a wee sum.

We were bound toward New Caledonia. I had not mentioned it, but I really wanted to immerse Peggy in a little luxury for our approaching anniversary. We have been on half rations for about a year now, due to the boat's needs. The boat comes first, and we get the leftovers.

When we were in Fiji the first time, we often ate at the Indian restaurants because it was almost cheaper than buying the food ourselves. But this time, Peggy needed to surpass even that economy and cooked beans into all manner of mysterious marvels.

New Caledonia is a territory of France. The French excel in many things, not the least of which is the taste of food as prepared in a fine French restaurant, served with flourish, all done to delight the sight and to please the pallet. My visions of bringing such pleasures to Peggy, danced in my head, and would bring to envious tears any epicurean worthy of the name.

Was I in the midst of one of such diversion of mind which caused me to trip as I was stepping off the house onto the deck? "I do believe that I've sprained my ankle!" I've never gotten even moderately hurt on a boat in all my years of sailing. Oh well, it's not serious.

I wrapped it tightly to give myself some added support and there certainly was no danger of my being unseaworthy, so I gave it no great notice. I didn't get much sleep last night though, more from the rolling of the boat and constant sail trim changes than the ankle's discomfort.

The course was to take us just south of Anatom Island of the country of Vanuatu. Had there been a port of entry here, I would have stopped to get some rest and let the ankle heal, but the Port of Entry was on an island way northward and farther than I wanted to sail just now. It surely was tempting just to pull in somewhere, but people have been known to be put in jail for illegal entry.

The US flag flew from the stern as I anchored, launched the dinghy, and rowed ashore. Neither yachts nor ships are often seen here, other than the trading schooner that plies the waters of these islands. As I stepped ashore and asked the only person in sight where I might find the Chief, I was directed to the school.

The teacher was not the Chief, but he spoke English. I told him that I wanted to present myself to the Chief and ask his permission to stay a few days while my ankle healed. The teacher brought me to the Chief. The ceremony of respect and recognition of authority was pleasantly engaged and permission was granted.

The teacher and I talked as we took our leave of the Chief. One thing lead to another as we walked along; when suddenly I was besieged by a conundrum. How could this poor "crippled" sailor walk all the way to the other side of the island with the school tomorrow and not be thought of as "healed" by tomorrow morning. And if healed, why was I still here?

The school was leaving tomorrow morning for a couple of days. They were going up there to see the petroglyphs, grooved and painted by their ancient forbearers.

How could I possibly walk all the way across the island — but then, how could I not?

I told the teacher that I was going. At least, I would start out. If it was in any way possible for me to join them in honoring the ancient people of the island, I was determined to join them in doing so.

I slept that night with my leg elevated to ease the mild throbbing and was up early and ashore. "Join us at the road going northward," was the instruction. I hadn't seen the road, but the fact that there was one had given me encouragement. There might even be a truck to come by and give me a ride.

The "road" was unpaved, to say the least. Unfortunately, there would be no truck. There were no trucks. There were no cars on the island. The "road" was a foot path down which the teacher led the twenty or so children scampered in joyous talk and giggles, followed by me in growing distance behind.

Happily for me, I saw that they had stopped to rest after a couple of hours of this trek. But alas, I no sooner arrived to join them, when they were up and gone again, leaving me jealous of the joy to which my walk muscles were so expectantly yearning.

The path was only inches wide in many places such as here. We had walked through forest bush and scrub, up really steep climbs and down slopes which I often slid down with varying aplomb, mostly accomplished in a three quartered sitting position using my shoes as skis.

One long part of the trail was at the very edge of a cliff that dropped straight down over a hundred feet or more. I remember thinking to myself that this would be truly dangerous if the path were wet from rain, because the few inches which was the path was only inches from the edge of the cliff, and the path was not horizontal, but slopped toward the cliff. I was glad that the path was indeed dry, rather than made of mud. As I looked down there, I felt an involuntary mini-shudder travel up my back as I thought of mud.

We were down to sea level again and amongst trees, two of which were mangos. Everyone was sitting around chattering with mango-covered faces as I arrived. At a nod from the teacher which I caught out of the corner of my eye, a couple of the girls each brought a mango to me.

Now I readily admit to being accurately described as preferring a table setting of pleasant plate and appropriate fork; for one dines with the eye before the taste buds. But when I finally came upon our group, I dropped down drenched with perspiration and puffing as I did so; accepted the proffered mangos and grabbing one with both hands, I tore the skin off of it with my teeth, crammed the running yellow colored juice covered mess into my mouth and holding tightly with both hands and teeth, I shook my head in the manner of any well mannered canine to growl silently and possessively of the prize.

Yet as focused as I was in my exhaustion and thirst, I knew exactly what one of the girls asked her teacher. It was spoken in her local language and answered by same. But her expression, tone, and gesture, as clearly as though spoken in English said, "Are all white men as weak as this man?"

"No," he said with emphasis. And he proceeded by repeating a couple of the names of internationally known sportsmen whose names I recognized as he retold in length what they had accomplished.

My smile did not get past my thought, as I leaned back against the tree. The smeared mango juice remained unnoticed and dried in time, leaving a mixture of salt and sweetness as a crusting mask which hid my recognition.

Undaunted, the children were up again and excitedly following their teacher, while parts of my person, not previously known to exist, presented excellent argument as to not being further harmed by this effort of getting off the ground! But there was that horizon thingy again. The need to see; to somehow get there, wherever or whatever *there* may be is the never-ending quest. And this venture was worthy indeed! I was up, and the pace was brisk!

The trail twisted about as its path of least effort had been created in the mind of some mythical creature wrought perhaps of a combination of goat and ghost, for there must have been a ghoulish delight if this specter was peering at my progress.

Ah, we were back to a beach again. I could feel a light breeze already. Maybe it will be stronger as we get farther from the jungle. With some luck, the bugs swarming around me to drink my mango-flavored perspiration might tire of flying against the wind and go back to the hellish place where such mini demons dwell. Yes, good! *"Be gone ye tormentors of the earth! A plague on your house,"* or if truth be known, much stronger and picturesque were the actual phrases that I had been accumulating for my use.

The beach was very narrow between jungle and sea. The sand quickly gave way to pebbles, and these, to perfectly round black rocks which spoke with increasing volume as the ocean shoved them around. The rocks averaged size between grapefruit and basketballs upon which we now traveled.

It would have been much less painful to my ankle were the rocks stable in their positions, but it was not to be. For with grueling frequency the rock would roll under my weight, an event not unnoticed by my anatomic scorekeeper. I found myself being comforted by the silence with which I endured this additional evidence of *non-islander's* weakness. And in the fullness of time, having paid the price of admission with full measure of blood, perspiration and pain, we arrived.

The children paid no great attention to what antiquity had toiled upon these stone formations. But I enjoyed the contrast of their youthful exuberance to the more sedate tracings of grooves in the stone in which perhaps teenagers of that time had enjoyed the fun of stretching their imaginations; and thereby seeing shapes and animals which were enhanced by chipping away little sections to join the gruves already naturally there. Someone had taken both fun and pride in the process. And likely may have been surprised to learn that a man would one day come from the sea and that he would pay such a price as this to look at the games which they had played.

The group was going on to another area unrelated to the petroglyphs, so I told the teacher that I would be going back from here. I did not understand his dismay. I thanked him profusely for the kindness of permitting my accompaniment and delight over the island's having this relic from the ancients. I waved to the children, and started off. I felt certain that I could get back before night fall.

I welcomed the rain. It would be much cooler now and with much fewer flying, biting beasties as well. About half way back I was really feeling exhausted. The ankle refused to accept the exercise as beneficial and rather persisted on a gentle reminder of an opposing reality. But I stopped short!

"Look at that!" I said to my surprised consciousness. "It's a cave."

I spotted the small cave on the side of a rock cliff. It would have been seen had I turned back to look around the corner of the cliff as we went passed it earlier in the day.

I went to the cave. And although no magic thunder shook the earth as I stepped inside, I found that I had entered a world cast back in time by thousands of years. For as my eyes adjusted to the darkness, I dared only to permit the gasp of breath to slowly enter my being, so that silence be kept here.

I stood motionless. I turned only my head, and that very slowly. A tiny fire had been burned in the center. There were ashes and a few unburned ends of sticks lay in an irregular circle around where it had recently been used. On the walls were painted several crude but clearly identifiable animals and birds. The paint color was only partially faded. Not at all like the almost indistinguishable colors of the petroglyphs which we had seen. All of this was present history, if I may voice an oxymoron; or was I hallucinating this?

At long last, I began moving about in this hallucination. I stepped carefully about. I looked at the rough artwork. I carefully touched it with one finger. I had no illusion from reality. I had no thought that I was in fact hallucinating any of this. I knew instantly and with immense pleasure, that the cave was currently used by fishermen as a place of shelter.

The fantastically unique pleasure, of which I now drink so deeply, is from the fact that I am standing with one foot in the present and with the other, where a thousand years has stood unmoved and invisible but to my eye. The entire island had known this day as being in present time, but I had that rarest of all experience, by having touched a time and space — beyond knowledge. Ah, how magic have been the days of my life. I am eternally enriched. How very far beyond price has been this day.

I wanted not to let go of the spell of this place, but alas I must do so and fully return to this island's present reality. With gusto I resumed my trek, in full enjoyment of my mind's jumping to all kinds of visions of the probable past, only to be reminded that one need but look around to see the past, for I am walk within it.

My firm grasp of reality just slipped again! No, this was not a specter. This was a man, an islander.

No one had been seen on our entire trek up here, but this fellow acted as though he had been expecting me. And as I came up to him, he spoke, of course, in the local language and gestured up into the jungle to where miraculously a tent had been erected.

We both went into it and thereby out of the rain. He had water for me to drink. I gulped it down. I was super tired again and indicated to him that I wanted to sleep. He simply nodded his understanding and quietly chose a place to also lie down.

I had thought to sleep through the night, but though with urgent need my mind yearned for its oblivion, even more insistently did the cloud of bugs buzz around my external belfry to the point of my dragging myself up to a standing position, bedraggled though I was, I announce my great appreciation to my host for the shelter of the tent, but that I was going onward.

The good fellow nodded his understanding and followed me back to the beach and watched as I continued down the beach until I took the trail that led up the steep climb into the jungle. I had given him a wave after I had gone those few hundred yards to where I started off the beach. I was somewhat surprised that he waited so long, but then figured that he was just watching to see if I would spot the trail.

This area was climbed by grabbing roots and rocks to help drag myself up. One does not just walk up a gentle hill here. But given enough exertion and appropriate panting, another of the trials was again thus endured.

An hour or so later I was astonished to catch a glimpse of the tent fellow way back on the trail. And later on I saw him again. This time the *penny dropped.*

The good teacher's dismay at my departure from them may understandably have been for my welfare. He certainly may have felt responsible for me and thoughts of my becoming lost and wandering the rest of my days in the island's jungle may have drawn pictures with the same pen that had recorded my *non-islander's weakness,* by picturing me as a hapless city slicker. And I instantly wondered if this good fellow had been urgently dispatched for my well being.

And then the mystery of the tent presented itself in my mind. Oh my, I hope hospitality had not required several men to be marshaled to the task of carrying that big heavy old canvas tent across the island for my comfort! Oh my, what a terrible effort may have been performed by someone. Oh how I hope that this wasn't done for me!

I caught the last glimpse of the fellow when I had the village destination in sight. Clearly he ever so discreetly had been keeping me in sight so that were I to have lost the trail, he could have been close enough for a rescue, while being ever so polite in the process. Such social grace is worthy of note and worthy of praise.

I might mention that slanting slope of the narrow trail at the very edge of the cliff which had my attention on the way out when there had been no rain. Now it was a muddy mess and had my full attention being paid to the *what if* game, as my left foot stepped as much as possible on the upper edge of the trail where there was some growth of grass occasionally, and the right foot took light quick steps on the mud. The waves broke loudly on the short rocky beach below as they looked up at my slow progress. My anticipation of this part of the journey had been much more colorful than the reality, though I had been pleased to now be beyond it.

Slow was my rowing of the dinghy back to the boat and back to the warm welcome by Peggy at my return. She could see all of the details of my experience in her first sight of my bedraggled person. I took a shower. There was some food and drink on the table. And then in her elegance, she simply lifted the sheet of the bed.

She smiled. I slept. Life is complete.

After a couple of days, I paid my respect and expressions of gratitude to the chief, prepared the boat for sea, and we were westward bound again.

At these moments when there is a merging of past and present by that strange door which when opened, marks the beginning of something, and when closing behind you, marks an end, we look in both directions. And as we pass through that door, for an instant we have had one foot in the present and one foot in the past. It is partially so with every door through which we pass, as having been in one room, [our past] we now step into the next one. Should some doors be left ajar?

Enough about such musings!

Fresh is the taste of the wind, and the *Osprey* spreads wide her plumage and with her eye on the horizon she carries us in comfort and anticipation.

We are westward bound, again.

CHAPTER 2

 DINING OUT

When the *Osprey* is loosed of her anchor's tether, sometimes she just soars over the ocean beneath her as when in her youth she had dreamed of falcons and their flights of lightning speed. This was such a time, as she revels at the feel of the wind beneath her wings, and throws plumes of spray back into the face of the sea. It is times like these that I almost catch her literal smile in the millisecond between the start of wiping the salt spray from my eyes and again having clear vision of her face. It's as though she wants me to think that she is really just a plank from a mahogany tree. Of course, I know the truth, he says with tongue in cheek.

I have long been at sea, but at least occasionally I still have a reasonable grasp of reality, for regarding this and other brief games of verbal ballet for fun's sake, I really am a very firm believer in ghostless inanimate objects. And it is just in fun that I sometimes yield to the temptation of playing at the game of a time when sailing vessels of the days of yore were thought to possess personalities of charm or witchery. We seamen are thought by some to be a bit strange anyway; but not all such as they are shown that magic, which dwells where we are thought so bold to venture forth.

The ocean's wave crests were hurled aside by the mighty flight of the *Osprey*. We sped toward New Caledonia as though all the earth had gathered its might to see our timely arrival at a French restaurant to celebrate the significance of marking another of our marriage anniversaries.

My perpetual sequence of sail trim, reefing and unreefing continued as the wind could not make up its mind as to what best would meet our needs and expectations for time of arrival. The wind had very much underestimated the *Osprey*'s abilities of speed. Contrary to its planning, we arrived at night.

If truth be known, I am no match for these three characters; the sea, the wind, and the *Osprey*. This passage had only been a three-day voyage, but I was really looking forward to some rest and recovery before celebration time. I wanted not to *heave to* amongst these reefs in all directions. The boat would be making forward motion, super slowly though it be, and although we had the sea room to do so, that *what if* game still plagued my mind, for we would be making leeway as well, plus the chunk of water that bore us was being moved about by the sun and moon pulling at it.

Seamanship has built into it a generous quantity of throwing all the possibilities up in the air and juggling the whole mess for an educated conclusion. The only inconvenience in this is the fact that one is perhaps also throwing one's well-being into the mix.

Yes, of course, I could have gotten an anchor to hold us off a reef to windward, but a wind shift could then swing us onto its neighbor. Some of our very experienced ocean sailing friends have lost their yachts due to just such yielding to temptation when the screaming need for rest has been too loud for the quiet voice of seamanly caution to be heard. Even three days without sleep can be debilitating when mixed with great exertion.

We *heaved to*. I awakened frequently through the night and found my way on deck to peer at the surrounding formation of the seas to confirm that none were being deformed by their approach to a reef. None had altered.

The interesting seesaw effect of first the small headsail stalling as the reefed mainsail filled and moving the boat forward until it stalled as the headsail filled, kept the boat in a very gentle and slow movement. One of the tricks is to set just the right quantity of sail to the wind for this to work properly. Under light conditions, a boat can be *heaved to* under full sail for such innocuous reason as just a whim of convenience as lunch is being made and enjoyed by a festive group of fellow revelers aboard for a leisure day of sun and fun.

At the appointed moment, with all of its glory and revealing luster, the sun made its anticipated arrival known, and neither shock nor surprise presented alarm. We had remained within the area of comfortable distance from danger.

Breakfast was enjoyed before sail trim brought us briskly into the southeasterly pass, just to the north of Ile des Pins. The waters were undisturbed by the wind as we entered. We sailed very close to the south of the island of New Caledonia and then up the westerly coast to Noumea and eastward into a lovely and fantastically quiet anchorage almost in the heart of town.

A very short row of the dinghy brought us ashore where just one and a half blocks away, a French bakery lent its fragrance a mile in all directions. Even those two folks aboard the *Osprey* needed no directions from the French speaking community to aid in finding the many delights created there.

The most pleasing of all was the early morning joy of its French bread. When still hot from the oven, this slender loaf is grasped in both hands and a generous portion torn off to melt a bit of butter while sharing its aroma throughout the boat. It is so profound a delight as to cause all associated brain cells who were fortunate enough to have participated in those memorable events, to even as I write today, find themselves clamoring to relive the immensity of that pleasure, simple though it may have been. It remains distinctive among the archives of our voyage.

Shopping in general is not a favored pastime of mine. But in new places I always tended at least at first to join Peggy in her searchings for our larder's need. On such occasions we are both sometimes surprised by our findings, such as on this occasion of our first time shopping in this French town's grocery store.

Peggy had been inclined to acquire a head of cabbage for a very specific culinary destination and found a real beauty. Its cost was accurately displayed.

Chapter 2 — Dining Out

The cost was ten US dollars, not for seven of them; this was for the one chosen by Peggy's knowing hand!

Under the banner of things that made us smile in quiet amusement so as not to offend any one, was our finding the peanut butter proudly being displayed in the very center of the gourmet section! To laugh out loud is impolite.

Our funds were mostly consumed by this time of the daily forward leaping of the calendar, so I awaited the time when we could walk to the local American Express Office and write a check for the cash with which to celebrate, by luxuriating with Peggy in the ambiance of a fine restaurant.

That time had not yet arrived, but in the meantime all manner of events continued to occur as the world turned. We met some Americans. This couple had been living here for some time and we were more than pleased to have them out to the boat as we became friends, and they were kind enough to drive us around the sights of the island regaling us with stories about their adventures here and some rather startling happenings.

I have only a second-hand accounting of this which normally would preclude its mention, except in this case I use it to set a scene.

Our friends had given long and detailed accounts of how they were followed daily by observers who were assumed by our friends to be in the secret service of France. They assured us that everywhere they went, even on mundane grocery shopping, that they were watched in every move they made as though they were dangerous spies or assassins, and that since as they said all French research vessels were spy ships, they were certain that we too were being watched by that ship.

***

It was a very big French research vessel which was secured to its private dock very close to where we were anchored. The warehouse had the ship's name in very large letters written on it, so no secret was archived there. Our presence was not secret either. We were flying the US National Flag from the stern of the *Osprey* and the French Flag in its place of proper honor at the starboard spreader, which on older vessels would be the starboard yard arm. So we were clearly known to be foreigners in their waters.

I found myself in need of a bench vise to properly hold a part of our kerosene-fueled cook stove to enable my repair procedure. I knew that any commercial ship would have such a utilitarian devise, so I took the part with me as I rowed over to the French research vessel to ask for the use of their vise.

I tied the dinghy to the dock, walked to the long gangplank, and coming to the deck I called out, "Hello the ship!" a couple of times until I got a response.

Conveying my need, I asked to use their vise and was cordially invited to do so. The task took no more than half an hour at most, and when completed I was told that the captain would like to see me. This is not an unusual request and I proceeded as directed and found him not alone in what may have been a briefing room. As I paused at the door it seemed to me that the woman who was talking to him was doing so with posture and gesture of speaking from an attitude of authority and importance.

My impression upon being granted entry was that perhaps she was the captain, which in itself could be somewhat unusual. But it was the gentleman who identified himself as being the captain. Therefore, the first impression left me to wonder what station of rank would be addressing a ship's captain in the manner as I had just observed.

Had I thought it at all likely that the captain would be found aboard while at his home port, I would have firstly asked to convey my compliments to the captain, whereupon one is ushered to him, and from him I would have asked the favor of use of his engine room's tool. It was a surprise to me that he would be here at all.

I was invited to a seat, offered coffee which I accepted, and politely inquired of as to what had brought me to this place and time; none of which seemed to be in pursuit of idle curiosity but rather pointedly seemed to be directed toward justifiability. Nonetheless, absolute politeness was maintained throughout our pleasantry and when the topic seemed exhausted, I bid them each great success in their endeavors, again expressed my appreciation for the use of the vise, having taken pains to show the reason for its need while jointly aware that the need could have been caused to gain access if that had been my intent.

Without having had those conversations with our American friends about their conviction of what they described as the paranoia of their host's countrymen, I likely may have been free of the paranoia of which I may have been partially infected. No matter how open minded we have always thought ourselves to be, the simple fact remains that we are as human in nature as anyone else, and unwillingly subject to even the slightest hint of anything so extraordinary as paranoia. I would have sworn an oath of assurance that I was free of any such ailment.

About mid-morning the next day, an unusually long open boat was approaching. One man in white uniform stood rigidly in the bow. Four others sat as a helmsman ran the outboard motor. They stopped.

The man standing saluted me briskly and said, "Captain, we are from the French Department of Customs. May we search your vessel?"

I invited them aboard with all pleasantries and when their boat was secured and all were aboard, I told them that they were indeed welcome to search the boat. I told them that I had only one requirement. When an inspection of something is completed, I require its return to the same place from which it was removed. I used the word require not request, although I knew that I was in fact outranked aboard my own vessel. No comment was made by them such as, "We'll see about that!" We sat back to watch the occurrence.

Each man took an area of the boat and began by looking about his area and then began a methodical search. The leader of the group who had saluted me upon their arrival did not assume a specific area to search but rather continued a general looking about. I had noticed with an unrevealed smile that the spiral bound note book was open at the foot of my bed where the radio and my Morse code telegraph key was also in plain sight. It had not evaded the scrutiny of our principle inspector, and with apparent practiced nonchalance he walked around the down-folded dining table, to the foot of my bed; looked carefully at my telegraph key without touching it, paused as he stood looking at the note book, and slowly picked it up as would a scuba diver on a ship wreck pick up a gold bar in disbelief of his enormous good fortune.

I could hardly restrain my glee in watching his raptured focus, because the wheels of his brain seemed to my view to be spinning at such speed that I expected his eyes to cross at any moment. He held in his hand a notebook whose pages were filled with nothing but line after line of code. There was page after page of nothing but jumbled letters written as words having no discernible meaning without a codebook to translate their secret meaning. He must have thought that he had in his hand the mother load of golden evidence of *spyhoodification*, if I may coin a phrase.

I am an amateur radio operator. And as such I am licensed accordingly. One of the requirements to upgrading the level of the license which I held, was a speed proficiency of sending and receiving the Morse code's dots and dashes.

Practice recordings of random letters at various speeds of transmission are used to help hone one's skill at this arcane means of communication; and the note book held page after page of my scribbled nonstop writing of jumbled letters mixed with occasional numbers and punctuation in a senseless sequence of my practice exercises. It looked like spooky stuff indeed.

Having turned pages of this, and having looked at my earphones and Morse code key, he slowly turned toward me and looked questioningly at me without saying a word. He had only questioningly lifted his eyebrows and appeared to be holding his breath.

I said, "Oh that!" I said it with not a hint of amusement in my voice, for I did not wish to confess the enjoyment which I was having at his expense.

Chapter 2 — Dining Out

After all, it was a private joke, and to have permitted its conveyance would have also conveyed my thoughts of the reason for their presence. So very offhandedly I explained the license requirement of Morse code proficiency and hence this practice book.

He returned the book to its place as he was called to the forecastle by one of his inspectors who had an uncertainty of procedure. He then came to me carrying a gallon-sized metal container. It was painted tan and had the word cabbage painted on it.

"Hold it!" I said. "That is food. It's dehydrated for longevity of time as we often sail in remote areas, and you will spoil all of it if you open those cans. If you feel that you must open them, I expect you to replace each one of them by immediate purchase and shipment from the US."

He shook the can. The contents rattled like the sound of small pebbles, not powder. Other cans were likewise shaken. None were opened, and after a few more hours of this, they re-boarded their boat and casting off, I accepted and returned his salute, and the event was concluded.

But please know that I hasten to say, that I realize nothing of any of the events of the last couple of days are in any way extraordinary and are by no means indicative of anything beyond the procedural norms of separate and unrelated function of governmental procedure and should not be thought of as special or unique, or spy-like, and certainly not sinister in anyway whatsoever. And the only reason for sharing the events with you is for your entertainment and laughter at my temporary infection of paranoia, as my words above have been pronounced with tongue in cheek. We met many people in the large church of our attendance, and as usual, the young men were pleased to greet me. I inevitably shook their hand with warm and vigorous sincerity, a mistake of which I was shortly to be edified.

At the time of our leave-taking for the day, a group of young male adults were standing by. One in the group had been designated as instructor. He stepped forward extending his hand, took mine in both of his, and almost doubled over as he brought all of his considerable strength into a painful vise-type grip of my hand. I didn't give them the satisfaction of showing my pain but carried on as I was talking in my imperfect French.

The lesson being taught to me was that of a proper hand shake as practiced in their French community, which is comprised of not much more than the touching of the hands which has often been described as being entirely limp-wristed and thought to exist by natural inclination amongst only a limited number of our countrymen. My thought of this nature has been forever enlightened by the painful lesson learned that day. Yet on occasions I still find myself carried away by enthusiasm early learned. I endeavor a more sedate clasp of hand, though I cannot muster that gentlest of all approaches of the greeting ceremony as performed by these truly skilled Frenchman.

* * *

The calendar unveiled the day of our triumphal march to the American Express Office. I had employed the local knowledge of our American friends, sworn to secrecy, to guide my selection of an appropriate restaurant to display in a formal setting, a marking of the many happy years of our marriage on this day of its anniversary.

I had made a reservation and had given certain instructions. We were escorted to our table already adorned by sundry aperitif of magnificently artful beauty and shortly to be confirmed of most delicate taste. The occasion was worthy of sumptuous decadence and the gourmet staff gave flourish to the skills of their challenged task.

To have kissed her cheek that morning upon her awakening would have brought a smile to her face. This would have been enough, but for myself, I wanted to add a special magic to my whisper in her ear. I wanted a floral fragrance to surround her thought of years gone by and of those that await our arrival. I wanted the most elegant of setting to launch us gently toward all those lovely horizons of our lives yet unveiled. Even as I knew that all of France would fear its inadequacy to such a daunting dedication; how then could I in my humility dare so grand a conquest! Alas, the petals of the roses which were cast before her, fluttered only in the eye of my mind. Yet lacking as my efforts were to bring grandeur to her presence, even so I was *wondrously rewarded,* for …….Peggy smiled.

***

We took our departure from New Caledonia soon thereafter, because the calendar was spinning its days swiftly toward another event of import. An event to take place much farther north in Vanuatu than Anatom Island, from which we had just journeyed.

We sailed out from the anchorage, which really was from the town itself, and had decided to attempt to take some fresh fish for our table. As we were approaching Ile des Pins I dropped a line over the stern and <u>immediately</u> caught a fish. The words fresh fish has a meaning in its fullest extent when there is a nonstop movement from sea, to pan, to plate.

I made the mistake of allowing another line overboard to be presented to the fish population, because no sooner had I done so as the boat continued its sailing, another fish demanded attending. This continued without an instant's interruption.

I counted the number of fish, multiplied by the average size, and found that almost as swiftly as the time required to tell you about it, I had brought twenty six feet of fish aboard. I dared not permit another line overboard for fear of yet another fish wanting to sail out of these waters. Those French fish seemed determined to take passage aboard this US yacht.

Peggy's food processing factory was in full flurry. Included in her extensive repertoire is the pickling of fish. The process results in marvelously extending the consumption period, and presents to the table a wonderful aperitif with which to spice the pallet.

***

We were bound for a short sail to one of the Loyalty Islands. The wind was howling behind us, and even with just a small jib and no mainsail we were still screaming along too fast.

We would be arriving too early. It would still be night time at our arrival. If this continued, we would need to sail back the way we were traveling to occupy the time. To do that though, we would need to be sailing to windward in very strong conditions against the oncoming seas in somewhat close quarters, with a less than ideal sail inventory. So if I could maintain steering ability and yet slow the boat down, I would try to do so.

I do not have a sea anchor as it is called. This is a parachute type devise which I have never seen as available to a short handed vessel. What I did have was lots of half-inch nylon line, which I very promptly launched as a drag to slow us down. I secured the ends of the line from points forward of the stern as a precaution against slowing the turning ability of the boat by the drag line fighting the rudder's effort at the stern.

Maybe I slowed the boat a little, but the boat generates such a huge amount of power at this speed that it may not have been slowed by much.

The taffrail log dial showed that the distance passed through the water was getting close to the distance of the passage, but as expected, the wind was slowing dramatically. Simultaneously, the first faint flicker of light reached the far eastern edge of our horizon.

And as the earth, oh so slowly turned her sleepy face toward the sun, our destination had also yawned, stretched a bit, and waved to us and to the day. Our efforts had conspired to success. Someone once said, "I love it when a plan comes together."

I will need to come way over to port to enter this narrow channel. So far in fact, that we may not be able to sail that high to windward, especially with our limited sail inventory. So I am going to motorsail through this channel.

Chapter 2 — *Dining Out*

It is not possible to know for certain just how high you can get to windward until you are there, but I estimate that it is going to be very close and it may not be possible.

The sound of the engine, though routine, is still a comfort in tight quarters. The gear was engaged, and the propeller churned the water, as I turned to port. We were now less than two boat lengths from the buoy's marking the narrow pass. The mainsail stood hoisted, as were both jibs, and all sheets were hauling tight. It was at this instant that the engine quit. I put the gear in neutral. I turned the key for starting. Nothing happened.

I had to maintain headway. I was as tight on the wind as I could get without stalling the sails. I was not going to make the entrance. I did not have enough speed to come about through the wind to jockey for a more favorable approach. If I fell off to starboard, I may not clear the reef which we were approaching to starboard. If I could get past the starboard marker of the channel entrance I could fall off to starboard enough to keep to the wind as the channel was tending to the right beyond the pass, but I could not get far enough to port to clear the marker. If enough speed is up, you can luff into the wind and get passed an obstruction. But we didn't have the speed.

I gauged the appearance of the water to starboard of the channel marker which was indicating the reef to the right and the channel to the left. If I could keep close enough to the wrong side of the marker, there may be enough water for us to miss the reef. I could see the coral of the reef. I could see how close it was to the marker. By the water color, I could see how shallow the water was on the wrong side of the marker. Everything was right on the knife's edge of possibility, but on the plus side of calculation. I held her course.

The bottom of the keel had to be just inches from grounding. But we were in! Another boat length's distance and I was able to fall off the wind enough to keep her sailing the rest of the way.

I chose an anchoring spot closest to the town for the convenience of possible engine parts procurement and had soon disappeared into the dungeon called our engine room. In the fullness of time I reappeared, having regained that lovely purring sound of our iron mainsail, the engine.

Friends had cruised here a year ago and their letter regaled the loveliness of several of the anchorages for their beauty and motionlessly peaceful waters. Far too many flowers bloom unseen, and it was several days before we were able to force ourselves to leave.

Almost due north from here is Port Vila. The main port of Vanuatu is in the capital city of Elate. From Suva, Fiji it is nearly due west and would have been our destination had I not wanted to treat Peggy to something special for our anniversary, which is why I had sailed her over this chunk of the South Pacific.

Had I consulted her on the subject, she may well have opted for a kiss on the cheek. She puts up with a lot from me.

CHAPTER 3

 OR NOT

A couple of days of plain sailing brought us to the shores of Vanuatu's capital city Port Vila. The small boat anchorage was very pleasant and quiet. We had been welcomed to the Isles of Vanuatu by the gracious and efficient personnel of the Customs Office.

We strolled about in the unhurried town which boasts some vehicular traffic. We were not at all surprised to see roadway crossing marks for pedestrians but were surprised by our later learning of its description as in the out-island vernacular of pigeon English, by which one was warned of the necessity to be certain to do the following: "Plac fo kat kros long rod luk alsame snak long si" translates to "place cross along road where looks all the same as snake of the sea."

Another somewhat similar pigeon is, "Suposum yu pela stop long dis big pela plac, yu pela mus walk long topside sea snake belonum dis pela plac." Which is referring to where safely to cross the streets of Port Vila. English translation: "Suppose you fellow go to this big fellow place; you must cross the street by walking on top of the back of the sea snake." Due to all people knowing that a sea snake is marked with black and white bands, this is of immediate local comprehension.

Pigeon English, with some variation, is broadly spoken throughout the western South Pacific in addition to the very greatly varying local languages of the island countries. Usually, these languages bear little or no similarity with each other, and pigeon is used with those not of one's own village. As an illustration of language variation, Papua New Guinea is reliably reported to have over 800 distinct languages within its borders. Note the fact that this speaks of languages, not dialects. I look forward to sharing some reasons why this is the case when you join us there.

As we walked, we asked folks if they knew where the church that we attend was located. It is such great fun for us to greet the local folks on such mutually comfortable grounds. Both they and we are relieved of the usual restraints of contact with total strangers and perceived social structures; such as those of village chief to resident villager, or as to a woman as differing to a man; and that of an islander to any stranger of whatever race.

Though not entirely unrestrained, it is at least happily ignored for the most part under the social umbrella of a church.

Most of our treasured experience and interchange that have occurred ashore have been the result of such conversations. Sitting at table with people in their places of residence or they in ours aboard the *Osprey*, lends the appropriate final melting away of unease, into a vicarious fellowship approaching that of family. Though our acquaintance may have commenced due to a church setting, religion has not often been the focus of our social intercourse, but rather it has been the natural interest for the opportunity of comradely introspection of persons of differing experience. It's fun for those on both sides of the table. Life experiences are exchanged, sometimes with raucous laughter.

There is one subject, however, that we did not broach.

A Vanuatu couple, whom we had met in New Caledonia where they were employed at the time, had absolutely astounded us by saying that they had just received a letter from the Vanuatu Government which informed them that the land which they had bought as a place on which to build a little house for their old age retirement, no longer belonged to them. Years ago, they had borrowed the money to buy that land in Vanuatu, and had recently paid off its mortgage. Immense contentment had accompanied that accomplishment, and they were now happily in the process of saving their money to buy the building supplies for a modest but strongly built house. Drawing the ever-changing little details of the house had been a joyous pastime.

But now, they were astounded at the proclamation from Vanuatu, that the ownership of the land had been taken away from them and returned to the person who would have been the owner had the land continued its passage through original tribal tradition. All European-type of land ownership title had been canceled, with total disregard to the money paid to the entire chain of persons, including citizens of Vanuatu. All land ownership title was declared null and void if not passed down via the lineage of ancient tradition.

They asked me what I thought about this. And I told them that I was absolutely certain that this was impossible. "You paid for that land to someone who was its rightful owner, and that person accepted the money he asked for it." I could not believe this was remotely possible. I spent years as a real estate agent. If a clear title is transferred from A to B, nothing can revoke it, *eminent domain* not applying in this case.

I was subsequently found to be totally wrong in that declaration.

Vanuatu had indeed thrown away its historic ties with all things non-Vanuatuan. The government had looked at the twentieth century and rejected it. Their conclusion was based of what was thought a better path for its people. This path, in my irrelevant opinion, was not one with a destination beyond today's very short horizon.

* * *

Within a few days we were off to the island which at the time of our sailing was still called by the European discoverer's name given to the place. We sailed to the Island of Pentecost, so named in 1605 by the Spanish Explorer Quros, to give recognition of the day on which he arrived. Our arrival was timed to coincide with the fabled land diving which occurs on no other island on earth.

Chapter 3 — Or Not

Who knows when this unique form of worship began? When did men first climb up toward the sky as high as they could and then dive off into space with jungle vines tied to their ankles to honor their god? How long have these gods lived in these jungles with these people?

We lowered the anchor where it would be free of coral. This is easy to do because the water is always so clear. We knew that we were in for a rough night. The swells were beating on the beach already and I expected it to get worse.

The sun shook itself free from its captor the ocean. The day was here. I rowed Peggy ashore, drug the dinghy up the beach, brought the dinghy's little anchor farther up and shoved it into the sand with my foot which now wore my walking shoes; locked the oars in the dink; and we started our uncertain search for a place and event about which we had only slight information.

Just up from the beach, we found a little dirt road. This means that there are vehicles on this island! How about that for luck? And a pickup truck was coming!

It had to be a startling sight for this islander to see the likes of us walking along this road. He stopped. In pigeon English he asked if we needed help. I stumbled through my pigeon vocabulary and miraculously he understood, and drove us to where a trail went upward on the mountain.

"Yu pella walk long dis one pella road, you pela stop altugeda plac belongum yu." [We will find the land diving at the end of the trail.]

We had learned that there were both Pagans and Christians living on this island. And we learned that both groups did the land diving. Today, the Pagans were going to have their annual high day, and our presence would be permitted.

I use the term Pagans because this is the term used by the locals in Port Vila to designate the non-Christians. I don't like the term. I don't think that this group of people thinks of themselves in any other term than as being persons of their specific village; which is as I would likewise wish to do.

This event is certainly not a commercial enterprise. This is not a "show" for which tickets are sold. This event is entered into with utmost solemnity and long preparation by the entire village, and rigorously so by the participants.

Though no other yachtsmen were there, three other none locals were. They had chartered a small sea plane which had "landed" on the opposite side of the island from us. We quietly talked together as we watched the arrival of more of the islanders.

We stood on a pinnacle of a mountain from which a long valley plunged. A row of mountains faced each other between which this valley cascaded ever downward until it dove into the sea. And here on this mountain's crest, at the head of the valley, and on the very edge of the precipice from which the valley descended, stood a majestic tree from whose mighty trunk great branches once had spread.

How long had time shared life with this wondrous tree? Surely its broad branch held the first man whose reverent dive is followed to this very day.

When in the fullness of time this mighty druid of the forest died, as had others before him, the people of the island must with solemn affection have asked the tree if they be permitted to build a tower for him to hold up to the sky. The permission was granted, for it is so to this day.

Chapter 3   *Or Not*

The tower is built of forest poles standing on end with poles closing the outer edges of the top and bottom as though building a box with only a frame. All four sides of the box are cross braced and lashed together with jungle vines to keep the box together.

It is made in place and lashed to the trunk of *the great tree*. What follows is a series of such boxes lashed atop each other and goes past the top of the tree by a great distance. The height of the tower reaches upward of seventy-five feet above its ground!

To stand at the top of the tower, to see the valley dive from under you all the way down to the sea beyond, would prove that you were indeed standing on the very top of the world.

More villagers were arriving. Except for the magic man, as the spirit leader is called, only women were in this group. They were dressed in what I assume was their most recently-made grass skirts. Several wore brassieres without shirts. They must have been from astonishingly affluent families because these were bought from stores. I noticed that the other women were not encumbered with any upper apparel.

Very soon the men arrived. They all wore "penis wrappers," which is the proper name for this apparel, and is so called throughout all the islands of the western South Pacific where it is worn.

The penis wrapper is a sheath made of finely woven plant material, into which the penis is inserted, thusly preventing the unpleasantness of being scratched as one walks through the jungle. There are differing styles of this device throughout the South Pacific. Here, a tassel extends from the end which is tucked into the belt whereby the penis wrapper is retained and is in a perpetual upright position.

The belt is a vine about the diameter of one's little finger, which is passed around a person's waist three or four times and then tucked under itself thereby retaining its tension.

By this time, the magic man was beginning the "blessing" of the tower with a great show of loud shouting and generally scaring away the evil spirits for the safety of the divers.

He was a small man of considerable age. He carried a couple of branches which were less than three feet long. The branches had leaves and were dunked into a pail of sorts, and with each shout he would whip the tower here and there with a great show of the spiritual power with which he was endowed.

I mean no disrespect caused by my wondering mind as I watched him. But my undisciplined brain kept inserting the picture of a Bantam rooster, which is a little fellow with a lot of attitude.

The magic man's posterior was festooned by a rather generous cluster of leaves, presenting perhaps a rather rooster-like appearance. All the men were likewise dressed in this additional everyday attire. Bushes grow everywhere, so it is not difficult to find this necessity. One must select a "V" shaped branching, because one side will drape over a man's posterior and the other side of the "V" is broken off, leaving three or four inches of it to tuck into the top of the belt. With a few such leafy branches one's posterior is efficiently covered.

I don't know if there is any other advantage to carrying these leaves around, but modesty must be an adequate reason in itself. The magic man seemed to me to have brought more than enough with himself, because he looked just a little over "feathered." But then again, this was a formal occasion. He continued all the way to the top of the tower, dispelling unwanted spirits with a flourish of threatening shout and thrashing branch. No self-respecting evil spirit would accept such insult.

Ever since the men started toward the tower, the women were chanting a one or two note song as they danced their encouragement. They were formed in three lines of fifteen or so people each and faced the tower. They held the hand of the one beside them, which had the advantage of keeping everyone in step. As they sang, they all simultaneously took two slow half steps to the left followed by two half steps to the right, all of which must have boosted the courage of the divers immensely. Thus the women too were further aiding the assurance of a good next harvest and the village's survival for yet another year.

I hasten to point out that throughout many of the islands it is the women who do most of the work including the labor of growing all of the food. The men may manage the fire in the "burn and slash" process of preparing a new garden area, but after that, their job in many places is to protect the women from jungle creatures, even though there are no tigers on any South Pacific islands. On some big islands, women are stolen by men from different villages.

There is a week or ten day ritual during which the divers must be cleansed. I cannot report all of this process. The only thing that stuck in my mind was that sex was prohibited during this time.

The young boys who chose to dive this year have their own ritual through which to pass. Not every male of the village dives every year. To dive *or not* to dive is the annual question. And the boy chooses the year of his first dive. One young adult perhaps approaching twenty years of age looked around after climbing the tower to his spot and suddenly found himself to be possessed by thoughts of a better application of his time. He hastily returned by taking the same route of his assent. The song of the "choir" continued without missing a beat.

One more piece of information is needed to complete your knowledge about the tower. Each of the square box-like frames of the tower has a dive platform extending into space which is about three feet outward toward the valley. It is about three feet wide, and it is held up at the outward end by a small vine from each corner. These small vines extend upward to the tower at about a 45 degree angle.

At each "diving board" two men await the diver to attach the liana vines to his ankles. When the diver steps out onto this extension, it sways several inches to each side, adding little to his comfort as he looks out into a seemingly endless abyss while trying to retain his shaky balance.

The lowest dive points are used first, and by the boys, since the vines are passed over the end of each platform. When the diver nears the ground and the vines are straightened out by the weight of the diver, the force breaks the small vines which hold the platform up and the breaking effort helps the diver by absorbing the first shock as the vines reach their extremity. Breaking the platform away also frees the space through which the next diver might pass.

The ankle vines have all been premeasured for each elevation. However, they are not specially grown vines without kinks and twists. It seems to me that the accuracy of the length measurement falls somewhat closer to an art form than to precision.

Nonetheless, each person who participates puts his life on the line. The attempt is to have the vines long enough to have the diver's head touch the ground in order to best impress the gods. The ground falls sharply away a few feet from the tower and that area is dug to make it soft enough that the head can slightly enter and yet not kill the diver.

When the vines have stretched to their maximum as the diver's head has reached the ground, the vines seeking to regain their coils, jerk the person upward with a violent snapping action. On his way down again he would smash into the face of the down slope closer to the bottom of the tower, where a couple of men are there to stop him. They also release his ankles from the vines, and move out of the way for the next diver to step onto his wobbly platform.

One of the boys very quickly reinserted his manliness after the snapping motion of his vines managed to have dislodged its position from within his penis wrapper. The young man corrected this happening with most rapid haste! The choir sang on.

Here still stands the great tree. And from his regal domain atop this mountain, as he commands all of the earth below him, I can see him smile upon his world and upon his people, and upon his days well spent upon this land. Were we to reflect upon our own time amongst our trees, I trust that contentedly we too may smile.

Chapter 3 — Or Not

To have been here, to have seen a man atop the world, to have seen him as he looks straight out into the empty void of space, to see him take a deep breath as he bends his knees and hurls himself straight out—arching his back to try to keep nothingness directly in front of him while his body keeps moving to bring his head toward the ground—to see him plunge ever faster, ever downward, until being snatched back from death itself; has granted me the vicarious feeling of that same rushing wind upon my face . . .

It took my breath away as perhaps a dozen men and boys chose to honor the gods in our presence.

Their tribute to the gods complete, these good people were returning to their village and we took our leave from our fellow observers. We left pensively to return to our time, to once more sit upon the magic carpet of this sailing vessel the *Osprey*.

We are getting better all the time at our leaping back and forth in our time travel, for we had no sooner regained our place aboard the boat when, with but one breath, we were again back to the year of our present remembrance.

The anchorage area had not forgotten how uncomfortable our prior night aboard had been. We seemed to be inside a washing machine as we were being thrown about. Our choice of a place to anchor had been predicated by our need to find the land diving location, not for the purpose of our comfort. The anchorage had not only remembered last night, but was determined to out do itself tonight. That goal was admirably accomplished.

***

With the faintest first light, we were away for a five hour sail to Ambros Island and a comfortable night's stay followed by another five hour sail to the Island of Malekua. The wind was piping up again as we chose our spot to set the anchors. And not surprisingly, it took on a bit of a roar as the rain deluged an entire ocean from the sky. I had set a couple of anchors against the possibility of this worsening condition, so we were well secure.

We had caught fish on the way here and Peggy, by some magic beyond the experience of mere males, caused a bounteous dinner to appear. About such magic I dare not so much as ask.

The next day was overflowing with pleasantry. Even the air was perfumed by flowers dressed in countless variations of color. Peggy wanted to go ashore and walk the beach. One's eye wanders over everything and we began looking for shells. We soon found that it became difficult to focus on this one pleasant task because as we walked leisurely along the shore, occasionally up to our knees in the water, the island persisted in having perpetually painted a picture of paradise more vividly enchantingly than the prior one. Life does seem to present each of us with an endless array of problems. To stroll though such art galleries, in which one's use of the word "Wow" as we again would say, "Look at that! What a picture that is of idyllic South Pacific," leaves us with the feeling of being challenged of appropriate vocabulary. As you would expect, the shells too were spectacular.

We had anchored within sight of a village. Social grace was not ignored. We presented the village chief with a large fish. Many reef fish are caught by the villagers but they are generally much smaller. We enjoyed our visit to his pleasant thatch-roofed house and were received by the village as honored guests.

Much unites these folks with the others of the Vanuatu Group of Islands, the most appealing of all is the ready quickness of their smile. Can there be higher praise?

We were leaving again. We can generally organize the boat for sailing in just a few minutes time and so it was today. The dinghy was already secured on the house as I removed the sun cover from the mainsail boom; attached the main halyard; attached the sail bearing removable mainsail track to the mast; untied the sail ties from around the boom; hanked the two headsails onto their stays; brought the anchor up to its bowsprit; cast free the sheets; raised all sails; secured all sheets; and as the rudder held her to the course, the sails filled, the boat leaned to her task, and we were off to find an island known by the name Espiritu Santo.

***

The Second World War had one of its closing events at Santo. Similar to many other islands of the South Pacific, the US here too had many varied types and quantities of equipment. Santo was a staging location and huge quantities of equipment were here when the war ended. Vanuatu was not an independent nation prior to, nor during the war.

The locals had remained as tribal communities having no national organization and certainly no money. For all of these reasons, the French Government who managed such thing here was approached with an offer for them to buy all of this mass of equipment for an astonishingly tiny pittance because the US could not afford the cost of transporting everything back to the States.

The French are reported to have laughed in glee, pointing out that since all of this stuff was going to be abandoned in place, why should they pay one cent for the lot? This equipment included such things as great numbers of the biggest bulldozers, fleets of trucks, and countless other equipment, all of which was maintained in condition for immediate use.

Whoever was in charge of this wealth of equipment took exception to being unceremoniously rebuffed and although earlier in the day mechanics were still greasing some of the equipment, the order was given to bulldoze everything into the sea.

The spot today is still called *million dollar beach*. Oh how this equipment could have built the island's roads and schools and harbors, and benefited France and the islands as well—at least it seems so from this writer's view.

We arrived after a pleasant seven hour sail and renewed our visas for a longer stay in Vanuatu.

The following day we met the local pastor of the church and his family. We shared a light supper with them and the next day he showed us where the *SS President Coolidge* had sunk off million dollar beach.

She had been a private luxury liner commandeered by the US Navy and converted to a troop ship. In October of 1942, she ran into a US Navy mine in shallow water off the island and was wrecked with the loss of only two lives. She was beached in order to save additional lives and as much equipment as possible. People actually walked ashore, though it is now sunken from sight.

For us, the specific present interest in the *Coolidge* is that she continues to pass things ashore such as the pair of surgical scissors which Peggy found at water's edge and still has today. Santo would have been a target for Japanese air raid because it was also a "rest and relaxation" center for the Army and had as many as one hundred thousand troops here where the locals numbered very few. But the loss of the *Coolidge* was not at Japan's hand but rather by our own.

On the Island of Aore, just one and a half miles away to the south, our church has a boarding academy. We may have stopped there just for that reason, but the fact that there was a slip way to bring the *Osprey* out of the water was the greater reason for our interest.

We went the very next day, but found the water too shallow for us to get the boat to its railway. Seven days from now the moon would show the fullness of her face, whereby that global lump of water on which she keeps her eye focused might bring a high enough tide to float us to the spot; and it was so.

I love a coat of paint on her bottom, especially when time has elapsed for the antifouling property of the last application nearing its exhaustion, and when it may be awhile before we again find another place to haul the boat out of the water. I had the paint aboard and looked forward to a nice clean and painted bottom.

Frank had scared me in the procedure of blocking the boat onto the railway carriage before hauling her out of the water. He had gone underwater, holding his breath while adjusting the blocks to securely hold the boat upright. The trouble was that he was using weights to keep himself down while working, which had no way to be released without a cumbersome sequence of untying several different ropes. If he were to be caught on something underwater he could drown before getting himself released. I dug up an old extra scuba diving belt and insisted that he change the weights to it because it has a quick release buckle for easy escape in the event of such danger.

The boat came safely out of the water, and Frank came up alive and safe to swim another day. I insisted that he keep the belt. There would be other boats. Frank's job was manager of the boat railway. He and I scrubbed the *Osprey*'s bottom, and the boat was left to dry.

As always, we found the conversations with the teachers stimulating and it was fun to speak to the students of adventures at sea during school programs for such events. And though conversations with us carry no reason for which to gather together, we are new faces and that is often enough in itself.

Throughout most of this part of the Pacific, these teachers were at their schools from far off places such as Australia; and though we were not from *home,* the cultural background was similar enough that a wish for a moment of nostalgia was given us the opportunity to convey. So everyone had fun, because nostalgia is not lost on us either.

The first day that we were out of the water, the school principal's wife presented us with a house to use during our stay. This move to shore quarters entailed little shuffling of goods from the boat, but each trip was accompanied by a whole host of very young children who wanted to help. Each one wanted to carry something.

So if there were three shirts and four pair of socks, eleven little children happily giggled their way from boat to house even if carrying only one sock. Everyone was happy, but Peggy's gift of balloons had the kids running all over the place ecstatically showing parents their first balloon.

The next morning, when the first girl saw Peggy come out of the house, she yelled out, "Pu pu woman balloon he come!" and others yelled to kids farther way.

But it was not followed by "gimme gimme gimme." It gave pleasure to the kids just to wave to her and smile at this lovely lady.

All throughout the Vanuatu Islands I had been having small troubles with the engine. Coming close to Port Vila, the engine temperature gauge started moving upward from the normal.

The drill is not mysterious; I stopped the engine and found that the belt which drove the fresh water cooling pump had broken. This engine uses sea water in a heat exchanger to cool the fresh water which is in the engine. Spare belts of all sizes are always carried aboard, and it is a simple process to replace one.

The engine assumed its appropriate temperature and after a few minutes of running during which time the belt has its usual tendency to stretch, I again stopped the engine, retightened the belt, and the customary process was accomplished.

But the question is, "What's the reason for all of this black soot all over everything in the engine room?" It's a mess. A few times into the engine room had me covered with the stuff. Not just my hands, but even my pants. Now

I am not inhibited or hesitant to go into the engine room naked. Skin cleans more easily than cloth. But from where is this stuff coming?

The cause was my losing the battle between iron and salt. The engine muffler was rusting rapidly to nothing. I had rigged a wrapping, but it was more like a Band-Aid on an amputation.

Into this picture stepped a lean lanky fellow from the Aore Island School's math class. He was the teacher. And as is so frequently the case, the Australian men are found to be very broad-based in their skills. He built a new muffler for the *Osprey* which served her well and long.

***

The school launch once a week transports some of the school staff across the short distance to Santo. A couple of stores were there and personal or school needs could be acquired. Mainly just for fun, Peggy and I went along.

We had lunch with a couple of people whom we spotted ashore. They were from fellow cruising yachts. There are not huge numbers of us. There may have been twenty or so of us at one given time, sailing a third of the South Pacific Ocean, though the safe weather sailing period tends to direct us toward similar areas. Please know that this number is just an approximation and refers to yachts of the same weather systems. Others would be starting into the Pacific from the east on any given year while still others would be leaving it westward.

We were talking in front of a little store. The store had a window in the front and I could see Peggy as she was looking at the contents of the shelves. All of the few stores were small. As we were talking, two local men were passing by, speaking very pointedly about a fellow who had just walked past us into the store.

"Those mountain people should not be coming into town like that!" said the one to the other.

Coming to town is generally thought of as a rather formal occasion to most of the folks, regardless of the sparseness of its stores or its paving. In fact, the yachting folks are criticized in many places for coming in short pants, etc. The gentleman in question had come down from the mountains without appropriate attire in the mind of the two men who were passing within our hearing. In fact he was entirely unattired. The more frequent term of description I believe is naked, for he had no covering or clothing of any kind whatsoever.

Peggy was in the store looking about. The naked man was in the store looking about. The three of us outside the store were looking in, to watch Peggy's reaction.

She had gathered three or four items and went to the counter where money was to be paid. The naked gentleman had found what he wanted and had approached the counter where money was to be paid. Peggy was the first one there. The naked man was next. There were no others in the store. Peggy paid for her few items. The naked man paid for his and he followed her out of the little store. Peggy came over to where we had been watching this, unaware of our attention. The naked man passed by us, going in the direction from which he had come, freeing us to comment about the event to Peggy.

The fact that she had not noticed the man does not speak to her lack of awareness. Rather it speaks to the fact of her having become accustomed to such varying attire of those in her surroundings that even total nakedness had not registered in her mind as noteworthy.

I was proud of her, but enormously amused as were our friends. The event was not even spoken of to our Aore friends upon our return, which I mention by way of emphasis that our personal concept of propriety might be just subjects to the perception of others. Wherefore, were the two local men who spoke of naked man's lack of attire to visit the mountains, they may be thought of as being ridiculously overdressed if they wore anything at all.

We were not the last ones to arrive at the Santo dock for the school's taxi to bring us back to Frank's island, Aure. Yes, that's right. Frank, whose other name is *White Feather,* was granted the fifty-seven-plus thousand hectors of the entire island, which would in times gone by have come to him via tradition, now is his by decree – all of it.

He and his wife Glenas are probably in their early thirties. We had become acquainted with each other before knowing of his recently altered status. We had spent leisure time with them talking about casual subjects such as we were doing this evening.

A few hours ago we had felt something hit the bottom of the boat hard enough that it actually bounced the boat upward slightly. Nothing had ever hit us this hard before, and we rushed on deck to catch a look at what on earth it was.

We saw nothing, and when we went ashore we were just about to tell our friends of this odd experience when the earth shook! It was our first earthquake tremor, and it was the prior one that we felt bash the boat upward ever so slightly. Our friends chuckled at our reaction. This was a very regular happening on this part of the planet, and we were indeed to become very accustomed to such events. Frank's seeing our mini-shook seemed to have shaken loose his reticence to bring up his problem. What specifically should he do with the island?

Briefly, let me say that we talked extensively. We walked the island and talked some more. I verified my possession of no expertise and could only convey what I would do here, where no Agricultural Extension Service existed to give professional advice to farmers. Viewing the fact that there was a small area in use as a copra plantation, I suggested that it be expanded and formed as I had seen many others planted: that cocoa be planted with all of the trees, and that a herd of cattle be commenced, and by what schedule bulls could be sold off as a progressively increasing cash flow basis which I did know something about.

His wish to talk with me did not result from any prior portrayal of immense wisdom on my part. I had spent many hours of indulging my interest in learning about the customs of the islands and about life as it once was lived. Frank and his good wife Glenas had regaled us with seemingly endless glimpses of things as they once had been.

Glenas had come from a different island. She was not yet as comfortable with us as Frank who may have previously urged her to tell us of this particular custom. She was clearly nervous. She was also embarrassed.

She prefaced her story by commenting that today people would laugh. Frank knew that we would not and, of course, we did not laugh. We saw nothing funny in it. Yes, it was an unusual custom as it is viewed by today's concepts, but we have a clear view of the obvious. Today is not the same as then.

In earlier times on her island, lookouts were posted to keep watch in all directions over the sea for any approaching canoes. The problem was an obvious one; are the approaching men hostiles or are they traders. Invaders were as likely as traders. The trading canoes crossed between the islands constantly bringing with them goods to trade for what the locals had grown or made.

As a proof of non-hostile intent, the traders to this island were required to lay face down on the sand as soon as they beached their canoe and in this position, the entire village walked across them, stepping on them in the process. We did not laugh. What more clear gesture could there be of non-aggression?

Frank began his accounting of a specific difference in today as compared to yesterday. Did I notice a fleeting expression of nostalgia? No, as I recall it, I must have been wrong.

"In the day" to insert our vernacular, if a man were walking along a trail and a woman happened to be coming in his direction, it was the custom that she step off the trail to not impede his passage. But if he noticed her body and was inclined toward her, at a specific hand gesture, she was required to recline on the path to receive him.

The Australian teachers of this high school accounted to us their astonishment that the girls came here with a comprehension that children were caused by invisible spirits. Pleasurable pursuits were not conceived as being of consequence. It seems plausible that the story of biblical Mary may have strengthened such a concept.

***

The church of our attendance was among all the other churches that first sent missionaries throughout the South Pacific Islands in the very early days. They were the last in this group to come to Vanuatu, then known by Europeans as the New Hebrides.

When our people arrived, they made themselves known to the other church leaders and asked if they would recommend any particular island to begin their presentation and were told that for several years now all of the islands had been introduced to Christianity except for one. And that everybody had been driven away from the Island of Malekula by those wild people who threatened to kill all of them.

These missionaries went to Malekula. But over the years they had only slight success with a few of the coastal tribes, and to this day, none whatsoever with the Big Nimbus people of the mountains.

When I learned that a sister of one of the local men employed by the school was married to the main chief of the Big Nimbus on Malekula, and that tomorrow he was going there, I knew that somehow I was going with him.

I had also heard about Malekula prior to our arrival here in Vanuatu. Against everyone's advice a tourist had gone there a few months ago. He had made his way up to the Big Nimbus area and had taken some pictures. He, of course, had been seen taking these pictures, one of which was of something considered taboo. The men chased him as he ran for his life. They caught him. And they savagely beat him to death, and he was left to rot in the jungle. However, he was not totally dead, he regained consciousness, literally crawled down from the mountains to the sea, and as good fortune would have it, was found by a trading schooner sailing him to where he could be brought to a hospital.

So okay, of course I'm bringing a camera, but I'll ask first before any picture. At this point, however, I'm the only one who knows that I'm going.

With all care and caution I broached the subject with my intended host whose immediate reaction was one approaching horror, but we talked longer and a deal was struck. I was going! Peggy was secure in the house. The boat was secure on the railway. The weather season offered no threat. Nothing presented a barrier at this end of considerations. I was going!

At the first rays of the sun we were aboard a fast launch making SSE ward for Malekula. Several of us were going. I was the only non Vanuatuan aboard. My host and guide had gifts for his sister which was to be our safe passage. I had gifts in hope that they might be presented to advantage and or as recognition of hopeful kindness received.

We roared onward. The sea must have been as amazed as I, to see me exceeding the customary five miles per hour speed of the *Osprey*. Several hours passed before we arrived. Not a moment was lost as we immediately, and with great haste, began our assent of the mountains. There was urgency here. We needed to get back with the aid of the sun.

The way was known. The path was selected with care. We began the climb. My panting began. We had gone neither far nor long, but I was panting. The trail was steep. In many places the strewn pebbles called more for skating than climbing. The trail was narrow and uninterested in the work it required for us to go straight up.

An hour passed followed by a second followed by a third. Four hours of maximum gut-wrenching exhaustion beyond endurable effort brought us to a stockade enclosure with a structure inside its seven foot high wall of small logs set on end shoulder to shoulder, with no opening between through which an arrow could be launched. Entrance could be gained by crawling on hands and knees through a small opening. Oh how glad I was to arrive! And how disappointed I was that we still had farther to go. An old man was at this outpost. Probably he was thought to no longer be of value where the others had gone. I wondered what might have caused a force the size of this fort to be dispatched.

I made pleasantries with the old man and left a small gift with him.

At long last, we had arrived at a very large compound enclosed in the manner of the prior one, except that about five separate houses were enclosed in this one. My host and guide called out at the "gate" which was closed from the inside with horizontal poles. His call was answered, he identified himself as a brother to one of the wives, reported his group of four, and we were permitted entry.

Only the women were here all busily engaged in efforts to keep the wheels of jungle existence turning smoothly as is the gift of women in most places of the world. The chief just now had only four wives. Each wife had a separate house. The entrances were of the traditionally crawl through design and therefore easiest to defend. We were not permitted entry into the houses and we made constant effort to convey our intent of utter respect.

His sister was just pouring water into the communal drinking containment. Water is brought up the mountain from a fresh water spring. The devise for transport of such water is a seven-foot length of green bamboo stalk about eight inches in diameter of which the horizontal growth section barriers have been knocked out. The bamboo is harnessed by vines on a woman's back in a vertical manner and extends beneath her legs. This is no small load with which to climb a mountain.

I was careful to ask permission before taking any picture. No I could not photograph the women, nor the houses. There was a very mangy dog lying on the ground in front of one of the houses. I asked if I could take a picture of the dog. The two women laughed at this ridiculous thing but agreed that this would be alright.

The women were dressed in traditional grass skirt plus necklaces of decoratively woven plant fiber. Some fading plant dye also adorned their bodies, for after all, these were wives of the highest chief of the Big Nimbus people.

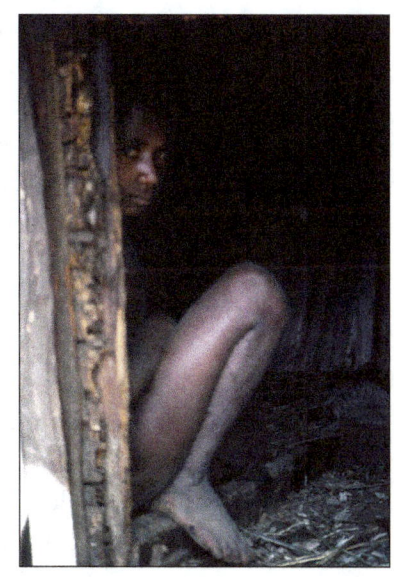

I might explain that the word on this island for penis wrapper is Nimbus. The people of the shore tribes are known as Small Nimbus. You will remember the couple whom we met in New Caledonia whose land had been taken away from them even though they were Vanuatuan? He is from Malekula and told us about the Big Nimbus and the Small Nimbus and the history of the island. He is a Small Nimbus member, and was very, very quick to clarify any misconception that might arise over these names by pointedly voicing the fact that there is absolutely no reference beyond the weaving of the penis wrapper itself, regarding this big and small reference. It references the size of the penis wrapper's design only!

We were at the chief's compound for no more than half an hour. The only man whom we had met was the old man at the first compound, and we met no others on the way back down the mountain.

On the way down our guide audibly gasped when he saw at the side of the trail a special placement of sticks marking it as taboo to go farther. He had not noticed it earlier and had taken us up in violation to this warning. So that is why all of his women were left alone. This information did not slow our departure, though well before now every muscle in my legs which had previously complained in a rather unmanly way, doubled their protestations. We at long last got to the boat! The engine started. We were off in haste and with relief.

While I was gone, Peggy had some excitement of her own. I had left the house at about 4 o'clock to load the boat and be of general purpose, having left Peggy comfortably enclosed in a traditional mosquito netting. This one hung at its four corners by eye bolts screwed into the ceiling and the entire lower end was tucked under the mattress at head, foot and sides. I had securely re-tucked my departure side.

Not long after I was gone but beyond my hearing, Peggy discovered that a rat had made its way into her enclosure, and excitedly stimulated by her voicing objection to his presence, the poor rat was crazily dashing about in hope of finding an avenue of escape.

Peggy couldn't find an open escape route either. And I can imagine an observer's uncertainty as to who was chasing whom!

All was well again, for behold, her knight in shining armor stood again between her and any threat of harm, as yet I stand today. All shall remain well.

***

We had managed to get to the railway, launched by the aid of a full moon, and would need such a tide to enable us to get back into the water. What if that was an unusually high tide that gave us enough water to get up? What if the next high tide was less and we are not being able to launch the boat? Would we ever get back into the water? We had been here three months thus far. Well, I guess we could teach!

I had met Peggy in our first year of boarding school and I have had the good fortune to have had the enormous pleasure of her presence for yea these many years, so the academy years were of special remembrance to us. We had a rousing school song. When it is given permission to do so, it can still echo, though more dimly in our minds. But with some persuasion, the words can even be remembered.

Such effort was employed at Aore. And by inserting its name instead of our school's name into the song, the tempo was retained, and the new words which I chose for it fit perfectly. So (here insert a drum roll), behold, a song was born, and perhaps a tradition may follow. I gave only a sideward glance to copyright infringement. These schools are many worlds apart in every possible meaning of the phrase, or does my hung-over school spirit favorably fog my spectacles? The school sang!

Frank had killed a water buffalo and brought a large quantity of "beef" to us. Part of it was kept ashore in refrigeration for us while Peggy went into high production mode in her skill of canning meat in jars using a pressure cooker. This is not her first time at this. And we know how benefited we will be in distant places to have this change of diet. Peggy is always happy to share her expertise with anyone. And her doing so is always to their very great benefit, for which I likewise am very pleased.

Today was the huge party! Vanuatu was celebrating its fourth year as an independent nation. National pride and patriotism was a new and heady experience throughout these islands.

All of the students of the Aore School were excited, and at the same time were a little unsure as to how such new reality should be cheered. The school food was planned to be festive. The staff was here from Australia and every Auzzie knows how to party. The *Osprey* people put on a fireworks performance by firing a number of flares high into the air to light up the night sky. No islander had seen such a sight in all of their lives. We managed a very respectable Independence Day celebration.

The moon continued its unhurried strolling around in our back yard, and when it finally chose to look fully in our direction it had brought with it enough water for our need. We were afloat again but not finished with our work. The plan was for us to move the *Osprey* out of the little lagoon where the railway was, to an area with deeper water from which we could take a departure when desired without the need of a special tide. We would need a good tide to do this though, as well as some sunlight to pick our way.

You may not have picked up on this fact, but rightly or wrongly, I am possessed of a certain quantity of perceived self-sufficiency. But when others wish to present a gift, one should not only accept such a gesture but express abundant appreciation of its receipt. All of this presented itself at five o'clock in the morning when the captain of the "Ronny" the school's water taxi, along with a friend, arrived aboard the *Osprey* to show us the way out through the channel. With the aid of their practiced skill and knowledge, we escaped the determined goal of the lagoon to continue its retention of a US yacht. After all, how many lagoons can boast of such a thing?

The shallow water reached up very close to us as its rocks and sand looked enviously at our new paint. The gift of their kindness was not only well received, but if truth be known, undoubtedly it was sorely needed. Thank you gentlemen for the great kindness extended to us.

When at last all work was completed, there were warmest expressions of hoped for fair winds to benefit our way, echoed with our thanks to all of them for their sharing time with us. Our departure had arrived. And with a proper salute to Frank and to the teacher of mathematics, we were once again bound toward the sea.

Well, almost bound for sea. We "checked out" of Vanuatu with the Customs Office at Santo and made for an anchorage northward on the island to await some wind with which to sail. The keeper of the earthly hourglass dictated that we should be there for at least a week.

* * *

The anchorage looked very inviting on the chart, and we found it to be even more pleasant than expected. Several of our cruising friends had also chosen this spot to wait. To our astonished amazement, there were about ten yachts there, and we took our time passing amongst them to call out a greeting before picking a spot to lower our anchor. Some of these boats we had never seen before. Peggy made lunch and we had no sooner enjoyed it when people started coming by to chat.

We cruisers love to talk. Maybe it's a recognition gained over vast expanses of time during long passages at sea that our personal experiences, focused so exclusively on just one other person, has brought us to the truly awesome awareness of the unique specialness of an individual person, be they of differing culture, differing status, or differing age.

I had launched the dinghy. We had gone over to Charlotte and Conrad's boat *Wisp* and were in their cockpit enjoying our selves when Conrad received an excited radio call. Dick, aboard *Tangarora* had a marlin on the line. We had met them in Fiji years ago. He wanted to bring that marlin aboard but had no way to do so. He too had just checked out with customs and was sailing the short distance to our location. Conrad told him to just keep coming and we would help him from a dinghy when he got here.

The boat arrived. The fish arrived. We launched Conrad's inflatable dinghy. It was much more stable than our nine foot *Dyer Sailing Dinghy*. We approached the boat, secured it to the shrouds; let ourselves drift aft to where we were facing the marlin still on the fishing line and held up to the surface of the water. It was not small. Wearing gloves, I grabbed it by the beak, intending to keep the marlin close to the side of the dinghy for Conrad to secure the rope around its tail.

It lunged at me in full attack. I sidestepped the lunge by quickly shoving the beak at the same time. The plan was to get the marlin in a position where we could get a lasso around its huge tail, the lower half of which reached way down into the water. The lasso rope was attached to the mainsail halyard for the purpose of lifting it aboard. It was with no small effort that we accomplished our task.

I take no pleasure in extinguishing the life of a fish even for the table as this fish was also destined. The majesty of such an old man of the sea, I would rather just admire. In awe I have watched huge marlin leap out of the water as they take their fish into the air, thrashing them about as they do in just the same manner as shown when they themselves are caught beyond comprehension by what had appeared to be food. I have watched a sailfish slowly awaken as the *Osprey* sailed silently passed it a couple of feet away and watch him slink downward, happy for his speed to enable escape were this huge apparition to peruse him. And we have watched whales play with their young, and other whales perform amazing antics.

Even so, we are all aware of the source of origin of the wrapped packages in our butchers glass enclosed presentation, and our focus returned to matters of the boat.

Part of the way to this anchorage area was with the use of the engine. Even with this short usage it began to overheat. Guys came aboard to discuss the problem with me. Jim suggested that we should follow the water flow from sea to engine. I had stopped at the engine. He went farther. The manifold was found to be full of accumulated debris which when removed with considerable effort, entirely solved the overheating problem. It's great to have a little help from your friends.

We were all waiting for favorable wind for our passage to the Solomon Islands, so as is usually the case, we talked. Dinghies were rowed about from boat to boat. Food was brought here and there as lunches or dinners were shared. Charlotte and Conrad stayed till 10:30 one evening as Peggy's casual comment records in her daily log. We are looking for wind, but there is no anxious pacing of the decks. Life is enjoyed.

A wind arrived and boats took their leave, the *Osprey* among them. However, upon leaving the harbor and making northward, the wind turned hard on the nose. Everyone pressed onward except us. There was another small bay area whose pleasantry seemed more appealing than slogging into the wind to the Solomons. The anchor secured us in an absolutely gorgeous creation of tropic paradise. Ah, how green is our valley.

CHAPTER 4

 The Solomon Islands

We were leaving the Islands of Vanuatu. One more day sail brought us to our very last night's stay here. It seems as though the fabric of time itself had opened a doorway through which we had sailed. Those few months seemed moments too brief to clearly focus our view. But those glimpses are seen by us with such grateful amazement that fortune had held to our eye so rare a telescope of time.

Our last night in Vanuatu was pillowed with gentle sleep. Only a morning yawn interrupted the smile that had awakened us. The sky was blue. The breakfast was lovely and leisure and able to even broaden our smile. The anchor nestled in its accustomed place aboard, and our voyage to the Solomon Islands awaited only the beginning flight of the *Osprey*. She granted us only one quick mental wave of departure to these Isles through which we have been so privileged to sail. She was ready!

The dinghy had not been launched yesterday, so it was secure. A sunshade had not been rigged because night had been approaching as we arrived here in our last anchorage in the waters of Vanuatu. We too were ready!

I started the engine, raised the sails, and the course was set which last night's look at the charts had determined. We were under way again.

The wind was light. We were motor sailing to gain some offing from the area of coral but were destined soon to take down the sails entirely. We mo-

Chapter 4 — The Solomon Islands

tored through the night as well. The next day was slow sailing, but the windvane steered the boat, leaving the two of us as happy observers engrossed in watching the drama of the passing sea life of porpoises at play about the boat.

The broad brush of breeze drew constantly changing shapes of the clouds above, until the sun chose to look beyond its horizon. It's fun to be lazy when the sparkle of the sea is competing with the sandman's sprinkling of dreams behind our eyelids.

We are at sea. There are no footprints here, where centuries have watched each other pass. No road sign is to be found here which says, "Turn at next right for Historical Marker."

There is no change of any kind whatsoever, since men had looked ever nervously about from the deck of an ancient wooden square-rigged ship. They were here on a day just like this one. And they had cause for fear, because they knew that here too, *"thar be dragons."*

Five pleasant days of slow sailing has brought us to the Solomon Islands. The traditional sailing route is to pass the Island of San Cristobal on its eastern side. It is the windward side, and is not encumbered by coral. But what if we chose "the road less traveled?" What would we find?

***

The island saw us at first light. A maze of coral stretched all the way from where we were to the island about six miles away. I started the engine, took down the sails and we started in. I was able to see well enough from the cockpit position for the first couple of miles of successful dodging of coral heads, but finally we had to revert to our serious coral avoidance procedure.

Peggy took the wheel. I went up the ratlines (the ladder affair secured to the wire rigging that holds up the mast). This gives me the elevation from which I have full view of the coral threatening to tear the bottom out of the boat if we were to collide with one. The sun was overhead now and would be tending behind us as time progressed, thereby giving best viewing into the water for dangers ahead.

Peggy is quite a distance from me in this process, and has the added disadvantage of having the sound of the diesel engine in her ear. She could easily think I had said turn left instead of right were I to have called out to her. So we don't do it that way.

To get her attention, I whistle and then point right or left, followed by raising the five fingers of one hand either one, two, or three times to indicate the five, ten or fifteen degrees of the compass the turn is to be taken. The signal for danger is a five or more whistle signal as my hand indicates to stop or proceed very slowly as I pick our way through a maze. I had no idea how close to the island we might be able to get.

It was 1:30 in the afternoon when we put the anchor down to one of the greatest welcoming of our entire voyage thus far. I remember seeing the movie *Mutiny on the Bounty* when the ship anchored at Tahiti. Dozens of dugout canoes full of laughing Tahitians came racing out to the ship. The scene before us was just like that!

People were running down to the beach, grabbing an end of a canoe, dragging it into the water, and with paddles churning, they came laughing all he way as they called back and forth to each other! Six guys lead the way. The six canoes were in a tie for first place! These were one-man canoes. Many of the others were larger and had several people each. Not long afterward, the women came, many with young children. What great fun for everyone, including us.

Most of the smaller children wore necklaces. These were different from any we had seen before, and turned out to be made of bat's claws strung together. Lots of people were coming and going all the time. Peggy and I stayed in the cockpit busily welcoming the new arrivals as we would be waving goodbye to the ones who were leaving; simultaneously we were gesturing to this one or that one to sit down over here or there. Everyone was talking at the same time in a language of which we only recognized that best of all universal sound — the sound of laughter.

As people came aboard, we gave each one a piece of candy, and a balloon to each child. Everybody was delighted. That two-second moment, as a piece of candy is given to a person, a moment of eye to eye contact occurs. No person is *truly* met without creating that invisible bridge. We had shown the early arrivers how to blow up the balloons, so the new arrivers always had several willing teachers. A joyous hubbub of laughter and language beyond our ken went on for hours.

We were later to learn that these people are a very isolated group. This part of the island is separated from all of the rest of the island by high mountains which encircle them. It is a very difficult trek to cross the mountains and only some of the men had ever done so. The people on the other side, who lived way over toward the eastern beach, had the regular arrival of the trading schooner to bring all manner of wonderful things to them. Some of the men from here had even gone with the schooner to places on other islands and had returned to speak of many things, including people whose color was strange.

Certainly none of the women had ever seen anything like Peggy and me whose skin lacked its normal color. But they had heard of such strange people. Actually, ghosts were ascribed as being white apparitions such as us.

Perhaps the mothers with small children, who wanted Peggy to hold her child, were doing so that some small fame might be theirs in stories to be told in a future age. But whatever the reason, without exception, each child screamed in fear and dread until safely returned to its mother. (Some of the expatriates told us that instead of children being threatened by being told that the bogyman would get them if they didn't behave, in these parts it was the white ghost who would get them.)

In very broken Pigeon English, these folks told us that occasionally they had seen distant sails far off to sea and had often wondered about what the people on such boats were like. All of their stories from long ago say, "Big pela canoe ime no come dis pela plac" which would have first referred to the great square riggers of yesteryear.

The days passed quickly. And these gracious folks brought many gifts of fruits and vegetables when our departure preparations had been seen to commence. As these gifts were presented, our words of thanks were spoken to each person with a tone of reverence.

Due to our unusual meeting in *this* time and place, of these people who are isolated on a few square miles of fertile land on a small island in the South Pacific Ocean, perhaps in an *other age* to come, even Peggy and I may again be spoken of — over a small fire on this quiet beach, overheard only by the listening stars; and perhaps at that same time, at some other corner of the world, someone may pick up a dust covered book titled *Where Whales Sing* — and once again someone may hear the *laughter* of these special people.

The island faded astern. The sun sank into the ocean. The stars were brilliant beyond compare as the *Osprey*, wishing to not disturb us, sailed silently onward. We talked quietly about these island folks as we munched on some of the sweet fresh white coconut which had been given to us.

I knew that Peggy had fallen asleep by the sound of her changed breathing.

As she slept, I quietly watched one of the shows — a few porpoises were darting about. I bet they too enjoy seeing the phosphorescence causing the others in the group to be covered with glowing light. Every detail of each body is clearly shown as though the light emitted from them. I could hear them snort a breath of air when they came to the surface. But it was those big areas of glow, way down deep, which were one of the proofs to the ancient seamen that here *thar be dragons*!

And at the surface of the sea, where time stands still just to watch — the *Osprey* could just as easily be flying a huge Spanish flag from her giant galleon's stern or be flying the black flag with skull and crossed bones, upon this changeless sea. Oops, I too had fallen asleep. "Was I dreaming? What was I dreaming about?"

We sailed slowly onward, and behind us Neptune brushed away our trail. Nothing marked our passage upon these seas. Had we actually been here? Neptune will never say. The sea has no evidence that we were here. But the gentle wind remembers, and ever whispers all things to those who sail upon these seas. "And I, I remember too," *says the reader.*

I awakened Peggy. She was looking uncomfortable where she was. I thought that her arm would be getting numb. She went to her bed. I took another bite of that coconut. I love that chewy sweetness. I looked at the compass lit by its red glow, and seeing us still on course, I followed Peggy below.

***

The boat heeled ever so slightly to her task. No distant storm reached here to ruffle the surface of our sleepy sea. No reef lay in wait to attack the *Osprey* on her chosen way. A little closing of the eye and folding of the hands, and perhaps to dream was the ancient poet's gentle call.

How like mystic voyagers is *our* quiet presence upon these waters — compared to the raging epic which these seas had seen not long ago when great iron ships had brought guns and men *to war.*

The island toward which we sailed is known by the name *Guadalcanal.* We were sailing the *Coral Sea* –which had been shaken to its depths by the thunder of those giant iron ships. All has now been made silent upon the sea. It is Neptune's decree.

I slept so soundly that I didn't hear Peggy awaken to prepare our breakfast. We even had freshly squeezed fruit juice this morning. And before she concluded this masterpiece breakfast, she had baked biscuits which she dressed in the peach preserves which were sent to one of the Aore ladies from Australia.

A gift thus twice passed is twice as sweet. Peggy does a great breakfast–and a great lunch — and you should taste some of her dinners! But then, you already know that I like her.

Not long after we anchored close up to the south shore of Guadalcanal Island, a fellow came up with his canoe. Almost without exception, such good folks have come to sell something to us, usually some fruits or vegetables.

This is as it should be. For them, we are an unexpected opportunity "knocking at their door." It is an opportunity for us likewise, for we do not have a corner grocery store available for our needs.

This gentleman had nothing in his canoe. We always invite anyone aboard who has taken the effort to come to us, and I asked him if he would like to come aboard. He said that he would, and said so in very acceptable English though spoken through a very bright red mouth.

This is one of the centers of the betel nut chewing area. The nut is chewed with a leaf and with lime. The process yields an astonishingly red result. This redness stains the teeth bright red as well as the entire mouth, forcing the other person engaged in conversation to carefully concentrate on the speaker's eyes lest one focus only on the speaker's mouth, which would cause him embarrassment. Constant expectoration is required with this enjoyment of betel nut chewing. Neither of us has had the pleasure of participation. The spit stains whatever it hits with this ugly redness.

Since our mouths were not red, the gentleman was aware of our non-use of this mild stimulant and hunger reducing habit so prevalent amongst the local population, and he was careful in the process of relieving himself of this perpetual necessity of expectoration. Aboard the *Osprey*, no one has ever been looked at askance for any behavior differing from our own. Rudeness would not be tolerated from anyone in our presence and has never been presented. Likewise, our guest was made to feel welcome, because he was.

He was a man perhaps of my own age and we spoke as brothers. Peggy soon offered us each a cup of tea which the three of us enjoyed pleasantly. I rather over-sugared mine to approach his sugar quantity, and we spoke of many things; haltingly at first, but as ease of each other grew, even so did the conversation. He now more formally introduced himself. He was Chief Reni and he was properly proud of his people and the heritage of these islands.

When I find myself in the good fortune of acceptance in the mind's eye of a guest, I always seek to learn about life ashore as it is lived in this time compared to times passed. I generally try to bring up my interest in the customs regarding marriage, birth and death. These topics seem also to open windows of general conversations and insights. This time was no exception.

Life here was lived in perpetual awareness of the spirits, the greatest of which is the shark. The shark is worshiped here, and its beautiful shape is celebrated by all present day carvers of wood in the Solomon Islands.

The chief may have wanted to weigh his words and or take special care in their choosing, because he announced that he would have the story of his people written for me ashore and would bring them to me in the morning. He was as good as his word.

In it, he recounted the fear that had been held by his people of those of the northwestern islands, for they were cannibals; and with big canoes they would bring large groups of raiding warriors; killing many people and bring the heads back to their islands. Big devil feasts, included killing and eating many pigs always followed. Even very young captured children were bought from the wariers for sacrifice to their gods and then eaten.

Many things were sacred to all of the people, including to the cannibals. The most sacred of which is the shark, but even one's canoe could speak yes or no, as shown by its rocking when no wave has caused it. If it rocked when asked a question, the answer is yes.

He tells of certain pleasures of which only the highest chiefs could participate with women. And that the devils will be angered if a fisherman were to allow certain fish to touch the ground after being caught.

I was very humbled and grateful to him for having his story written specifically for us. *The words of the chief can be found in Appendix C.*

***

That afternoon, we moved a short distance to quieter water. Comfort is always sought. The water looked inviting from afar and "Wow," a modern house was here. What a surprise!

I launched the dinghy, tied a long length of rope to a tree, rowed back to the boat, brought the line aboard, and pulled the bow of the boat toward the front of this lovely house. This securing system for the boat is only used when the water is deep and steep to the shore. By the time I had gotten this done, the owner had come out from the house. I asked him if we might be permitted to tie to his tree and was immediately and enthusiastically assured that we were very welcome to do so. I invited him aboard.

The Humphreys had lived in the Solomons for over thirty years, which he told us in his flowingly beautiful British accent. For many years he had served Her Majesty's government here, during the time of England's protectorate of these islands.

Our talking was unhurried. It was getting to be late in the day as he was taking his departure, so being late; he invited us to come to the house tomorrow for morning coffee.

Our evening aboard was very pleasant and the next mid-morning we were greeted as we came ashore. Peggy had brought a pumpkin pie, made either of pumpkin, or of acorn or Hubbard squash whichever we happened to have aboard, all of which are interchangeable.

They had not had pumpkin pie in years and thoroughly enjoyed it, as we enjoyed the coffee in properly decorative china cups, and the biscuits (in America called cookies) were proper and most delicious.

The morning vanished without notice and the Humphreys accepted our invitation to tea (in America dinner) aboard the *Osprey*. Our days are not divided into those which we enjoy as to those that we don't, but rather by the different types of pleasure of which we are granted. I constantly marvel over this, for we are very simple people, neither seeking nor deserving more than a passing nod.

I don't know how much of this island is owned by the Humphreys. They did tell us that he had built the house himself. And oh, how perfectly lovely a setting in which to enjoy the richness of one's advancing years.

They each had their favorite activities. He cherished his library and among many other interests that gave her pleasure was the approval recently given by her to the rooster for his behavior.

The chickens were there to supply a steady availability of eggs, and in her early perception, the rooster was there without interest in the hens for any other moment than for his brief service. The conversation that she and I were having was somewhat away from the house. The chickens were close to where we were talking, and I had mentioned to her that her rooster certainly was a beautiful creature; and told her that as a child I had always admired them. I was city born, but they seemed like magnificent things, though known to me only vicariously from books. They appeared to be so varyingly marked in the differing coloration of feathers that I have always listed them among my favorite things to see when opportunity presented.

She said that her opinion of this rooster had changed. She said that she had been studiously observing the chickens for over a year before she noticed what was happening. The hens and the rooster would be busily scratching the ground and pecking here and there, all of which seemed to be with total self interest; until she noticed that every now and then the rooster, having apparently just unearthed something special, would make a distinctly different quiet call and immediately a certain hen would raise her head in excitement and run over to him, look where he had just been scratching, reach down with her beak and grab something.

The rooster would have been standing right where he was and watch her accept his gift. Thereupon, she would hurriedly return to where she had been busily scratching, and he too would return to his efforts.

Hanne was fascinated to see that a concern existed on the part of the rooster to the hens, and had since seen him call others to also share a special treat. This was not associated at all with his service. She was delighted by the discovery and by the rooster's interest in the hen's pleasure. And I was delighted to note a pleasant interlude of enjoyment experienced in the life of a retiree, in their adopted land, on a beautiful tropic island, in this far away sea. And I was delighted, not only due to the time available to her to have achieved this discovery, but also in the talent honed to have understood it. There may be a scientist who disputes the results of these observations; I choose to take pleasure in accepting her conclusion. What gentleman would do otherwise?

Yet with all of its allure, we choose to "sail on," (Seeing these happy folks had presented thoughts of our own retirement to come -- or are we in it?).

The day before Peggy and I left their island, we spoke with the Humphreys of our leaving. Charles had asked to keep our guest book over night. The next morning, Hanne told me that others had stopped here before us, but that Charles had not taken the time to write in any of the other yacht's guest books before, other than just a brief comment. She was taking pleasure in the fact that this time he had looked up the exact words to a specific poem as a tribute to us.

In their behalf as much as ours, I pass those words to you:

Chapter 4 — The Solomon Islands

The Humphreys, Tavanipupu Island, Marau Sound, Solomon Islands:

I have never sailed the high sea in a sailing boat, but I should imagine the experience to be akin to that of flying alone in the skies. The latter is well described by a young Canadian *Battle of Britain* pilot by the name of McGee.

He was killed in action a short time later. I first came across his verse during my war-time years as a single engine pilot and was impressed by its beauty and profoundness. I hope you like it.

Oh! I have slipped the surly bonds of earth and danced the skies on laughter silvered wings. Sunward I have climbed and joined the tumbling mirth of sun-split clouds and done a hundred things you have not dreamed of wheeled and soared and swung high in the sunlit silence, hovering there, I've chased the shouting wind along and flung my eager craft through footless halls of air, up the long delirious burning blue I've topped the wind swept heights with easy grace where never lark nor even eagle flew. And while with silent lifted mind I trod the high untrespassed sanctity of space, I put out my hand and touched the FACE of GOD

Hanne and I have enjoyed your short stay in our little haven. We would have liked you to have stayed longer, but you have commitments and new places to see.

Fair winds, wonderful sailing and keep off the reefs.

Charles and Hanne Humphreys

* * *

The capitol of the Solomon Islands is the city of Honiara, about thirty five miles up the coast of Guadalcanal from where the Humphreys live. Those thirty five miles included some jungle barriers but the *Osprey* rather enjoys sailing to that of jungle treks. So for us the distance was easily passed. We were going there to formalize our entry with the boat into the country, and we paid the $100.55 which they called a "light fee" for a two month visa with the boat in presence.

Aqua Vector was at the yacht club when we arrived for our visa formalities. She was not hidden from view. A yacht of seventy-four feet of length, and weighing in at fifty three tons, ketch rigged, and newly built for Neal in New Zealand, is a remarkable sailing vessel whose presence is readily noted.

She was modern in every way. Neal Nunnelly, the owner had an unabashed love affair with this vessel, as well he should have. It was an impressively crafted vessel in every way.

Everybody has problems occasionally and Neal was no exception. In this case it was electronics. His navigation system had failed and the crewman who knew celestial navigation had run out of time and with all but one crewman had flown back home.

As I have mentioned, celestial navigation is all we have, so it was nothing at all to introduce him to the easiest of the procedures, the noon shot. This acquires latitude at which one is sailing, and since he was bound for Australia, he need only sail WSW until gaining the desired latitude at which he wanted to enter Australia, and then just keep sailing due west until he arrives. Without either knowing the math to solve the spherical triangle which is exceedingly cumbersome, or having the sight reduction books and very accurate time, longitude cannot be well determined. But I have a little trick by which even this can be done without calculation if a current nautical almanac is aboard.

So each noon time we would be practicing a sun shot with his sextant, and as is the case with everyone, the results get better each time. After a week or so of this he was ready. Many months later a letter caught up with us confirming their safe passage. He is remembered warmly.

We had the great good fortune to meet John and Caroline Kaliuae at church. We talked together and enjoyed the exchange so much that they invited us to dinner at a hotel. What a lovely time! After dinner they took us home with them to see a movie about the Second World War. Here we were on Guadalcanal, right where the US Marines had landed during the Second World War. We were anchored at the spot. And we could see it from the house, where we watched John Wayne and company reenact the invasion of Guadalcanal. Being here gave us an eerie reality that was chilling. Peggy's uncle JW had charged up this very hill.

As we were preparing our departure from their house, John presented something to me that he had found in his garden. It was a hand grenade from that time. I looked at it. I looked at John. And then with a grin on his face, he took his other hand away.

It had been covering the *pin*. As you know, unless the pin is pulled out, explosion cannot occur. The pin was out. But he immediately showed me that there was no explosive in it. It was just an empty rusted grenade which was being given to me as a memento of this place and that time.

***

We returned to Honiara from John and Caroline's house only about ten miles away, and were back to the boat. "Peg, let's go to the Florida Group. We could go from there to Marova Lagoon on the way to Australia."

She said, "Well, the people on that German boat certainly thought it was great!" And we too found it to be so.

The sea was rough, but the short day sail to The Floridas brought us to a sequence of anchorages with perfectly still waters of such quiet tropic splendor, that ten days were required to pass before forcing us away.

As in most of these smaller tropic islands, we didn't see one car, not one commercial enterprise of any kind. But we did see the shoreline of our little anchorages festooned with flowering plants gracing a hundred hues of green on a hundred different shrubs and bushes beneath the coconut palms. The trees are all bowing slightly to the west. All of their days, the tradewinds have pressed upon them their duty to do so. It seems that even a tree can learn if given enough time.

These were very lazy days for the two of us. We lived quietly and peacefully here. Without any practice, we were a part of this place. Even as that bird was want to move about amongst the loveliness that mantled the shore, we too moved every couple of days by simply lifting the anchor.

In a brief unhurried couple of hours, when coming upon yet another spot of splendor, I would let the boat glide to her chosen spot and silently lower the anchor, for here tranquility and life were one.

The boat was no more than a boat length from the shore, and we were so fully engrossed in all of our surroundings that as we both watched that magnificent blue butterfly approach the branch of a bush on which to land, I knew that the bush didn't really lift that branch slightly to make it easier for that fellow to land and stay awhile. But harmony does seem to be the order of the day. And tropic grandeur is the garment in which these islands are clothed.

To be immersed so deeply within this portrait of perfection, even the air we breathe is delicately touched with the fragrance of flowers, surely it must always have been so but—what's *that?*—that thing, which rust is trying to remove from this perfection! It's part of a sunken war ship piercing the artistic canvas of our lagoon. A grim reminder of the past! And, *what's that?*—they are the cold eyes of a saltwater crocodile, the first that we have seen on our voyage. A grim reminder that today is not without the macabre either.

The spell is broken. Will we ever find it again? Will enchantment be forever lost? Had we actually noticed our being spellbound? Are we even aware of any loss? We know that the night sounds were quiet ones. We know that sleep again performed its incomprehensible mystery. We know that it was just as amusing to awaken trying to yawn through a smile as it was yesterday. The world has not changed, so our mind looking around and finding this to be true, declared it to be a wonderful day. And it was so.

Peggy enjoys finding sea shells of all description. And she permits my companionship in the process. Occasionally, my perpetually irreverent mind, will see us as a couple of barnyard chickens going about pecking here and scratching there and then rush on to search again a little farther onward. Well maybe *rush* is not the word to properly convey our diligence. The chicken analogy can only go so far. I found some nice shells, but Peggy is the real pro here!

The usual array of boat maintenance and repair is cared for upon its presentation. I had repaired the dinghy, made a gasket for the manifold, and did a small sail re-stitching job while we were here in the Floridas, all of which was carefully being supervised by a whole host of kids leaning over my shoulder most of the time.

No other yacht intruded in any of the *Osprey*'s personal lagoons. In this one, a palm trees reached out toward us. Some of the trees must have been half blown over by a storm in their youth which caused them to grow almost horizontally for awhile and afterwards bend them suddenly upward at about a 45 degree angle almost reaching the boat with gifts of coconuts.

We do not pickup coconuts on the beach or elsewhere, not even if there is no village in sight. All of an island is divided amongst the villagers where there is value to be found. That includes every tree. Everything is owned by someone. Copra is a cash crop. It is comprised of the partially dried white meat of the coconut. There are no fences. There are no signs proclaiming *warning no trespassing*. And indeed, trespass may not be comprehended. But respect of property certainly is known here and likewise by us.

Well we have stayed longer than we expected. We aren't accustomed to limiting our time by months, and here in the Solomons we had only two of those, so it's off toward Honiara again for a visa extension and also for a provisioning of Peggy's stores of which fresh is always best.

Leaving Honiara, making toward the *New Georgia Group* of islands, has the cluster of *The Russell Islands* about a third of the way. The Russells show the typical results of having been pushed up from the deep sea floor and give all of the appearance of having been the mountain peak thrust up with only its top breaking sea level. Where the ocean has worn away this upper edge, a barrier of coral has grown which now protects the island from further erosion. And over time, even this protection is enhanced by the gradual formation of small barrier islands upon the coral. Very careful coral avoidance must be taken in all such common areas, and even with such care, an astonishingly high percentage of yachts, manned by very experienced seamen, come to grief in such places.

The Russells present absolutely nothing unusual of which I am aware. Virtually every island group in the South Seas is replete with the same hazards. And very few of the vessels lost are the result of carelessness. Those of us, who have been fortunate to have sailed on, have done so thanks to not having been exposed to the exact set of circumstance which took our friends down. I am anxious to not portray ocean voyaging as a dangerous venture. The sea has, however, been not inaccurately described as unforgiving. To my eye's view, the greatest dangers are from fatigue, and from those hazards at the perimeters of the oceans; that stuff called land, or rock, or coral.

This is the bedrock reality which is rooted in the brain of all who sail the sea. It is too obvious to be actually thought of via studious thought process. It simply resides. And it was present after we had left Honiara.

The wind was not strong when we sailed. But somewhere, a storm had thrown this sea around which now has found us. This sea was rough, even though the wind had not arrived. Visibility was worsening. If this keeps deteriorating it will not leave enough light to safely enter. Was that automatic *situation evaluation* going on undirected within my head? And without being aware that the entire matter had already been discussed and decided upon, I discovered that I had decided not to stop at the Russells.

The wind died. The iron mainsail was engaged so the steering was to be by hand instead of by the windvane. The night passed, not with total drudgery, even though I was certain that the night was considerably longer than usual in passing, in spite of my evidence to the contrary.

The rain had eased. The visibility had increased. And in the fullness of time, and right on schedule, an island had thrown a mountain into the sky to dare us not to see them. Well, with an invitation so grand, how could we refuse?

The land of the great warriors stretched out before us, with Vangunu Island almost touching the big island now called New Georgia Island. Here were the "Northwest Islands," spoken of by the chief in the south. Here the mighty cannibal had struck fear through all of the Solomon Islands. All knew that it was the power of their god of war that made these men invincible. It was my plan to talk to the descendants of those warriors. I wanted to learn of that time. Was it the shark god who led their fathers of old? But I had learned that the shark was worshiped by <u>all</u> of the Solomon Islanders.

Not all conversations with locals are without omissions or embellishment. I like the opportunity to read national history about such topics to broaden my view toward fact, such as a couple of such accounts which came to hand. My motivations are not scholastic, and we do not travel around through the islands of the South Pacific for any cause other than the marvel which we encounter, and for the drama of the *call of the sea* — which is a catch all phrase used because to describe it otherwise is too voluminous and risky for our claim of sanity.

We entered into the Marova Lagoon between the barrier islands, at about 08 degrees East Longitude and 29 minutes South Latitude, with intent to look at the bay on its north coast for a favorable anchorage. Another adventure of the *Osprey* has begun!

* * *

As with many of our ventures, this one started in church too, because here our meeting of people is <u>beyond</u> the nodding of the head and touching of the hand and briefest of eye contact. This is due to our being strange strangers. The people in a small church in a tiny remote US town who suddenly find two people in their congregation of twenty, who look different than they and are circus acrobats having arrived in a horse drawn wagon with surreal pictures of trapezes painted on their wagon, might cause one to look at these people with curiosity.

This analogy fails on the one point of esteem. Because we were wrongly, but always, viewed by the membership in elevation very far beyond any possible due.

Owen and Trish Ringrose, and their three daughters were at church. We had known that they would be here; because we were now at the Batuna Community, where a church headquarters and church boarding school for the entire Solomon Islands is located.

We knew all of this because while we were in New Zealand, we had met this family, and they had told us that they were going to this place as missionaries. Our popping up out of the sea to meet them again was an unexpected surprise, and the cause of even a complimentary excitement expressed upon our walking into the church.

After church we were whisked away to their house where excited talking related the pleasure and delight which the family was having. We happily gave focused listening with unpermitted interruption to each of the children's stories, even though each one of them tried to excitedly interject some omitted detail offered by a sibling. We heard the youngest one first. It was great! Maybe too infrequently the littlest ones are not fully given an opportunity to be actually and fully heard. It was great fun and the camaraderie of the entire family was a delight.

We met many of the folks to our great enhancement of social interaction. We shared time during dinners at many residences; from the most humble to that of the church leaders whose houses were not of luxury by any stretch of the imagination either. Only the difference of house style differed somewhat. But each person was the same of interest and pleasure of acquaintance. Only their life experience differed. And each family felt welcome aboard, as food preparation with sundry mild spice and presentation was enjoyed in the vastly different atmosphere of an ocean sailing yacht.

It is always a gift of such immensity; to be accepted into a community of persons. It is a gift of such elevation and of such personal quality which so many throughout the South Pacific have granted to us, yet it is never diminished by its previous experience.

Owen and Trish needed some supplies from Honiara and as was the custom had scheduled a local small taxi plane to take them. Since they were going to be gone for two days, they invited us to use their bedroom in their absence. We had been shown the house when we had first arrived and had noted that they had a waterbed. Well that sounded appropriate for us. So when invited to come ashore for a night, especially to be enjoying a waterbed for the first time, I was interested to "try it out."

Our constant muffled giggling threatened the success of the outcome of our *trying*, as we continued sloshing about. But two days later, when asked by the Ringroses about our enjoyment of the bed, no one saw the brief side glance that Peggy and I secretly passed one to the other as we both nonchalantly thanked them for a delightful night's sleep.

The *Osprey* was not as fortunate. Someone entered the boat in the night and stole my wrist watch and a Nikon single reflex camera. I reported the matter to the school principal. He announced the theft at a school assembly. Peggy and I had told some stories to the school and we were in fact held in certain esteem by the students.

The school was in an instant buzz. Someone had seen X with a camera. Inquiry was made of X. The camera was returned but the watch was not. It was reported to have been accidentally dropped overboard when the thief was hastily leaving the boat. The brother of the boy who had done this thing came to me. He said that his brother was visiting him at the school and was now gone, but that when he would catch him the next time, he said, "I'll kill him!"

"WAIT wait wait!" – "No, no, <u>NO</u>!" And what followed was my pointing out that the camera was returned and I gave lengthy assurance that I forgive the boy, etc. and that I require that he no longer plan payback against his brother, and that no shame is on him or his family, and that I hold no anger over this. It is finished. — Well, he accepted my requirement without enthusiasm, but I am content that the brother would not be violently pursued at some future time.

The weather remained radiant. The island remained glorious to be seen, as was its astonishing bird life. We had a wonderful time. But it had also been a long time since we had been to any place where an American Express office was located. So our cash was depleted. There is no AMEX office here in the Solomons. So the church headquarters was kind enough to cash a $500 check for us. I hope this revelation doesn't get anyone in trouble for violating church policy. Is that why I have not mentioned the name of church denomination which we attend, (he says with tongue in cheek and glint of eye). I need not, but do hasten to point out that funds did reside in the bank to cover that check. Peggy has always managed all of our expenditures, and due to her proper grasp of our purse strings, these funds as all prior or subsequent cash usage has been judicious; with some few but notable exceptions during our marriage, such as buying airplanes or real estate of which at one time I had thought to possess special knowledge. And although these things were not purchased secretly, they were not on her priority list. Boats fell in this category as well, and the *Osprey* was not the first, though only two preceded it.

It was a fond farewell expressed between us and the Ringrose family, and the teachers and several students, as we rowed the dinghy back to the *Osprey*. We were almost immediately underway for a couple of hours sail to another little island. We met another gracious family with whom we got instantly acquainted. Sometimes it just happens that way. And when it was learned by them of our interest in the shark worship, the wife, joyous to have information which we were seeking, said "Well, my parents are Shark Worshipers." And I had my source of reliable information.

***

There are many important events which occur here at the death of a man, especially if he is someone of high standing. He is buried in the ground as soon as possible. However, before his death, he will have told the family how long the grieving period shall be during which time the oldest son must keep ashes on his head. And that a feast is to mark the end of the grieving time which will be for all of the people of the family including those from distant places. However, the eldest son must continue to wear the ashes for a month or so after the feast.

Then, the son will go to the grave and say, "I am your son. I have come to take your head." whereupon, he will dig up his father's head to bring it to the place where the Spirit Leader calls for the Shark. This is the place where he makes worship to the shark at the required intervals and is where the Spirit Leader gives offerings to it. This is a place of extreme taboo. No woman may go there. And since I didn't ask if I be permitted to go there, in a full reversal of all of my prior behavior, I went anyway. I tell myself that no one told me that I couldn't.

The place where the son brings his father's head is at a very narrow projection of land from the shore. At the very point of this sand is where the priest calls the Shark. There is a narrow path on which he walks. It goes straight to the end point of the land. On each side of the path and close to it are cairns (rock piles in pyramid shapes). These rocks are about grapefruit size and are piled about three or four feet high, not coming quite to a point. Atop each of these many cairns a miniature house is mounted. It is about eight inches wide, eight inches at wall height, and about twenty-four inches long with rafters and a ridge pole about six inches above the walls. The sides of the house are covered by woven fiber. The roof is thatch. Both ends of the house are entirely open.

The son will place the head of his father in the center of the house facing the opening which points directly to where the priest worships the Shark. The preparation for the father's worship house, are done by the son during the grief and preparation time. He must firstly gather the proper rocks. The cairn must be approved and blessed by the Spirit Leader. The construction of the miniature house must also be approved by the priest before the time of digging up his father's head.

I stood here. I stood where the priest calls the Shark. From where I stood, I could look back into the little houses. I could see the recent and the ancient skulls, *as it were*, looking back at me. I did not ask them how long they had been here in their silence. Yet I wondered about the millennium that some of their sightless eyes may have looked at where I now stand, and I wondered what their lives may have been like. And I wondered about the sound of the echo of laughter which they would have shared with their children those eons ago.

But other echoes are *heard* here too. There were bad times. These people were devil worshipers and cannibals as they roamed this sea in giant canoes; a time when even young children were sold as living sacrifice. A permanent red stain is upon such history. But such stain is the result of devilry and of a time gone by and is not passed down through the DNA. So if we must remember, let us all remember to never return to such dark times. Let us all beware.

Here and now, these times are good times. There is laughter everywhere. Nothing is so complete, as the joyous laughter of a child. As we move about this island with the boat, children often showed us their treasures as we walked the beach. It might be a stick of drift wood, or an oddly shaped rock or a lovely little shell. We would always stop at such occasions and look with equal rapture at such wondrous treasure and turn it in all directions in our hands with appropriate oohings and ahhings, all to the total appreciation of each child, for their entire world is one of marvel.

Peggy was the person approached to buy things. Even here it seems that the woman is known to hold the power of purchase. There were necklaces, baskets, little carved turtles and sharks and *Nusa Nusas* being offered for her to buy.

* * *

The Nusa Nusa is now a nationally recognized icon, rather like the Statue of Liberty is for the US. The Nusa Nusa is a figurine which was the ancient symbol of the god of the people of the Marova Lagoon Islands here in the northwestern area of the Solomon Islands.

These were the cannibals whose Great War canoes raided all of the surrounding islands. These were the warriors who took back to their villages the heads of the slain. These were those whom all the other islands feared, for it was their god who was stronger than the one protecting the island of the people being invaded.

The god of these terrible warriors was the dog god. And their Great War canoes had a figurine mounted on the front of each canoe which was carved as having a man/dog head with hands that carry a skull. So the logical final result was, "If you can't beat them, join them." And all of the islands of the Solomons took the dog god as theirs.

Everybody was traveling around with the same Nusa Nusa, but everyone also had a figurine for their canoe whose hands carried a bird, which safely indicated that they had come to trade, not to attack.

Peggy finds in our boat's guest book, that during our thirty-five days in the Marova Lagoon, 110 people visited the *Osprey*. Each was given something, if only a drink of Kool-Aid. And at the Island of Telina, to everyone's absolute delight, Peggy made pancakes for twenty people and for us. What a breakfast!

John Wayne lives here. John Wayne's reputation is spread throughout the entire country at least by all those with whom we discussed carvings. Everyone spoke of him with near awe. Oh no, this is not the Hollywood actor. This is a local man, also of our church membership, whose craft is known as magnificent art as proclaimed by everyone who knows his work. And here he is. He has come out to us in his canoe and introduced himself to us.

He knew that we were coming in his direction, and knowing that we were members of the same church as he, he was looking forward to meeting us. He had brought some fruit with him on which we were all munching happily as we talked of many pleasant things. He had many children, and asked if we might have some mosquito netting which he might buy. Apparently his brood had outgrown the present mosquito protection barrier of their sleeping accommodations and he needed an enlargement.

Peggy not only knows what we have aboard, but she also knows where everything is! And sure enough we had some which we happily gave to him. Later in the day we came ashore to meet the family and to see John's present commissioned work. One of his specialties is intertwined sea life in an intricate upright spire of amazing sculpture in wood. We spent the day together.

We met many other interesting folks at church. Many who overcame their shyness visited us aboard the boat. One of these was Steven. He brought some shark carvings to us. Even though sharks are not worshiped by the Christians such as Steven, they still hold the position of highest beauty form in the eye of the people. And indeed, the shark to me too is a creature of beauty in form, but its reputation spoils that for many, Peggy and me included.

He told us that he had hoped to trade some carvings for some plastic dishes. So Peggy showed him that we had some plastic dishes (not my favorite for sure) but they were exactly what he was longing for, and Peggy had a set for eight. His eyes glistened in anticipation as I indicated that there was a carving that I wanted done. I described it to Steven. Peggy liked the idea of the exchange and Steven said that he could do it and would happily receive the dishes for the work.

We had a full set of china dishes aboard which were for our daily usage and had never been broken thus far on our voyage, so we were not going to be eating out of coconut shells at the loss of those plastic things.

Steven was ecstatic. He said the carving would be ready in a week. We didn't have much time left on our visa permit, but a week still gave us time. However, he did not have a suitable piece of wood for the job. He wanted *kerosene wood* for the carving and we would need to sail to another island to find some.

We left immediately. And in less than an hour of motoring we had the anchor down again and Steven and I went ashore to find a tree that had an appropriate shape. This was not a matter of strolling around; this was cutting our way through brush and undergrowth with a machete. And still Steven would not be satisfied. We went back to the boat. Moved to another section of this uninhabited island and tried again, this time successfully. We cut a dead branch that looked good to him, cutting it a little longer than necessary for the project, and we returned to John Wayne's island where Steven could begin his work at his own island house. He started by cutting out the basic shape, which he then brought to the boat to fit it to the intended place where it was to be mounted. The next day he returned for the final fitting with some of the porpoises already started, but wrongly so.

The wheel house has a curved overhead (roof) which has a very large aftward-sliding hatch which uncovers the entire cockpit well to just aft of the wheel position. A curved frame of the over-head forms the shape to which the sliding plywood hatch is attached. And it is to the face of this curved frame that I want the carving of the porpoises attached; showing them in various positions amongst the waves, all of which must be on the forward face of the wheel house frame, not the top where one usually thinks waves and porpoises to be.

Although I had explained this to Steven, he must have had visions of beautiful plastic dishes dancing in his head and on his table, but fortunately he was caught just in time to change the design. After all, to bring to a vertical surface a horizontal scene and make it look as though it is part of the horizon which carries onward away from you is quite a trick to require the eye to perform without awareness. But I got it into his head the second time around, and he—by that magic with which true artists are endowed—brought back exactly what was in my mind. It was perfection. Nineteen porpoises, I just counted them, are cavorting about through six waves on a curved piece of *kerosene wood* just over three feet long and four inches high. Some of them are crossing in front of others, all going from left to right in the direction of travel such as we are accustomed in writing. And thanks to the great work of an artist by the name of Steven, on the South Pacific Ocean Islands of the Solomons, now there live in perpetuity, nine ever smiling porpoises created from his hand. Beautifully done Steven.

The unnoticed nod of our heads in passing these porpoise, and a smile of which even we ourselves are unaware, are none the less a constant tribute to the artist from whose hand porpoises swim across the mantle of our fire place. They have chosen this place for their play when the *Osprey* could no longer serve as host.

Peggy insisted that Steven accept a set of silverware from us, to go along with the dishes. The twenty dollar bill which she included left us just enough money with which to fill our fuel tanks with diesel for our departure to Australia. As it turned out, in a few days we left the Solomon Islands with twenty five cents with Australia as a frail thought of a far distant horizon from here. But we were not gone yet.

* * *

Everyone knew where it was. It was a Japanese war plane, still intact, and under water in the lagoon. I wanted to see it and was surprised to see it in such shallow water. The water was only about twenty-some feet deep and of course the water was perfectly clear. Every detail of the plane could be seen from the dinghy. I swam down to it, aware of the crocodile seen a few days earlier. Crocodiles were becoming less of an oddity.

I could tell from the surface that by US designation, it was a Zero; a fantastically maneuverable fighter aircraft. Its position looked as though it had landed there by intent. I reached the plane easily. By all appearances it could have ended its flight here yesterday. Only the paint seemed slightly faded. Between breaths I swam around it, first at the trailing edge of the left wing. I felt the aileron. They still moved slightly. I got another lungful of air and dived to the tail section pulling myself down the leading edge of the rudder and swam along the fuselage downward on the right side and briefly under the right wing to see the painted red sun duplicating the flag of Japan. The next dive brought me to the tight one man cockpit. My feet were straight up, my head straight down; I was in front of the open cockpit which I entered no farther than my shoulders before that ever insistent demand for air forced me back up to today.

I chose to not go down again. In my hand I held a small piece of that day. It was a piece of jagged metal that I had kept bending until it broke. I don't know why I wanted it. Was it because I too have slipped the surly bond of earth in a plane no larger than this? I am ill equipped to ask such questions much less to answer them. But there were recalled moments down there—nothing mystical in any way, but things remembered in detail. While holding my breath underwater, when grasping that aileron, I vividly remembered it. I had planned to land on the other side of the mountains. But when I came to the mountains there was a long cloud bank as far as I could see in both directions as the mountain range spread. The tops of the peaks were covered. I flew higher. However, above the clouds now, I could only see more clouds stretching to the horizon beyond the mountains. I flew farther over the mountains until time told me that I was beyond them. I still had fuel to turn back when I came to it. It was a hole in the cloud cover. I could see the earth below. I dove for it and then started a really tightly left turning spiral downward, barely able to keep at the edge of the opening of the clouds. There is nothing worse than hitting a granite cloud. One is busy with procedure during maneuvers of any kind, but these are moments of time that fix themselves in our mind, even such simple things as these can be as vivid in our memory as the ecstasy of a first kiss.

With a couple of strong strokes of the diving fins and pull of the arms, I came over the stern of the dinghy and rowed back to the *Osprey* and to Peggy. I kissed her cheek with a salty wet face, hosed myself with some fresh water and soon, sun dried; ravished Peggy's lunch as we talked about the war plane and about the day. Peggy had seen the plane from the dinghy but not from the water. Somehow, she is comfortable with just my unexpected kiss upon her cheek. Today is not yesterday. The war is gone, and life is good, even

The Solomon Islands   Chapter 4

though our permitted stay in the Solomons is drawing swiftly to an end. We need to be bound for Gizo.

* * *

We lowered the anchor in an appropriate spot in the tiny harbor of Gizo, a port of entry and departure. Tomorrow the Customs office would be open and our clearance for Australia will be issued. I put the sunshade awning up for added comfort while Peggy was busy waving magic wands about, to create our dinner. We ate in the cockpit with the side windows rolled up. The harbor was calm. The breeze was gentle and comfortable as we looked about at the life of Gizo.

Little could be seen of people moving about in the small town. While on the other side of the harbor, we had a perfect view of a very small community comprised of maybe fifteen houses. The houses were built over the water. They were built on stilts. One walkway, also of course on stilts, came from the shore and joined all the houses together.

The houses were very small. I watched a young man perhaps in his twenties walk down the walkway. He was very slender and walked rather listlessly it seemed to me, as though he didn't actually have anywhere to go. I watched him. And I asked myself, "If I had been born in one of these houses, how on earth could I get from there to here?"

Sure, there was Gizo. But there wasn't much in Gizo other than government people transferred here from Honiara. The concept of pulling one's self up by one's boot straps seems impossible. How could I ever get out of such a place? I felt that I would simply not be able to do it. I watched the young man. I hope he finds a way, or finds contentment where he is.

Contentment can be found. There can be great joy in bringing home a fish to proudly place before one's wife whereby a special treat of cooking aroma and taste brings broader smiles. And when there is no fish, a shrug of the shoulder when warmed by a smile can mean, "Maybe tomorrow."

Just as easily as I can place myself in his house, I can just as easily see that the only difference between us is where we happen to find ourselves born. We both feel the same emotions. We share the same sunrise. But oh my, that few hundred feet of distance between us is a chasm that were I he, I could never cross.

I was relieved when we were checked out of the country and I had the anchor back aboard. The scene of the stilt houses had come with a shudder up my back. One island remained on our departure course. It was the last island of the Solomons which we would see. Having checked out, we would not be going ashore, but to anchor is legal. And it gives us a final place of preparations for another sea voyage. The chart showed a well protected anchorage about a hundred or so feet wide and a few hundred feet in total length.

We made toward the island a short distance away. And as we entered, we were astonished to see men climbing the steep grey stone cliff face of the fjord like walls surrounding us. These walls were only thirty or so feet high but the men climbed by finger strength in tiny crevices and little foot holds while collecting bird eggs to the very apparent objection of the parents. The eggs are considered a delicacy. Some of the men stopped at the boat to offer to sell or trade something for the eggs, but we respectfully declined.

In the morning, we completed our final preparations for sea, and as the anchor nested in its accustomed secure position for a voyage, the Solomon Islands and its people took permanent residence in the dedicated area of our minds reserved for fond memories as the Islands themselves now began to sink below the horizon into the sea.

CHAPTER 5

 TOWARD AUSTRALIA

It was a great breakfast. Peggy knew that she wasn't going to be rushed. We had slept well in this quiet little anchorage on this our last island of the Solomons. Wondrous glimpses of the ancestors of these good people had been shared with us; as well as the joyous events of the present day life of these folks who enjoy their days upon these tropic isles of The South Pacific Ocean.

Thank you for including us in the lovely events of your daily lives. The people of the Solomon Islands have been graciously kind to us during our stay, which was far more brief than we would have wished.

Pancakes with fruit preserves can launch a glorious day! And a sparkling day it is with which to start our voyage to the biggest island on the planet. It's a *continental* island!

We had been sailing comfortably though a little slowly. The wind was perhaps seven knots from the east. Not one cloud was in the sky. From the cockpit, I was walking forward on the starboard deck when I sucked in a quick half lung full of air. And just as quickly, while holding that almost gasp, I looked from *it* to the rigging above my head. The *it* was a steel nut laying on the edge of the cabin top.

Things like this do not just fall out of the sky—they have come from doing a job at the end of a bolt! As my head was turning upward, my mind fingered its way through the file record of such things aloft and had found only one place where a nut of that size belonged. So in the millisecond required to look upward, my head had already been instructed where to look. So I was not surprised to see that it was indeed off the bolt which secures the spreader to the mast.

The wire rigging for the mast which runs from the sides of the deck to the masthead holds the mast upright on the boat; and the *spreaders* on a mast, by pushing the wire out from a straight line, causes great pressure to be forced against the mast from both sides, thereby keeping the mast straight in the mid sections. We could possibly lose the mast overboard by breaking it if a spreader were to come down during hard sailing.

Attached to the mast there is a U-shaped bracket with a hole in each end and one in the center which receives a bolt passing through it and through the mast and through the U bracket on the other side of the mast which keeps them attached accordingly. The spreader is built with a steel projection on both sides at the inboard end which attaches to that U-shaped bracket by a bolt which in turn passes through the U on the mast and the brackets on the spreader. The nut which secures the starboard side spreader had worked loose up there out of sight, and the bolt was already out of one side of its bracket and half way outward on the last side.

Fortunately we were on a tack which had the pressure on the opposite side spreader, so it was going to be easy to solve this problem by going aloft, reinserting the bolt, and replacing the nut which happily had not gone overboard. I grabbed the nut and put it into my pants pocket and went below to where Peggy was, showed the nut to her which instantly changed her expression to serious concern. I told her about the starboard lower spreader and what we were immediately going to do about it.

Having left our last port of the Solomons over a day ago, we certainly were not going back if not required. The sea conditions were very moderate, so I can certainly go up in the boatswain's chair without danger. I'll take down the mainsail which will enable my legs to be holding around the mast while freeing my hands for working. The two headsails will keep the boat underway and the windvane will keep the boat on course; whereby we won't be getting broadsided by the waves which could set up a rolling motion to give me problems aloft.

We will attach the mainsail halyard to the boatswain's chair to get me up there, and Peggy will use the electric anchor winch which Bob and Jane gave to us, to effortlessly do the job of lifting me. The whole thing is going to be a piece of cake!

I silently cheered Bob and Jane all the way up to my perched position. We used to do this in ports with a five fall block and tackle system by my pulling myself up as Peggy took up the slack of the line around a halyard winch on the mast. This held my weight between pulls. It required team work at the call of, "One two three PULL." That took some work on my part because I was lifting my own weight in that process. This, however, was going to be effortless and great! And having mounted that anchor winch on the aft end of the house above the bridge deck, made a wonderful place for Peggy's comfort as well as for her security during any heavy weather conditions, much less for the gentle conditions of today.

I called, "Okay" to Peggy, when she got me to the right height and she tied the halyard off on a cleat. I confirmed that I would need no other tools than the ones already in the pail which she was going to send up to me using the flag halyard, and as she was coming forward to send the bucket up to me, I swung out to check the spreader attachment at its outboard end where it is affixed to the shroud. I was feeling so pleased that this simple little problem was being resolved so effortlessly by the power of electric energy from the batteries instead of the use of all the tackle as used by the old square sail driven vessels of yesteryear as we had previously been required to do. Ah this modern world does have its advantages. As I was being effortlessly levitated up the mast I said, "I like this!"

Such were my feelings as I pushed myself outward off the side of the mast to check the condition of the attachment of the spreader to the standing rigging. I should have been paying attention to the obvious rather than enjoying my reverie, because as I swung outward my weight pulling off center on the masthead instantly (of course) caused the boat to heel sideways – and I went right past the end of the spreader and the standing rigging, out into space – and the farther I swung, the farther my weight, which was being carried by

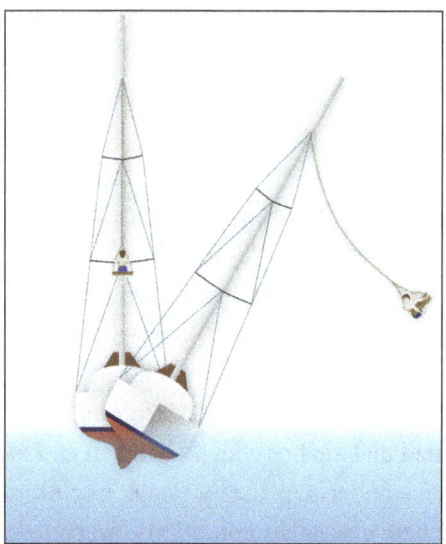

the height of the mast as a fulcrum, swung the boat rapidly farther over sideways until her ten tons of righting effort not only stopped me from being dunked into the water way out here some thirty feet away from the boat, it snatched me back as it righted itself as though I were at the end of a giant whip with a handle fifty feet long and at the end of a whipping line twenty-five feet long, being snapped by a fellow with an arm having ten tons of power.

My posterior was off the plank which comprised the boatswain's chair seat from which I was falling off backwards. But I had clamped one leg into a bend which caught the plank of the chair behind my knee and held it there. The other leg had been thrown straight up into the air as my back was about parallel to the horizon.

The problem was that I was now flying back toward the mast in a way which would have offered my head as a battering ram against the mast. Somewhere in the depth of my soul I must have felt a concern for the wellbeing of the mast, but I must confess that my only recognized concern was for my skull. Were I to impact the mast at this speed, at the very least I would be knocked out of consciousness and therefore flung from my grip into space—but there was no time to contemplate anything other than prevention, and immediately started twisting body and all movable parts in wild gyrations to get myself turned to face the point of impact in order to stave off some of the speed to whatever I was about to hit.

The first of these efforts brought me to the mast where I had just enough time to let go of my seat with both hands to slow my impact by cushioning the speed of the hit by the full effort of pushing with all my might against the mast as my arms were bending at the elbows just before my bashing into the mast with various parts of mainly my upper body. There was just enough time to quickly grab the halyard that carried me as I was thrown out again by the quick roll of the boat only to be snatched back again toward the mast—this time smashing into the wire rigging with my shoulder and upper arm because I couldn't get myself twisted around in time to partially fend off.

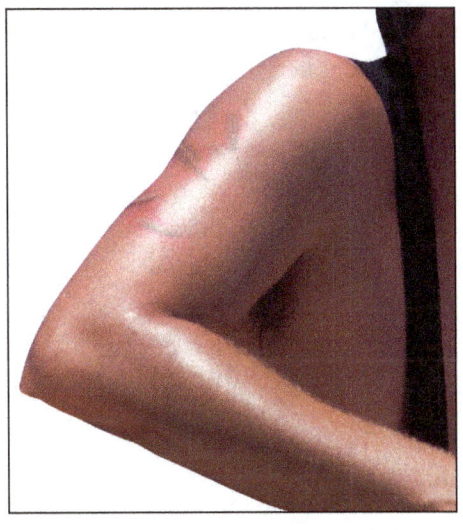

I had lost count of the repetitions. I was being pulverized. I had been whipped about like this however, for probably no more than half a dozen times when I had the good fortune to finally get myself twisted around into a perfect approach from which I could fend off to a speed of survivable impact and yet be in alignment to also then get both hands to make contact simultaneously enough that I got a grasp of the mast.

It would have taken a "jack hammer" to have loosened that grip. The boat settled down from her rolling. Peggy, who had been enjoying this show no more than I, sent the required tools up to me and the matter was resolved with no further drama.

I used a cotter pin from our parts supply to prevent the nut from future misadventure, by inserting it through the hole in the bolt for its purpose of providing a barrier to retain that nut. When the mast was rebuilt and enlarged in New Zealand, this cotter pin was somehow overlooked. Its absence was not noted by the skipper who is ultimately responsible for all things. I am humbled accordingly. And right now I also happen to be bruised and battered a bit.

Actually, the impact of the individual strands of the wire that make up each of the standing rigging cables were each clearly imprinted on my hide where the bone had stopped the compressions of hide and tissue in those impacts.

But all things considered, my skeletal construction was not impaired and the bruising of muscle and tissue is a short lived inconvenience. The entire event lasted much less time than you have taken to read about it and the illustration on the previous page may give an even quicker view of the event.

Peggy did an overview of my person and finding no gushing wounds, she divested herself of the words which she had been unable to voice due to her having held her breath between gasps. But I smiled, so she smiled, and all was well. We put the tools away, raised the mainsail; and although the grace with which I moved about for a day or so may not have gotten me into the Bolshoi Ballet Company, the boat was doing all of the work anyway and comfort returned to its accustomed reign aboard the good ship *Osprey*.

A couple of days jam-packed to overflowing with the leisurely life aboard an ocean sailing vessel, crowned with nothing but pleasantry and passion, followed one day after the other. Each day of ocean cruising is always a heady day.

The bruises were long forgotten. Only delight reigned supreme where all was right with the world and no dangers lurked to dismay; for I had chosen a course that would pass all reefs and islands well clear; and in fact I had added to that factor by a considerable margin. After all, what can it matter if we reach Australia on day X or day Y? A secure course, most free of hazard, is always the choice.

This was the fifth day after having left the last of the Solomon Islands. Night had quietly found its way to this part of our water wonder world. The moon was brilliant and almost entirely full. The sailing was gentle and caressing. The temperature of the night lost the battle for perfection being waged by our environment to see who could claim the highest posture of perfection, because equally has all factors of our surrounding united to achieve that rare occasion of *uniquely perfect experience*. The beauty beyond compare of a cloudless starry night to grace a glorious moon; a pleasant sea breeze wafting a lovely ocean-cruising yacht along her chosen way; two persons wed by bond and soul to inhabit such perfection within themselves as well as this entire world where literal perfection also securely reigned, is to be found only in tales which begin with the words, "Once upon a time."

During the twenty-nine day crossing of that big chunk of the South Pacific from the Galapagos Islands to the easterly most of the Tahitian Islands, I read a small book and afterward was jealous of having lost those couple of days because it was at the expense of having lost the experience of that part of the voyage.

Peggy had recently acquired a portable "Walkman" tape player with such exquisitely magnificent music, that when she asked me if I would like to listen with earphones while on watch, I thought that I might even surpass the magnificence of our surroundings by this added enjoyment–as though perfection can be exceeded.

I stepped from the moon-filled night into the cabin below and took the Walkman from Peggy's hand, covered my ears with the earphones and was enthralled by this little device transporting me to the front row of a marvelous performance of a truly great orchestra. It was beauty in the extreme.

And so it was that after just a few minutes time that I stepped back out into this other world, having actually added to the experience of my sensory perception capacity. Someone else's words once said, "My cup runneth over," for it was truly so–when in *super slow motion* I was slammed into disaster!

I was still fiddling with the Walkman as I turned myself in the process of sitting down on the cockpit starboard seat, turning so that I would be facing forward. I was still fiddling with this thing as I brought both legs up toward the cushioned seat. But before my feet got to the cushions all of the electric currents carrying data to the neurons that jump around between my brain cells all carried a joint shout yelling, "***What's that ?***"

It wasn't that things were moving in slow motion, it only seemed that way because the brain was functioning in super fast survival mode! And even the processing of the various procedures of its millisecond leafing through past memories to identify what the eyes had sent for information was being clearly followed in real time awareness, apparently for the purpose of wanted help from any source to identify what appeared as an unknown and therefore a possible threat. And it was indeed a threat – a threat to our lives!

The process of the brain went like this:

A. I see something strange.
B. As my head turned in the process of sitting with the eyes focused on the Walkman, peripheral vision had seen something white.
C. It is long – too long – it is strange. The first file found a similarity and said, "It's a really long bed sheet."
D. Rechecking all files, "Why would a bed sheet be here and in the water?"
E. "It's too long for sheets"—

And here normal brain systems returned, for the observing of this brain function had all occurred in microseconds. My feet had not yet reached the cushions as I spun around, leaped to my feet as my eyes focused on a line of white about two feet high.

I was on the starboard side of the boat looking from right to left, toward the direction of our travel. The white line continued unbroken. As it reached forward it rushed increasingly closer to our course. It curved toward us. And as my head spun to look forward I had already identified what it was!

When my head finally finished its super slow motion turn (for so it seemed to my brain) I saw that we were right now rushing into whiteness which was right now directly in front of us and as my head continued its turn I could see that the whiteness was also to the left of our bow as well – and we were already entered into the whiteness with the forward most part of the boat!

"Peggy! Quick!" Somewhere during these milliseconds I had removed those earphones, had done something with the Walkman, processed all visual inputs, of course needed no discussion time with my brain cells who were all continued to yell, "Go! Go! Go!" because I was already in survival mode and I was going!

I had started the engine, cast off all sheets on the way to the ratlines, and up I went to get the best view possible to find a way out of the coral reef which we were by now totally surrounded, which was reaching with greedy claws to tear the *Osprey* to shreds!

It was night! But the moon was bright and had refused to allow a cloud to pass between us to darken the way! Peggy was at the helm and with my call she had turned the boat to hard left and engaged the propeller when I called for propeller with slow turns just to keep forward movement or fast as called.

I could, of course, see no water depth. My call of right or left turn was based only on the way the waves curled over the coral ahead of us in their whiteness. We were surrounded by whiteness. We were in the midst of the surf. We were in the midst of the coral reef itself. Peggy made no sound. She turned the boat as I called for it, and gave a short blast of propeller thrust as called; and we snaked our way through what seemed an endless maze.

I could watch underwater with my minds eye as the hull passed within inches of one coral disaster after another, with the propeller spinning so close to the tops of other coral. It gnawed at the pit of my stomach!

The projection of my mind's view of the underwater reality of our process as seen only as related to the seething of the sea and the choices being made with such limited information, while utter disaster or survival itself turned on each out come, was chilling. Time stood still, as though each star was mesmerized by the drama being played out by two frail creatures seeking to survive.

And then it happened!

An actual smile was clearly visible on the face of the *man in the moon*. At long last we had cleared the reef! This coral was many miles from any surface land.

An explanation of this event:

In coastal navigation where the tide runs into a land mass and rushes currents hither and thither, tidal effects are calculated and considered accordingly. But for these years of ocean sailing where the small islands pose no slowing to the endless tidal lump of water being pulled upward by the moon and sun, tides are of no significance and therefore are ignored.

But here, just south of the gigantic Louisiads Lagoon of New Guinea , that lump of water which has freely been traveling across the vast South Pacific Ocean undeterred, now runs into the Continent of Australia and it can't go through it. The shortest route is to go over the north portion of it. Water has piled up on Australia's east coast and the following tides are shoved northward along this huge lagoon and then through the Torres Straits. The currents are horrific and northward.

I had set a course with a margin of safety well to the south of where we would pass clear of the southern extension of the Louisiads by many miles, but alas, I had (to our near peril), failed to properly attribute this current's effect on the very slow speed of our progress which therefore had this extremely long grasp upon us and our course, and which therefore had inexorably continued its silent shoving of the *Osprey* northward of our chosen course so that even my huge safety margin of course selection was not enough.

Having spoken to some who have lost their boat right here, it is seldom that just one condition or event was the cause of their loss. Even such a small thing as a momentary interruption of normal vigilance, such as listening to grandly glorious music in this instance, prevented an otherwise early observation of an approaching reef and thereby its normal evasion procedure can cost the loss of a vessel or even the lives of those aboard. Music is no culprit. Breathless white-knuckled steering at sea is not called for either. The point here is the simple fact that even innocent events can accumulate to suddenly change the intoxication of pleasant enjoyment to absolute disaster; and where one moment a beautiful, proud and capable ocean cruising yacht can grace a scene, she can also vanish from it never to be seen again.

But it is so with all things and all life. The closer that true disaster has stood in way of our course, the more aware we are of the simple joys which it could take away– the sight and sound and touch of one we love, the sight of the boat braced against the wind as her motion eases her through the seas, the sound of the whispered wind and the touch of the tongue to your sea-salted lip are, however, not lessened by specters such as these. It is rather the entirety of every event presented throughout our lives, those of all shades and hue, which lavish the savored choices that we make. I only know that it is thus for me. And so, I smile.

A couple of days later, the good ship *Osprey* passed securely through another majestic wonder, this one seen even from outer space. It is the Great Barrier Reef. It is a marvelously magnificent living entity. It teems with life. It is vibrant with the beauty of color, of shape, of coral and of inhabitants.

We were in the waters of Australia. We were on the threshold of yet another and different experience for the *Osprey* people. We have arrived in Australia!

CHAPTER 6

 Down Under

The voyaging cruisers of the western South Pacific mostly seem to choose Cairns, Australia to wait out the passing of the cyclone season—which obviously occurs six months after the northern hemisphere's event, and is the reason why we too chose Cairns as our destination. Actually, the islands near the equator are also mostly unaffected by cyclones, but yachts have been forced to leave during this period due to visa time limitations. And even when a new visa can be obtained, one may be required to fly to another country and obtain the new visa from its embassy there. We had this happen to us a couple of years later. And then there is the cruising permit for the boat which has on occasions required the sailing to another country before renewal.

As we have mentioned in the past, at certain times of the day, cruising vessels with amateur radio equipment aboard, meet on a certain radio frequency for the purpose of contacting each other, and or to report positions at sea in order to receive weather forecasts for that specific location.

Prior to our departure from the Solomons, we had monitored the passage of two Americans aboard their Chinese Junk making from Papua New Guinea to Australia. All of us with armature radio could recognize the voice of Joyce. She never missed a radio schedule. Unfortunately, she and her good husband Stoney, (an apparent informal delineation of his last name), were having some difficulty. A steering problem was plaguing them in the area of the Great Barrier Reef plus, after recording the light flashing sequence of a lighthouse at the reef, they could find no such light signal in their book of navigation lights for Australia. Among many other things, the book states the latitude and longitude position of a lighthouse. They were desperate to identify this lighthouse so that they could not only know for certainty their location but to also know if the pass through the reef was north or south of the lighthouse, or if the lighthouse was warning that no passage was safe here. Our concern for them also lay with the fact that Stoney was reported to be considerably weakened by a serious health condition. Joyce, though being the perpetual voice on the radio, may have been thought rather less expert in seamanship.

We never heard a resolution of the lighthouse identification problem, but we were greatly eased of our concern upon hearing that they arrived safely in Cairns and were moored at the Cairns Cruising Yacht Squadron where we too were bound. We were subsequently to find ourselves in somewhat of a dilemma when we too approached the Great Barrier Reef. Our skies were perpetually covered by cloud after we left the Louisiads astern, so no celestial navigation was possible and as you know this is our only navigation availability other than "Dead Reckoning."

I had no absolute certainty of our exact location, so being at the north of the small island where we failed to be able to identify a lighthouse, I chose to move cautiously westward, prepared to come quickly about if the reef suddenly presented itself. It didn't, and we passed through what turned out to be a very sizable opening which happened also to have been the one used by Stoney and Joyce, as we were subsequently to learn.

The entire long length of the Great Barrier Reef is an almost unbroken sequence of separate reefs with very infrequent small atolls occurring; but there are openings of various widths that are to be found. These passes through the reef may be separated by considerable distances.

There is a very great hazard which we were to find at each of our subsequent returns to Australia. The Australian coastline was never seen from our deck level before we were at the reef, wherefore no warning of its great danger exists before one is actually at the reef. Even the great good Captain Cook had trouble here.

A few days of sailing southward brought us to the approach of Cairns. This too was a pleasant sail and the reef afforded us reasonable comfort as we slept each night at anchor within this vast lagoon.

At Cairns, we presented ourselves to the authorities of Customs and Immigration, and then carried on into Smith's Creek, setting an anchor in water that was without ripple much less wave. Our comfort by virtue of the ease of the boat's motion was at last assured. This was going to be a very pleasant interlude as we were to watch the land and people of Australia as the passage of time occurred. We were going to get acquainted with some Aussies!

Bob and Jane, of the US yacht *Brown Palace*, who had been here a year or so ago, had written to us about Cairns. And the information of significance in our memory was that their letter said, "While you're there, be sure to look up Olgert and Margret Upiti."

We asked the yacht club folks if they knew them and discovered that everybody knew them! They were an Australian couple who were members of the yacht club and were living aboard their sailboat right here in Smith's Creek. We rowed over to their boat and introduced ourselves as friends of Bob and Jane who were fondly remembered by them. They graciously invited us aboard and we reciprocated by inviting them to dinner aboard the *Osprey* a few hours hence. The yachting community does not often encumber itself with distant social scheduling.

Dinner with friends is entirely encompassed by the mutual enjoyment of the comradery. Although the hosts endeavor to enhance the pleasure of their guests by palatal pleasures, it is the simplest of pleasures which attract us; such as the most lovely of all transformations occurring upon our planet, by which an acquaintance morphs into that most marvelous of all creation—a friend.

Without exception within our experience, yachtsmen are gregarious creatures. Ocean cruisers by definition deprive themselves of this human tendency, which may speak to our enjoyment in meeting folks when we do pop up out of the sea into a community of other people's bustling lives.

Chapter 6 — Down Under

Peggy's dinner was a creation of pride and relished by all of us as we spoke of many things, when though none of us had moved, the slatted door to the engine room creaked slowly and ominously open. We each saw the first movement in silent unison.

All eyes were fixed on the mystery, when without missing a beat I said to Peggy in a very quiet voice, "Do you have anything left over for Robby?"

And then continuing in a tone of secrecy I said to Olgert and Margret, "One of the wee people lives in our engine room" which I had to immediately follow up with a conspiratorial grin to mark the end of the jolly farce.

But how often does a door just open by itself? This has not occurred on its own in any country visited by us thus far at least! What mystery is this?

We four had been lazing back in the comfort of our cushions totally unaware that the tide had changed. It was now running out which means that the boat had swung around and silently caught the mud with the deepest aft reach of her keel and had been stopped there.

As the water continued to recede, the good *Osprey* very slowly started settling by the bow, pitching the boat ever so slowly off her even keeled normalcy, until the engine room door did its opening trick with only the invisible hand of mystery upon it, plus the now altered direction of gravity's pull.

Only briefly did the mystery remain, because we all instantly were aware that we were aground! And although our guests were immediately concerned, I managed to be a millisecond ahead of their saying so, and their being contented that there was no harm here, I further assured them that the rudder was in no danger either.

Their being required to get into their dinghy from this odd perch was part of the fun and hearing from them years later about their remembrance of the wee fellow who was our crewman gave us a second grin which oft times is more pleasing than the first.

Our joint friendship remains as the lingering taste of the bounty of one's favorite meal. Very often we accompanied them to the machine shop which they owned. I love things like machines. I think that a steam locomotive engine is a thing of absolute beauty. Though I must hasten to point out that as a machinist I have no firm grasp of reality. But Olgert was patient and inclined to teach, so I spent many joyous days on all manner of projects for the boat while maintaining a running conversation on totally unrelated trivia. It was great fun.

Margaret and Olgert first met each other in Melbourne, Australia where she was born. Olgert started his life in the small country of Lithuania and stepping off the ship which brought him here he saw the northwestern coast of a land that went on forever. He got a job. It was to build a fence. The fence had already been started. He was brought to the end of it. He looked back along the fence that had been built so far. It was perfectly straight. It went into the distance out of sight down into small valleys and over the following small hills. It went straight over the distant horizon.

He was given the posthole digger and told to start. He asked how far he should go and was looked at as though he had asked an odd question and was answered simply with a wave of the hand toward the next horizon. Piles of posts and slats had been dumped in the same direction.

Olgert took his work seriously! And very carefully he back sighted the line of the standing fence for each fence post to the perfection which I saw in everything that he did in the shop. He is a man greatly admired for everything which he does. I watched as many visited him in the shop. Many Aussies came, both young and old. And as friends of their adult son's came just to talk and or show their pride of a new "mountain bike" or tales of current adventures, Olgert was always ready to stop what he was doing to listen and or advise.

Margaret had her own projects which she brought along to the shop. They were a team. Margaret was the secretary for the yacht club. So when there was to be a yacht race from the clubhouse to Green Island out by the reef and special urging had been expressed to the visiting cruisers to join in the event, we felt obliged to add our name to the list even though we are adamant non-racers with a non-racing designed vessel. We have never raced the boat, but never has always seemed to require the skill of crystal ball gazing into the future which is beyond our firm grasp anyway.

The day came. I had hoped for some muscle in the wind, but it was just a very light breeze. The *Osprey* is not lightly built. I wanted to appear to be taking part in the event but in a less than competitive way, and managed by intent to be last to cross the start line. The skipper of the boat ahead of us, with much shouting at full lung capacity for the crew of eight to do six things at the same time and to do it faster, was not in threat of our passing him. I rolled my eyes at Peggy. In fact, these race events are generally taken to be really serious things to most of the membership.

For the convenience of all of the spectators, the start line extended from the yacht club to directly across the creek to the mangroves on the opposite bank, a couple hundred yards away. We would be tacking to windward as we approached the start line and would be crossing the line at the mangrove end. The wind was so light that the *Osprey* would not have sufficient speed to tack through the wind.

I would need to hold the jib to the wind as tacking commenced thereby to push the bow through the wind in order to gain the new course; which is why I asked Peggy to steer the boat through the tacking maneuver because I needed to be up on the bow. Normally I can tend the sheets from the bridge deck which is just about four quick steps from the wheel.

I told her to just hold the course that we were on until I said "Okay," at which point she could tack the boat. This requires the wheel to be turned so that the boat changes course by about ninety degrees. We needed to hold the present course as long as possible in order to gain as much speed as possible so that we could get the boat tacked with as little delay as possible.

I watched the mangrove-tree-covered bank getting closer. There was deep water right up to the bank. When we had gained as much speed as we were going to get, and with the bank coming close now, I turned to Peggy and said, "Okay, tack," and she started turning the wheel to the left as I looked forward to watch the boat tack just short of the bank as anticipated.

But the boat was not turning fast enough! I saw that Peggy was still slowly turning the wheel instead of doing so quickly! At this rate of turn we might hit the mangrove trees! I shouted "Turn!"

As I said, we have never raced the boat. And at sea, all course changes are done with small slow turns of the wheel, and although she knew that to tack she needed to get the rudder to turn full over to the opposite direction, there was nothing which I had said to indicate a different turning speed. So what she was doing was based on all prior experience.

Please know that I have never raised my voice in all of our years of sailing. So understandably upon hearing me yell "Turn," her first reaction was to think that something had been done wrongly and needed to be immediately resolved, wherefore, she immediately and with all the speed that she could muster, turned the wheel in the opposite direction (none of which I saw happening for I was watching the mangroves still in the hope of clearing) when to my horror I saw the boat turning in the opposite direction than anticipated.

The boat sailed at ninety degrees directly into the mangroves. The trees caught her first by the bow stay, with leaves and broken branches falling all over the deck including on me as the bow finally crunched through the mangroves which were growing out over the water, plowing through everything until the bow hit the bank with enough force to have her raise the bow a couple of feet above her water line as she slid to a crunching halt accompanied by the sound of crushing large branches and snapping smaller ones.

The yacht club spectators were perfectly situated to have a full view of the entire event as it occurred directly in front of them.

Both Peggy and I were speechless. I managed as quickly as possible to disentangle the boat from the clutches of the mangroves and clear away the debris off the deck. I shoved the boat out from the bank by pushing against the larger of the mangrove branches within reach which we had not destroyed, and still without having started the engine (which is just not done in a race), we crossed the start line and carried on to the finish line at Green Island.

I felt truly and entirely humiliated. Peggy knew that I did not blame her, but also knew how embarrassed I was as a visiting yachtsman to bring a known ocean sailing vessel with all flags flying to such unspeakable disaster. What a laugh! And what a picture of the US flag fleeing the Aussies by trying to hide in the mangroves.

We saw where Olgert and Margaret were anchored and chose a close proximity to likewise do so. They knew nothing of our occurrence.

I wrote out the event and we rowed over to their boat and had them read it. I told them that I felt rather inclined to tuck my tail between my legs and sail off over the horizon to another harbor southward, but Olgert suggested that he just pass the note to the club newsletter officer and that we just forget about it, which we did.

We were later to learn that the club spectators had assumed that our steering had broken, and had cheered our quick remedy and our continuing the race. I have wondered in the past, how many wars have been waged due to overblown reactions to what otherwise may have been ignored. At worst it had offered an opportunity to express derision, which was beyond the gracious dignity of the Cairns Cruising Yacht Squadron's membership to engage. I doff my cap.

I remain secretly proud of the fact that Peggy's reaction displayed that gentlemanly behavior and proper etiquette have previously always been shipmates with us aboard the *Osprey*. Never again has a shout been heard!

Progress toward accomplishment of our boat projects continued at a reasonable pace. I take pleasure from the appearance of fresh varnish properly applied. It seems rather like jewelry which sparkles the presence of a lady. And the pace took a giant leap forward, upon receiving word that our son John was getting a military plane "hop" to Australia for a visit with us.

He would be spending a couple of weeks. (If a request is lodged by an officer in active military duty for a seat aboard a plane on duty flight to, in this case Australia, on a "space available" basis, there is the possibility of joining such a flight. These arrangements are of course subject to cancellation at the last instant.) This was going to be fun for all of us and very significantly memorable as destiny was later to reveal.

Shortly a side mooring became available along the banks of the mangroves. These consisted of four points from which to secure the boat. There were pilings ashore to hold the bow and stern at the bank, and heavy moorings with float lines to secure the bow and stern between them which together hold the vessel off the mangrove bank

The same piling and mooring used by us was also used by the vessel ahead and astern of us, and a Chinese junk owned by Joyce and Stoney used the two which we now shared, securing our bow. So we now knew that we could see them returning and could then greet them accordingly. Our several prior attempts to find them home had failed.

It was Joyce whom we finally saw boarding the junk. We made ourselves known and asked about Stoney whom we had not previously met either. We were told that she had just returned from the hospital where he was very unwell.

We talked for some time which gave Joyce some small chance to unburden herself, which happened also to tell us that she was very uneasy about her visiting the hospital and seeing Stoney in this condition. Thereafter, it naturally fell to my accompanying her pretty much on a daily basis; and it became my good fortune to have the pleasure of becoming known to him as a friend. Most unfortunate however, it became evident that he did not expect to survive from his present condition. We did our best to ease his concerns over various matters, talking of many pleasant times and places from which conversations he would on occasions drift off into sleep, a sleep from which in a few weeks he did not awaken.

The junk was sold. Joyce flew back to the states and was shortly heard of on the radio from her RV bus. Life goes on as it must.

* * *

Our son John was indeed coming. We, were excited! This was going to be fun! And Peggy and I started talking to Aussie friends for suggestions of a tour to see part of the country close up and personal. We chose a bus trip into the wild north territory.

With the major boat projects completed, we were still going daily to Olgert's shop. Margaret always launched the day by brewing an abundance of coffee. Olgert's honored privilege was to, upon sitting down with his cup of coffee, broach the topic of the morning, whereupon it was my honored privilege to argue the opposing postulation. We always argued with great earnestness and always in the manner of two gentlemen lawyers, never with time limits for rebutted arguments. It was great fun!

We had given John the phone number of Olgert's shop. He called upon his arrival in Sydney after having arranged his travel to Cairns, so that we would know how and when he would arrive. And arrive he did, and with great fanfare and smiles by all of us. We introduced him to all of our friends, both yachtsmen and Aussie, exchanged stories in our evenings, and feasted on all other bounties of life! It was a joy!

When one has a sailing vessel, it is obligatory that some sailing be done on such occasions. And so we were soon off to explore some of the great barrier reefs of Australia. I watched for shallow coral from a perch on the ratlines as John steered the boat. Snorkeling was next on the agenda. The water was wonderfully clear. The coral plunged to great depth between its colonies. Its form, its shape, its hue differed dramatically as one looked in any direction. And the bifocal kaleidoscope of swirling color swayed and arched and dove as clouds of tropic fish in perpetual motion flashed silvers, and reds and greens and purples of all shades before our eyes in a never ending bedazzlement of sensation! How very unworldly are such places!

To be privileged to even briefly dwell in this world of inner space is not unlike that of any future outer space adventuring astronaut. John seemed changed by the military somehow, or was he just aged a bit by this thing called time. Whatever it was, he seemed more engaged in conversing on what seemed to us to be a greater scope and more interested grasp of concept. But then, of course, parental pride is not a totally new and isolated fact, as perception is defined by its participants as reality.

We sailed back to Cairns and our mooring, for tomorrow we're off on another adventure!

Friends drove us to the appointed place in Cairns where the bus was to be, and there it stood, unattended by either a driver or other passengers. We walked around the bus. It was washed and appeared ready. The paint which looked as though it had been recently reapplied was itself the color of dust with light green stripes, and at the time we had no idea how appropriate the dust color was, when out from the little shed building a crowd of people came rushing toward the bus carrying their stuff all rushing and talking at the same time as the driver herded them along. Well okay, I may have exaggerated when I spoke the word crowd.

The bus had four rows of seats, a double seat on each side. Everyone's stuff was loaded into compartments under the bus; seats were chosen, and with a warm welcome from the driver we were off toward the unknown.

The windows presented the world to us which had been surrounding the city of Cairns. We sped along on a beautifully paved roadway. The sparse but semi-tropical landscape swept past us when with nothing more than a "here we go" yelled from the driver, the bus leaped into space, dropped a foot or so down onto the dirt from the end of the paving onto the "roadway from hell" as later named by our fellow passengers.

So this is why this trip is only offered during the dry season. It would be impossible during the rains! And soon the ruts in the road were hurling us about as the bus lurched first left and then right and then farther right. It seemed that our speed never changed! But I was amazed at how much thinner the seat cushions had quickly become.

Each lurch was vigorously accompanied by loud shouts of mock glee, all in the very best of good natured fun. This was a good bunch of people. The driver yelled again, and with wonderful timing, for just before actual blisters were ready to form on our blisters, the bus stopped—almost!

It was a river. It wasn't really very wide, but what had everyone's instant attention was the fact that there wasn't a bridge! We could clearly see the dirt road continuing on the other side toward which we now apparently intended to go; because the driver seemed to have contented himself anyway, that the water wasn't too deep for us to not be swept away. And as the tires threw a deluge of water up to the windows through which we could no longer see, we all simultaneously lifted our feet off the floor!

The driver was correct in his evaluation. We reached the road on the other side and half an hour later we saw a gasoline station and general store combination where we stopped to everyone's delight. Without exception we all poured out of the bus, stretching and bending and talking at the same time. The driver had been immersed into the body of our close community and behaved in like manner as the rest of us.

There was a restaurant of sorts inside and we sat or stood around drinking soda or coffee and or having a sandwich at one of the tables amid the hubbub of further getting acquainted with each other, because conversation was almost impossible on the bus. All of its sundry construction seemed noisily to conspire to exchange places with other parts of the bus, which is to say that there was a wee rattling aboard.

At the sound of the voice of our leader, we all instantly and willingly obeyed. When all were aboard, the driver started the engine! Well, that is to say, he reached forward toward the dashboard, turned the key, and as we, he was ready for that familiar roar of which we indeed had become so very fondly accustomed to have abuse our ear drums. No one moved. Not a finger moved. Not an expression of any face moved. For a brief moment not one breath was taken.

All eyes moved in unison with the driver's hand as he again turned the starter key with the same resounding silence as before. The driver did not gasp! But in a rather unsurprised tone of voice, and with an apparently practiced tone of instruction announced that we were all to step outside and push the bus for a rolling start. Wherefore, having heard our leader's voice, we got up from our seats, walked out in an orderly manner and took a firm gasp of whatever protrusion the body of the bus offered; the driver, with his head stuck out the window at his left, gave his call to us to "giddy up team" rather as voiced to a sturdy team of horses.

The bus's engine lurched to life and we were all proudly re-boarded, enjoying some heavy breathing from the exertion as the bus again formed the required gigantic cloud of dust that continued to follow us from the distant horizon.

And so it was that we band of happy travelers bounced along for a least a couple more hours before we got that flat tire. I had noticed with approval those extra wheels carried on the roof of the bus. But if truth be known, I really didn't think that we would be using them. This land traveling seems fraught with dangers!

The bus driver, having warned us about the presence of a host of various poisonous snakes and tarantulas, invited us to wander around at cautious leisure while he changed the tire. Well off the road, a few trees offered shade and were the destination for several of us wanderers, where we also found a very small shallow creek. This was the beginning of the rainy season, so hence the presence of the water. And remembering the river which we crossed, I could also understand why this was to be one of the last bus tours of the year, as the river would soon be impassable. John was having a ball. This was all somewhat different from the areas of home where he had been accustomed to travel. And if the sparkle in his eye were not noticed, the grin, which was now a permanent part of his face, was not to be missed and it gave us pleasure.

The landscape of Australia had taken on an ever-increasing harshness for what one from elsewhere is accustomed to consider welcoming for human beings. Although we were still in the coastal fringe of the continent which rings the interior desert where few but the aborigines linger, even here the desert appeared to be encroaching. Structures strange to our eyes pierced mysteriously upward from the earth. Some of these structures are said to gain a height as much as thirty feet (nine meters), especially in Africa. Most which we saw were less than half that.

These were called anthills. Made by what was called white ants, which are in reality termites that eat mostly dead plant material such as wood, leaf mulch, dirt and even animal dung, plus farming a rather extensive fungus-growing garden. Much of this activity has the byproduct of various gases including methane, and these giant mounds are built as chimneys to vent gases and also very critically to ventilate the colony by which the temperature is maintained to within one degree all day long. I am very impressed! We saw thousands of these mounds.

We had left Cairns at 9 in the morning and our scheduled arrival in Cooktown was set at 4 PM the same day. We arrived. We didn't check the time. It didn't matter. We had arrived. All was well. At the rustic little hotel, we were expected, and having taken leave of our friends, and having shaken the hand of our driver, we settled in for a rest to be followed tomorrow with a few days of exploration which we were to find was interspersed with the occasional involuntary reaching toward various parts of our anatomies to unobtrusively massage portions of which were unaccustomed to the gentle beatings received from the bus which seemed to have an inappropriate expression of glee on its face as we left. Can we ever know the actual line between reality and perception? Actually, that was said with the proverbial "tongue in cheek."

The morrow dawned. And our anticipation mixed well with breakfast fare all trucked in from afar. This was Cooktown. And yes, it bore the noble name of the good captain himself for reasons which we were certainly interested to learn. All Cooktonians of course knew everything about this and eagerly shared their knowledge, most of which was quite similar to the tales as related by the prior person.

Usually, the more intense the listening, the more bounteous the embellishments, all offered with fullest sincerity and probable correctness. For good Captain Cook had been here a long time! His voyage inside the Great Barrier Reef as he came up from the south had been with considerable troubles. They had slammed into the coral reefs several times over that long passage and were now taking on sea water as fast as they could pump it out. So they sailed the boats hard onto the quiet beach here and labored long and hard between tides to finally be seaworthy enough to continue onward.

There is a prominent hill here at the town. It is very close to the shore. And the reef reaches very close to the shore here as well. So it is perfectly understandable that the good captain would have climbed the hill to get a good look at the best course to get him farther northward without undoing all of the repairs that had been done here. Everyone with whom we spoke was also certain that he had done so and simple logic was on their side.

I needn't tell you that the next morning Peggy and John and I climbed the hill. And it was quite a climb and quite a height. And it was indeed rewarding to anyone future-bound upon this sea. A few years later, the scene still lingered without any diminishment to my inner eye as we too were to pass this way—directly in his wake and safely so.

I had found enormous and instant enjoyment upon my visits to the Topless Bar which was its name. The décor was Australian frontier and interesting in every way. A light lunch was served daily with the ubiquitous presence of Australia's famous beer. For those of differing palate a variety of beverage was available from the ever present waitress staff who seemed ever to bend to a customer's pleasure. The unusual name of the establishment was due to a tropical storm having blown off the top of the building. It was always fun to go there.

Alas as always, the rug of time was pulled out from under us too quickly. The bus was to be ready for our departure the next morning. And Australia sent a dozen or so kangaroos down the road ahead of us for the first half mile or so, as an appropriate lingering look at Australia's Northern Territory.

Along the way, occasionally a pink and grey tree would suddenly rise from the earth and circle about in a loud magic display. They were huge flocks of galahs which entirely mask the tree which momentarily hosted them. They are a pink and grey cockatoo, joyous to the visitor's eye, but represent a pest to the farmer.

We passed a little pond in a marshy area and there majestically stood a tall lone Jabaru, motionless as he watched all his surroundings. He is a long-necked wader with a very big strong looking blackish bill. White cockatoos with heads adorned by yellow crests crowded the air, as thousands of parakeets flew together in their gorgeously varied colors. Australia may have dust underfoot in places, but occasionally the very sky is filled with squawking tiny rainbows who sing their own anthems of possession.

The homeward-bound bus started without failure and the tires retained their fill of prerequisite enlargement. As we charged through the bridgeless river no one raised a foot, for we were seasoned Aussies, a claim not voiced aloud where it might be overheard. I salute the Australian. He has a vast land to conquer and to tame, not at all unlike our earlier western frontiersmen of North America.

The *Osprey* and other friends seemed to approve of our return and very shortly stories were told of the north, as John had a last night of cherished togetherness as a family. We took him to a commercial plane bound for Sydney and he phoned that he had arrived in plenty of time for his return flight aboard the military plane. We did not know at the time that this would be the last that ever we would see him.

There remained work to do on the boat into which I immersed myself as Peggy went about her tasks which included among many others, the donning of a backpack by which application our "daily bread" and other necessities arrived from town to the boat. She was also busy writing letters home to friends and family and I whistled as I worked, oblivious that anything was amiss.

Peggy hid her growing thoughts from me with either terrific skill or due to my blindness, I cannot know which; though I had thought myself completely aware of her mood and need. I knew of the increased exchange of letters between her and her mother, but I was caught completely by surprise when she told me that she had decided to fly home. This was unexpected, especially viewing the fact that our visas and cruising permit for the boat were soon to expire and must shortly require sailing the boat away from Australia.

I told her that I understand if she felt that she had to do this, and that I could easily single-hand the boat to New Guinea. But she very much did not want me to do that. We had a friend whom we had met in the islands who was crewing on a different boat and though Peggy preferred that I write to her to find if she was available I asked Peggy to write the letter so that the woman would not feel that she was asked to interject within a family problem. Peggy wrote the letter. However, our friend was committed to crew farther for her present yachtsman, so Peggy left Australia leaving me with an uncertainty as to my plan which looked as though it would be as a single hander making for New Guinea.

Peggy's flight left at the appointed time and I carried on with my work on the boat. Advertising for crew is a common event in newspapers and yacht club bulletin boards. I did not do so, perhaps due to my persisting shock.

CHAPTER 7

 LUCY AND NEW GUINEA

Just before my leaving Australia, two girls came to the Cairns Cruising Yacht Squadron by bus from the Northern Territory where they had been working. They were adventurous girls and one was a sailor.

I invited both of them to take a look at the boat to see if they would feel comfortable going to sea with her, as well as to let time help to determine if they felt at ease with me. They both loved the boat and though they both wanted to go, Lucy, who made it clear that her name was pronounced as Lucie rather than as a gambling term, was the only one who had a passport. They felt that they should not delay my departure by waiting for a passport to be applied for and issued, which would require an undetermined length of time. So Lucy won the contest and in two days we were off.

Clearing customs and immigration, we sailed to Fitzroy Island and anchored to await a favorable wind with which to make toward New Guinea. But after a couple of days of this and still no wind, and with Lucy getting more and more anxious to be underway, I agreed to leave.

The sailing was oh so slow, but Lucy was delighted. She was going to sea for the first time in her life on a real voyage, and when Australia fell below our view and only the South Pacific Ocean occupied our world, she was ecstatic.

Lucy was a sailor and yearned to learn navigation. So out came the sailing charts again. I showed her where we were and where we were bound and showed her our course, asked if she would like to do the navigation, assuring her that she could give up any time that she might wish, and that I would get her out of trouble if she had any; and with a perpetual grin on her face I didn't look at the charts until we made landfall. My eye on our progress was surreptitious, but maintained.

I had seen a flicker of reaction at my having said "if you give up." It was a pure Aussie reaction, where to give up is just not to be entertained! We sailed for close to a week before a coastline presented itself. And the closer we came, the more poor Lucy bent over the charts. She could not recognize a thing. A full day passed as we drew closer. She was growling at herself in mounting frustration!

"I want to do this!" she almost yelled, and finally was forced to ask for help, an effort as great I suspect as any she had ever experienced.

I showed her the direction the land formation was, as it stretched north and southward out of sight. Our destination's shore line, though also N & S was only a few miles like that, and at the headland of a big bay. North of the bay was such a coastline such as this. South of the bay was the immense lagoon of the Louisiads. Given a few other indications from the chart, we changed course southward.

Our intended destination was Samarai, a small port of entry on the eastern end of this large bay. Lucy's navigation had brought us several hours north of the bay, but not to the end of her rage. We were sailing rather close along the north of the bay as we watched the glorious greens of the landscape. Lucy watched. Her eyes flashed from one scene to the next! The farther we went the faster she breathed! Her fists were clenched!

For another hour this mysterious anger continued, until a peak of emotion seemed to be reached as she very quietly said, "Those $%^&* bastards. They all told us that all of the rain forests of the world are gone and I'm seeing rain forest from horizon to horizon. They said that tar balls cover the oceans and I saw none!"

I told her of my years of ocean sailing, and the thousands of miles which that represents, and the percentage of the planet that covered; and that I had never once seen a tar ball at sea much less ever found the waves covered with them.

This passionate young woman justly felt betrayed. It eased her rage somewhat to hear that my opinion at least was that the people whom she had listened to for all of those years undoubtedly believed everything they had said, and were themselves unwitting recipients of exaggeration. It was an interesting start to what was to become a really fun adventure.

Samarai is not a bustling metropolis and not greatly unlike parts of Australia's Northern Territory. But Lucy had originally come from the Canberra area where the lust for adventure had brought her across her continent and now eastward to the very foreign country of Papua New Guinea. Canberra was never like this, at least during recent memory of the last hundred years or so. Customs and Immigration welcomed us in fluent Pigeon English which was almost identical to what had become regular usage through most of the islands as far away as the Solomons.

We didn't linger here, for though a quaint little town, adventure and exploration called, and was answered, and was found. We walked silently into the richness of a rain forest gowned in green with hues of countless shade and texture and shape — from ground covering ferns to huge trees which create a canopy far above; and when you add a mix of tropic birds and blazing flowers hosting brilliant butterflies some of which are gigantic in size, a feast of fantastic life and vibrancy boggles the mind at first view. I never tire of it. I marvel at it and I am humbled by it.

In the evenings we talked of many things which included her fascination with China since her grandparents had been missionaries there. So I promised her that I would sail her to the *China Straits*. But in the same breath with a very small chuckle I reached for a chart and showed her that the name of the waters directly in front of us bore that name here in PNG. I'm not sure that there was an outward reflection detected on her face from my small comic indiscretion regarding China. We sailed on.

Chapter 7   *Lucy and New Guinea*

I don't know whether during Lucy's time spent in Australia's Northern Territory she had been introduced extensively to the Aboriginal culture or whether she was just naturally comfortable with others, but there was an even flow of respect by her which was as genuine as mine as we mingled with the local folks here. It pleased me.

Lucy was having a great time and was an excellent sailor. The *Osprey* sailed through the China Straits and to many islands, and as always we anchored in the area of a village and therefore always had a perpetual offering of fruits and vegetables for which to trade and thereby also to having the pleasant opportunity of meeting the people who were always invited aboard.

For Lucy's twenty-third birthday celebration there needed to be something to mark the occasion, so I baked her a rooster cake for which Peggy had a recipe aboard. And thanks to Peggy's detailed recipe, it was a fine birthday cake indeed. Years ago we had named the recipe with this title because it required no eggs, which is not an uncommon situation aboard a cruising sailboat.

Two days later, we came around to the sheltered side of this rather high-hilled island, to choose a quiet water anchorage when to our amazement a huge square rigged sailing ship was there. She flew an Australian flag and clearly had tourists aboard. We motored close up because we were planning to hail her, but they saw us coming and were already at her rail waving us over. They were as surprised to see us with a US flagged yacht here in New Guinea as we were to see them! They told us that a party was planned for that evening and enthusiastically invited us to join them which we did. Lucy had not been invisible to anyone, and it's not shocking to discover that a truly beautiful woman is indeed very welcome at any party.

A dozen or so locals were there when we arrived. Some of the men had musical instruments which may have been village made, and the women were with them to put on a show by arrangement of the ship. I have heard that the swaying motion of island women's dance has been thought by some to be rather erotic. The show was great! The party was fun. And not long after Lucy and I were shown one of the cabins, and after Lucy had talked animatedly with each of the Aussies and the party was finally ending; the locals took their leave and Lucy and I followed not long after.

We were anchored a short distance from the square rigger and waved them farewell the next morning. We enjoyed the day here and spent another night before we too sailed away to another island cove.

I was looking at the chart of the area in the direction of travel for the next few days and started looking more closely at an interesting little river. I have more than a passing interest in jungle-type rivers. Peggy and I explored one in the Tahitian Islands with the dinghy beyond where it seemed possible to go.

The chart showed that as expected, the river would not accommodate the *Osprey*, but it was full of turns among mountains and went a very great distance into its island. It appeared as though this would be more than just a few hours up river and then back the same day. And not surprisingly Lucy wanted to go along. When we got there, the anchorage was without surge possibility and with superb holding, but I did not want to leave the boat unattended for more than two days and a night, so that was the plan.

We launched the dinghy, took along an extra tank of gasoline with oil mixed in for its engine, a good supply of water and food, the usual personal necessities; and after a hardy breakfast we locked the cabin of the yacht and were off.

Oh what a magnificently painted tropical jungle into which we now entered! How easily have we gone back in time, where mankind has moved amidst this forest primeval has been no more invasive than any other of its creatures along their chosen paths. This is the forest primeval.

Here, are the hearts that beneath it live as time has always permitted. Here, reaching for the sun are the giants of old in their garments green and distinct; as the young trees push impatiently upward in their shadow. Vines and ferns crowd the ground while flashing colors fly about, sometimes in unharmonious screeching, perhaps in rebellion to the strange noise of our outboard motor which they would have never heard before.

Chapter 7   *Lucy and New Guinea*

The river water was not as clear as the sea. But the steady almost rush of the current moved around its boulders as revealingly as though they had stuck their heads up for a gasp of air to breath. I love these passages around bends of the river where time has not taken occasion to look.

Hidden from the river are trails through the jungle where generations of folks have walked as their father's feet have walked before them while eons of time have passed unmarked. And as we turned this next bend in the river, and as we saw this specific scene of thick impenetrable jungle—a question is asked by my mind. "Has any other person ever in history been to this spot? No one could bring a canoe up this stream. Are we the very first humans to see this majestic and glorious sight?"

We don't need to think of ourselves in any way other than traveling up a truly beautiful wonderland, but to even imagine such a thing as being a possibility, much less as being a likelihood, seems somehow to add an almost awe of our surroundings. Ah how the aura of this place pushes our mobile minds to even higher plains of pleasure! Life, our own and that which surrounds us is truly a wonderment.

Magic moments became hours, and hours became mid day and beyond, and there arrived on schedule a reminder of food. Ahead, a sandbar reached outward from the starboard bank. I ran the dinghy up on the sand. We got out, pulled the boat up farther and looked around for a pleasant spot in the shade to have lunch. How convenient and surely grown especially for us, was this accommodating tree to have provided those stout roots which bent out from the bank. They even formed back rests for us.

Let's look around! We had seen that there was a large opening in the jungle canopy beyond the left bank, so we climbed the eight or nine feet of almost vertical bank up to the ground level and found that this spot had been cleared for growing something. Whatever it was had already been harvested, but of instant interest was a little shelter hut about nine or so feet square. The roof was of thatch and quite recently done. It looked very capable of shedding a shower were one to come. The walls were of woven fiber and the floor was covered with dried plant leaves clearly intended for sleeping comfort! Wow, what a find! Just the sort of thing that a tour guide company would advertise as a setting for rustic romance in far off New Guinea!

We brought our few things to our hideaway. I left the oars in the dinghy, as well of course as the outboard motor attached, and placed the anchor firmly amongst the big tree roots; not because there was concern but just because habits are followed automatically. And after our late lunch, we took the remainder of most of our day light to explore the close proximity of the jungle into which we could not deeply penetrate; coming away with a marvel about what we had just so brief glimpsed.

We had brought a pup-tent shaped mosquito net with us. These things are equipped with long nylon ties which hold the tent down firmly as well as other ties to secure it upward to form its shape. I had extra cording to use which reached to the roof ridge and else ware as required to hold up our *in-house-tent*. We covered the "bed" with some towels, and our sleeping was thus arranged without difficulty. Supper was a delight. And as though on queue, a nearly full moon hurled its brilliance now beyond the jungle canopy, into our thatch covered shelter, and bathed a New Guinea jungle in sudden silent silvery shades of whispered mystery. The thick fullness of the jungle canopy had kept out even this glorious glimmering until that very moment. It was an enchantment. And just about that quickly, all of the promise that a tour guide advertising might have hinted about, became reality. And not long afterward, we slept well and soundly.

But we were awakened – suddenly and fully! There had been no thunder or lightning to advertise the rain but it was here! A deluge poured from the sky! No wind blew. It just *rained!* And an hour or two later, the river took on a voice more like a roar of mighty waters than the gentle little river of our acquaintance!

I went out to look. I took a flashlight with me because the entire moon had been swallowed by this blackness. I went to the bank of the river to check on the dinghy. It was nowhere to be seen. I moved the little light of my flashlight around down stream but couldn't see very far through this deluge. I saw nothing of the dinghy. But I saw that the water which now raged here was about four feet from the top of the bank.

There was nothing to be done. We would probably need to walk our way out. Our supplies flashed through my mind, and whatever it was going to take, we would do it. Lucy and I both knew that we could not take full stock of our situation till morning so we went back to sleep as the rain now had suddenly stopped as though someone had turned off a fire hose.

Morning arrived. And after a yawn or two, followed by the requisite stretching of an arm here and a leg there; and after the chuckled complaints about hard mattresses; teeth were brushed using the water from the pail which had also granted us a swallow during the brief night. But our looking out from under our thatch-roofed castle at these unique surroundings was enough to again arouse a primal response to each other's personal presence here, from which we emerged back into the reality of thoughts about how we get ourselves returned to that century of time from which we had only one day ago departed.

A very quick walk to the edge of the river bank before dressing, joyously presented our new day with the sight of our upside-down dinghy. It obviously had spent time underwater, where it may also have been spinning in the current in its underwater performance of a ballet.

The oars were gone. The fuel tank was gone even though it had been connected to the engine via its rubber fuel hose. Also the extra fuel tank was gone. But the boat seemed relatively undamaged as its anchor line had held and the tree still stood in whose roots the five pound Danforth anchor had been placed. The presence of the dinghy was such a better prospect for us than trekking by foot through what was to be very tough going indeed!

The water still surged in its downhill race to the sea, but its roar was becoming more and more a song sung in our memory, as half the flooded water which had pushed against the banks now was already mixed with the taste of salt for which it seemed a few hours ago so anxious to savor. Nothing else seemed to be changed, though a mist hung over the jungle. And all of yesterday's birds had shaken themselves free of unwanted rain and had begun clearing their throats to hear which one could make the most noise. Some of it was even melodiously beautiful, but perhaps the word screeching would not be totally unkind to describe the loudest voices.

Even this sound was orchestral now that we had the boat, and beauty again clothed all of the world which moved before our eye. A wet sheen was painted on every leaf, on every rough hewn branch and bark. On the reds and yellows and blues of all flowers had formed round worlds created by droplets of water each displayed its own rainbow within itself.

Each leaf, each tree, each droplet on each flower, each of these—as it were—called out saying, *"Don't miss seeing me! This entire show is just for you!"* For whom if not for our eye is this beauty shown?

Though the license of poetry is borrowed here, the truth is that no other eyes will ever see this precise scene for the jungle is ever in change. This did not cause us to feel in any way special ourselves. But neither did it elude the majestic grandeur from our deeply moved emotion. Many creatures cannot even detect color, which we all know is just a slight difference of the frequency vibration of light. We have been immersed in a grandeur.

Entering this magic forest yesterday, we had thought that we could never again see anything as beautiful. But beauty had out done herself again. We would have been speechless had we not been in need to plan the next part of this adventure for here indeed, we were up the literal creek without a paddle.

But each word we spoke, each laugh and thought, needed to detour around a smile. It was going to be a fun day.

Back at our thatched shelter we gathered up our stuff and cast a last look about. I had of course noticed this carefully stowed pole attached to the inside of the shelter. I had not been able to guess its purpose, but it would be very serviceable as a stout double-ended oar with the added potential of withstanding thrusts against hazards to the dinghy and therefore to us, as with white-knuckled grasp of our "oars" the white water rapids were shortly to rush us toward the sea.

I took the large pole. But I left money in the form of a two kina note carefully but obviously woven into the wall at the inside of door opening. It also spoke our thanks for the use of the accommodations. I still wonder if he noticed that the pole was missing, or just if he was amazed that a storm had blown a two kina note into his hut and secured it so perfectly for him. But then, the jungle is known to be a place where great spirits roam.

We carefully stowed all of our stuff aboard the dinghy, turned her bow toward the *Osprey*, and launched our destiny toward the sound of crashing waters. We were committed!

It was a toothed creature, this surging bedlam of growling white water. It had fangs. I needed to keep the dinghy from being crushed by an impact into one of these boulders as we flew along. Not only could the boat be destroyed, but we would be hurled into this maelstrom and tossed about as leaves and perhaps be bashed into these rocks to unlikely survival at the really treacherous sections. This was not a task to be taken lightly with no thought, but if we didn't think that it could be done with reasonable safety we would not have done it.

The reason we chose to do it now rather than postpone it was due to the fact that when we had come up stream, we were required to get out and drag the boat over several areas without sufficient water to float, and now knew that we could well and truly zoom over those prior shallows. And well, maybe there might possibly have been just the slightest hint of being challenged by thoughts of rushing rapids as we pushed the boat from the bank, because above the lingering roar of the river, the jungle also heard two people's simultaneous top-of-the-lung yell of, "Yaahooo!"

What a rush, in all sense of the word. We leaned our weight first to one side and then the other as Lucy shoved at rocks with her stick and I with the pole, and then we would "row" with all of our strength to gain positions of entry farthest away from the approaching white water as we flew along from one area to the next! And as total exhaustion set in, we suddenly fell back onto the seats, for what to our wondering eyes there appeared–the broad waters where the *Osprey* awaited! We were back!

It had been a wild experience with many a shout of "Yahoo" and or "Look out for that one," all done with giddy grins plastered on our faces. Yes, it qualified for the designation of a fun adventure, and it was also great to be back to the comfort of the *Osprey*.

Three months had flashed by unnoticed. But on several quiet occasions Lucy had managed to mention her absolute fascination with all things Chinese. I did not dwell on the fact that I had for several years unsuccessfully tried to get a cruising permit to enter China with the boat.

I wanted to offer to the Chinese Universities the opportunity of the English language students to come two at a time to the boat for a week or two as we sought to travel up the Chang Jiang River. The students could enjoy an unusual venture in an English speaking environment, and we would have the benefit of fully comprehended conversations with the folks of the river villages.

Though Lucy may not have known it, it was not going to be a Herculean task to conjure up interest in my mind about sailing to China.

We were sailing back to Samurai. It was time to be leaving New Guinea making for Australia—or China. Which direction are we going? We anchored in preparation of checking out of the country and Lucy was quick to get ashore for something. I didn't ask what and in a couple of hours she was back.

She handed me an envelope without saying a word. It was from Peggy. I read the letter which had been sent to general delivery to hold for my arrival. Lucy waited. "She's miserable and wants to come back to the boat." And with those words she knew that China was not to be our destination, though by now I too was ready to go.

I've since wondered if Lucy had read the letter first. Because, even though she knew that I was a non-drinker, she had returned with a bottle of whiskey to presumably divert disappointment, for had Peggy been happy with a job, we would have carried on to China.

The sail back to Cairns was the fastest overall speed thus far ever achieved by the good ship *Osprey*. Never had a passage been sailed with as much gusto as the waves dissolved in clouds of spray as we zoomed along our course which the windvane steering system held to perfection as we watched this show of ocean prowess. We slept well, ate well, and laughed at the least excuse.

With landfall in sight, Lucy told me that she would be ready with her things when the boat was secured which I said was okay if she wished, but was not necessary. A couple of weeks later, she was gone.

It was a good voyage for us. But we were an embarrassment to each other when with friends of our own ages. So with a mixture of feelings, the story of Lucy and the *Osprey* has come to a close. I hope her future life is worthy of her.

CHAPTER 8

 Peggy is Back!!

Wow, it's great to see her walking into the airport terminal, and a joyous hug said welcome home. I had borrowed Charlotte and Conrad's car to bring Peggy and her baggage to the yacht club. We stopped at their boat to thank them and return the car keys, but we didn't stop to talk. Peggy needed some sleep after this eighteen hour trip. And my sleep was as contented as hers.

Australia needed to take two full turns of the planet before we stirred around much aboard the *Osprey*. But after the third such trip, Peggy and I were off on a road trip of our own to see more of this fabled land. And this time, we were going to get very acquainted with Charlotte and Conrad's station wagon, because it became our house; our bedroom, our dining room, and our magic carpet aboard which some of the many faces of Australia were to pass before us.

The car was worthy of its service to us, as it had been practicing for this over the past considerable number of years, even as our personal vintage has likewise become distinguished as *mature*. And as our unabashed and loud singing of "Waltzing Matilda," sung in Australian with words such as billabong, was raucously being rendered by us; the car retained a much more dignified sound of ever-thrusting motion within its cylinders. By comparison to us, it was the sound of a gentle purr.

The "tableland" of the state of Queensland, is the general elevation of the country in this area. From this elevation the land tumbles downward toward the sea. The decline cannot be described as being a cliff because it is much more gentle than that. And at the bottom of that decline of elevation is a wide expanse before actually reaching the sea. The city of Cairns with its harbor is on this plain, and the distance up to the town of Kuranda on the tablelands is 34 kilometers by train. Cairns and Kuranda are joined by a scenic railway which has no other destinations.

We took this little trip with our son John while he was here. The mountainous formations, with roaring waterfalls and picturesque old train bridges were great to see. It is part of Australia, which too often is thought of as being all arid desert. Our assent to the tablelands by car took considerably more mileage and was equally impressive.

As soon as I saw the family I slowed the car to watch them. They paid no attention to us at all and just kept on as though they were the sole owners of the road. The parents were leisurely proceeding along ahead of us as their offspring cavorted about a short distance to the right. What a delight to watch them!

These were some of the original inhabitants of Australia. They were here before the great sailing ships came from England. They were here before even the Aborigines inhabited this land. These were kangaroos enjoying a pleasant afternoon! What a feeling of having truly arrived again in Australia! There were kangaroos, right in front of us on this little dirt road!

I pointed and said, "Look over there Peg! There must be over thirty of them! Wow, look how they jump! I didn't know they could go that fast! I think they're Reds." I don't know why I was whispering.

The Big Red is the largest of the kangaroos. I had looked up some information about them and was surprised to see them this far from the inland area of the huge dry center of the continent but then, we had been traveling for several days. Talk about speed – these guys can go to forty miles per hour!

The Big Red is not always red. Here in the eastern range the males are usually a pale red to brick red, while the females are generally a bluish grey. The males weigh around sixty kilos and stand two meter tall; the females rarely exceed thirty kilos. She will have one young (joey), though she can nurse more than one. The joey will stay in the mother's external pouch for six months after birth, but afterwards often climbs back in when it feels threatened.

How uniquely different we always find the world to be, except for the people! We seem all to be the same. Some of us have less pigment in our skin than others, but that seems to be the only briefly noticeable difference. Many of our customs differ in various areas, especially where travel has not mixed us together very much and where being educated may in one place be defined by such important things as knowing the difference between which fruit is going to kill you or not and such useful reality as building a proper hut; while in another place it may be defined as knowing the name of the fourth king captured by the third emperor of such and such (history buffs' forgiveness is here beseeched). And I render full and proper homage to education which has brought medical and all other science to where it is today. I poorly voice the regret felt in what sometimes seems as such blindness in my community to the education of survival, of the immense and broad base of the curriculum for life in which only your hand exists; where no grocery store is poised from which to buy; where clothes are not bought; where doctors don't exist; where you grow or kill what you eat. I am in awe of such people, be they in my community with its convenience or in every community which we encounter.

I doff my cap, especially to you women of the earth. You are a wonderment to me. You are a mystery and yet, with my total blindness, it is homage with which I kiss your hand.

Our road trip has just begun, and I am already enthralled by this land without end. We have a map. It seems to cover an entire planet from this close up vantage point. This is—Australia!

We are not the first to be here; nor were we of the great sailing ships the first. They brought prisoners from England, fellow white people of their own land, who were cast ashore here. Many ships came over the years with the considered dregs of their society. Yet it is these folks who raised their heads, shook the dust off their shoes, looked at these horizons and said, "This now is my land!"

They made the tools which they needed, and with a fierce determination still evident within their descendants, they tamed an entire continent and deserve our salute of praise which I readily give.

But they were not the first people here. Before them walked the Aboriginals of this land. Were they the first? I surely will never know. But there appears to be none who are known with certainty to have been before them.

Very shortly after our arrival here, I had the great good fortune to meet a woman who, with her husband now deceased, had been a Christian missionary to these good people for thirty years. They lived with these people, working together, laughing together and at times of sorrow, crying together. She and her husband were welcomed after time, and lived as extended family with the Aboriginal People.

It was my great honor to spend many, many hours with her in long discussions of insights which only such long-term intimacy can glean.

The ancient stories of the Elders are secret and sacred, and if such things were to have been discussed, they would not find their way to this writing. The society, present and ancient, is rich with symbolism and ceremony. These are an honorable and ancient people; wanderers mostly of the quiet places of the Northern Territory where 32% of them still abide.

As a nomadic people of wanderers, I expected them to be very muscular of leg, but find them to be astonishingly slender of limb to the great extreme. Although our encounters with the Aborigines have been greatly limited, I never saw an exception to this fact either personally or in any of the extensive photos of which I have come across.

Over a third of the country is reported to be dessert, but Peggy and I are only at its borders. However, these big red wanderers are mighty of leg indeed. The

Big Red kangaroo jumps some fifteen feet in a single bound as he is traveling beside the car about ten feet away. What a sight!

We saw a wallaby, two fork-tailed eagles, and thousands of lorikeets with their fantastic color-contrasting feathers, and "hordes" of Galahs, both of whom formed clouds of flashing colors which zoomed about in the sky. They were a never ending delight.

We knew that we were approaching a settlement of some kind, because a typical outskirts community was presenting itself. Houses were being seen in close proximity to each other. Right here for instance there were very nice one story modern houses lined up beside the road. Each building lot seemed to be about 150 feet wide and maybe twice that in depth. The houses on the east side of the road had driveways that were moderately steep going up to the houses. Mailboxes lined the street. There was one house that even had a small sign which named the property.

"Peggy! What did that little sign say back there on the lawn? I've got to go back!" And sure enough – it said, "Platypus Pass."

I drove up the driveway to the house, knocked on the front door and said, "I'm sorry to disturb you folks, but we saw your sign on the lawn saying *Platypus Pass*, and might you be able to tell us where we could go to see platypus?"

"Sure, in our back yard! You're welcome to drive the car in back and stay as long as you like." I told them that we were camping in the car of our friends who were on a different boat and that we would like to stay the night if it wouldn't disturb them. They were very gracious, welcomed us warmly, showed us where the swimming pool bathroom was for our use, and told us when and where to see the platypus. We settled in for another great unique experience! This time the great Pacific Ocean was entirely overshadowed by a backyard creek. Peggy whispered, "Look – look! I see one. It's to the left of that big root sticking out from the bank!"

What a sight. This thing was just going back into the water! Wow!

We had brought some platypus facts with us in the hope of maybe getting just a glimpse of one. The description sounded unbelievable:

The platypus has a muzzle like a duck's bill; a tail like a beaver's and lays eggs and suckles its young. It lives in burrows and finds food in rivers which it locates using electrical impulses. The male has a poisonous spur on his hind legs. Its feet are fully webbed and are its swimming propulsion. It is found nowhere on earth except in the eastern regions of Australia along fresh water rivers.

This guy was busily following anciently established routines of daily habit, of which we possessed not the slightest clue. But busy he was, as he seemed in a rush to climb out of the water onto the slope of the little river's bank for just the briefest moment—before rushing back into the water where he now proceeded to swim about rather lazily it seemed with his head out for breathing comfort as he maintained a constant surveillance of the general area.

They are very thickly furred in dark brown which is made to appear almost black when wet by the river water That duck type bill, on an animal-type head looks totally incongruous to us whose first reaction was, "Now that's something that only its mother could say is beautiful." But just imagine how ugly they must think that we are!

It is said that they are born with teeth in that duck's bill but that they soon are expelled. Its tail is not as wide as a beaver's. It has course hair on top of it and sparse hair underneath and is only used for steering while swimming, not in aid of swimming. It also serves as fat storage used as nourishment during periods of winter time when its food source is depleted.

The bill is blue grey in color and is flat, soft, rubbery and somewhat flexible. It is filled with nerves and therefore affords great sensitivity for the capacity to feel and uses its bill to acquire food and find its way around under water. There are two nasal holes on the top of the bill, very close to the end, which enable the platypus to float with its entire body submerged except for the end of its bill. This is one remarkable creature.

We slept on our air mattresses in the back of the station wagon, content in having seen an actual platypus and had seen him up close and personal. We had been no more than fifty feet from him.

The folks on whose place we were camped were very solicitous of our comfort and pleasure, and had invited us to swim in the pool with them, but we were over anxious not to appear cheeky as the expression is here. But I now regret not having done so because they may well have wanted to hear about these two creatures who like them had noses instead of duck-type bills. But to us, our sailing around was a perfectly unremarkable thing. And although it is certainly nothing of immensity it may have granted a diversion for them had we exercised greater acuity.

Morning came, and before we had eaten any of our breakfast, there were platypus! "There's one over there! And another one over there! This is fantastic!"

Platypuses are primarily loners. So this must be a family! The water wasn't very clear, so when one popped up over here and dove down again and when one popped up over there we assumed that it was likely the same one. But there had to be two of them cavorting about, and we had numerous sightings of them in sundry attitudes and behavior! It was an absolute joy to us to have been so close to all of their activity this morning! And our hosts were delighted by our ecstasy and bubbly chatter about the experience as we thanked them profusely for their gracing our memory by our having seen Australia's platypus; a memory by which we are forever enriched. With great fondness do these folks reside amongst our treasured memories, as yet another Australian couple by whose hand a door was held open into a passage of time through which this fascinating platypus creature has passed into our experience. What a fitting name for their property, "The Platypus Pass." Thank you for this profound glimpse.

We took our leave with mutual waving of warm and respected farewell, as the old station wagon drove down the long driveway and turned homeward. For home is where the *Osprey* awaits. How lovely to have Peggy back and to have clear sailing ahead.

This road trip was a cathartic experience. I have never felt as though there was erosion of our firm grasp of reality. We clearly are not sea creatures. Here, we can stop the car and walk about upon the land – not so upon the sea. Here, we are fellow kinsmen though they be bird or beast. Here, there is a familiarity even with something as strange as a platypus because it dwells within the grasp of our hand.

But the *Osprey* is a space ship which is alien to all of the realms that swirl within its fathomless darkness where neither bird nor beast, nor mankind itself can exist. And though, to be cast upon that world of water is, each time again to taste the heady challenge of a gamble in which you have bet the maximum, can it be wondered why our arrivals back upon the land as fellow inhabitants is very different indeed from casting off upon the unknowable abyss of the sea?

Sweet is that taste of voyage-arrivals upon our tongue, even as our departures may approach that of a rather intoxicating elixir.

When we use the term *seamen* referring to ourselves, we could more accurately precede it with the word *temporary*. But upon our good ship *Osprey*, which we endow with all of our knowable reckoning of need and security, mixed affectionately with some small skills learned over time, exposure, and the general craft of yachtsmanship, we do so in full knowledge of our debt to many others. My personal debt is to Susan and Eric Hiscock, who stand among my personal favorites with such books as *Cruising Under Sail*.

As we reach for the stars in whatever endeavor we pursue, it is our good fortune to stand upon the shoulders of giants who plowed the field before us. It would be an unfortunate failing to not be aware of where we stand, for herein lies reality, and therefore humility cannot be escaped.

***

The trip back to Cairns was rich in the sights of vibrant wild life which remained totally unaware of our loudly expressed pleasure of witnessing the wonders of a paint brush which splashed colors through the sky on the wings of wondrous birds. But we were also surrounded by a whispered reminder which we could not ignore.

Over the ages the winds have bent the strong old trees which huddled together against many storms. If they could walk about, a stout cane need come to hand. We share this storm season together. This is why we have chosen a secure place up a twisting river for the *Osprey* — just in case a wind such as that which has bent this small forest, were to return. They find this place frequently, slamming into Australia more often southward from here. It is the fickle nature of weather whose spurs jab us to greater hurry in our return; and the closer we get, the more urgent is our concern even though the car radio's weather reports remain unthreatening.

At last, we have gained the city limits of Cairns. The yacht club is next, then the car keys are given back to Charlotte and Conrad with our thanks, and then again at last to board the *Osprey*. It's always great to be back. The *Osprey* also smiled. Looking at her from a distance, one might be forgiven for thinking that she is just a few chunks of tree. There is a mutual granting of security between us; when close ashore, she needs our protection. At sea, we need hers.

She has brought us here and to many lands. And *beyond here*, she has also shown to us – the stars.

Our most familiar star awakened us to a new day, bright and beautiful, and reawakened us to the tasks yet unfinished. I removed the Edson Steering gear and had it ready the next morning to take with me in Olgert's car for a careful overhaul at his shop. The topic of the day was sails! I had been gathering local information about sail makers in Australian and international. Olgert had gotten his sails made in China and I wanted to know why from China and how happy he was with them.

This is the way we worked at Olgert's shop. It is true that we worked. But it would be untrue to say that we did not talk, for we did so incessantly! He was delighted with the sails, with the quality of their construction, and that each sail arrived exactly as ordered, and more cheaply by far than from any other source found by him in a dedicated search.

I had been doing a lot of reading on the subject of making our own. I had found a proper sewing machine on the market for the job but was truly daunted by the creation of various amounts of draft required for each specific sail. Before I had traveled far on my mental trip along that road I knew that I was out of my depth, but had hoped to gain some confidence as I tried to learn. The reverse was the case. But our need for new sails was to the point of being critical! I wrote to Japan and to China and to the US for estimates, and waited.

We met new people at church as well as every other place we went. We went to a concert in the park one day. It was being performed in a lovely park outside of the business district of Cairns. It was crowded with standing room only. We were in the back.

Sitting on a park bench in front of us was a gentleman who began a conversation with us during intermission, probably because of detecting our odd pronunciation of words, he concluded that we were Yanks. He was interested in pronunciation, and proceeded to criticize his fellow local Aussies' pronunciation of the name of our host city, Cairns.

The Australians, as is the case with Englanders, preference to not pronounce the Rs in many words and place some on the end of words which are invisible to some others. He proceeded to say the name of the city as the locals pronounce it, instead of the proper way, which he also pronounced.

He said, "They say Cans instead of Cans."

I said, "Hmm," because, I could not distinguish any slightest difference at all. I hurriedly changed the subject to commending him for the performance of the concert, as it was his wife who was its maestro.

**

We met John and Julie aboard *Caspie,* a very small sailboat, who were building a new and much larger boat in a fenced field outside of Cairns. It was a steel hulled, junk rigged boat by a naval architect on Chesapeake Bay. I had met good Mr. Calvin and was very interested in his designs and in this design specifically, so of course I wanted to see how John was doing on the project.

They invited me to come – gave the directions to find them – and I was immediately caught up into the project. So in the middle of everything else of our projects for the *Osprey* and our departure preparations for New Guinea, I had the added fun of helping John, who otherwise had only Julie and their young daughter to help with some heavy steel plates.

It was about this time that Haley's Comet was arriving. The radio informed us all that the best time for us to see it would be at 2 AM tomorrow morning. At the sound of my alarm clock I rushed on deck, looked toward the indicated direction and found that I needed to climb half way up the ratlines to gain enough elevation to see over the mangrove trees. And there it was, Haley's Comet in all its glory after having spent generations of earth years since last it came our way. Now there's a voyage for you! I rushed down and told Peggy! She must not have heard me because she just muttered something and turned over. (Was she trying to say that she had a head-ache?) No, she said that she didn't want to get up. But that didn't make any sense—this is Haley's Comet – of course she wants to see it! I urged her up, which she did with half her energy and half mine. We got up on deck and to the ratlines by my supporting a third of her weight but the next problem was how to get her onto the lowest rung which is four feet off the deck. One must first grasp the ratlines from underneath for support if wished, and then step up onto the top of the cabin roof, and while still holding onto the ratlines, swing one's self outward into space, pull yourself upward with your arms and get a foot onto the lower rung, and then with a thrust of the right foot, gain an upright position on the ratlines to then begin climbing in the manner of using a ladder.

Peggy was not speaking in any audible word usage of any language of my acquaintance. She sounded and acted as though she was half asleep, but I knew that she would not wish to miss this moment because after all, who would?!!

I got her onto the ratlines. "Okay Peggy, you are on the ratlines." I was behind and under her. In fact I had quickly shoved my arm under her posterior as she slumped toward a sitting position. "Okay Peggy, now we are going up one more step." She grunted something unintelligible and did nothing. I took hold of her left bare foot and shook it a little and said, "Okay Peggy, lift this foot up to the next step and up we go!" Again the mumble, but no movement.

I had no choice now. So ever onward and upward, and with my 80% effort and 20% of hers we could see Haley's Comet!

I said, "Wow, look at that!" And this time she responded, but with a gigantically yelled groaning utterance which astounded me! We were in an anchorage area of many boats and I expected a dozen spot lights any minute to reveal a woman in her night gown trying to escape from her husband who is in his usual night attire of absolutely nothing!

I closed my eyes to the brilliance of the lights, but none came, for which I was grateful; but though I have given up on Haley, I've now got to get this woman down from here when I found another situation. As Peggy had hollered, she slumped downward and was sitting fully on my arm the fingers of which had grasped a ratline and were tiring due to loss of circulation. And worse than this, one of her breasts had fallen out of her night gown and was now between the ratlines. In the midst of all of this, there also came the ever awareness of the crocodiles with whom were shared this specific area.

I prevented so much as a scratch, much less harm to any of her tender parts, and I got her down by saying, okay this is your hand, we are going to put it here and then likewise the foot movements, and even managed the swing off the last step onto the cabin roof, (to the disappointment of the crocodiles). I got her back onto her bed inside the cabin.

I was very worried about her strange condition of a total stupor from which I could not completely awaken her. In the morning at her usual time of awakening, she was fine. I brought her to the hospital where this was diagnosed as a low blood sugar condition. She remembered parts of the event. She remembered my trying to awaken her and not wanting to awaken. She remembers parts of the climb up the ratlines, and some but not much of meeting good old Haley. And the entire event has been reduced to the jest of Peggy having been affected by the dangers of the dreaded *comet dust,* which ages ago was actually thought of with great apprehension.

* * *

While back here in the land of reality, Olgert gave us one of his jibs to try on the *Osprey*. It was one which had been made in China by the company for whose cost estimate I had written, and I was very interested to test its set and draft. On a good day for the test with wind in the 20s, we set out toward Fitzroy Island and put that sail through a vigorous test of performance. It was sheer joy! It was a little undersized for our boat but compared to what we had been sailing with, (that jerry-rigged, double-headed sloop which itself is a contradiction of terms); a jib that somewhat resembled what the *Osprey* was intended to have, brought us back to Cairns with grins on our faces. Peggy is always nice to me. When I grin, she grins too, (or is she laughing at me again? I give her plenty of cause.) It looks as though China is getting our order for sails if the price is right!

Christmas is here. Though we are accustomed to having warm weather at Christmas, here in the southern hemisphere its summer time in December as the usual festive anticipations are a-swirl all about. Our close association with Margaret Upiti, Olgert's good wife, assured us of all the great fun planned at the yacht club for the Christmas and New Years parties and events; plus all of the church activities almost required starting a formal appointment calendar. It was a great time, approaching that of a family, as so many of us with like interests and adventures were all simultaneously gathered together, by which vicariously we all sought to be with those whose names were the same as ours. We did so in recognition that we were all known by the name *yachtsmen*. I don't think that it was being rationalized this way by anyone here, but a kinship was present among us. And perhaps it was this fact which softened the smile, moistened the eye, and granted specialness to the touch of the handshake or the gentle hug of departures.

Chapter 8   *Peggy is Back!!*

Robert and Joann sat at our table for awhile. They lived ashore in a rented house and had a rather small boat; sailed to Cairns from their home farther south from here. Robert had been assigned his medical internship in the Cairns hospital. He was not very long out of med school but carried that enviable title of Doctor, earned as is always the case with vigorous and applaudable effort.

It is always interesting to me to learn the vastness of varied family settings that have brought people to *the water world*. We talked here at the yacht club with Aussie sailors from towns large and small.

One of the ladies had been brought up on a very sizable wheat farm far from any water. As a child she had grown up looking way up there at huge farming tractors which had even dwarfed her father (who in the eye of a child is the biggest personage on earth). The settings from which we all have emerged differ to infinity and our skills now reside within persons unrecognizable from earlier time. A point in case, there was a time when Robert didn't know how to tie his shoes. But a "few weeks later," I told him that I wanted him to cut my back open.

A lump had developed below one of my shoulder blades. It was about the size of a grapefruit – well, maybe a peach. Actually it was about the size of a peach pit or maybe a walnut, well okay, maybe a very small grape. In any event it didn't belong there so I wanted it removed. He looked at it, agreed that it should be removed, said that he had never done something like this, but if I would come to the hospital at a certain time, he would cut it out.

I arrived at the appointed time. It was a couple hour's walk. I waited, and at the appointed time Doctor Robert found me in the waiting room. With a furtive look around of which I did not permit my observed notice, and in an appropriate side room, Robert performed his first surgery.

The reason for his looking about as he did, was to see if anyone was there to note what he was doing. And indeed, he was subsequently found out due to his sending the extraction to the laboratory for determination of the matter of its composition.

The reason for Robert's secrecy was over the fact that an intern was not permitted even such small surgery as this. Happily he was only tongue-lashed for his breach of protocol and didn't really get into trouble. I left to walk the three or so miles back to the yacht club, assured that the lab results would be shared in a few days.

John and Julie's new boat building location was on the way back and I was in pleasant thought about the project and planning to stop for awhile, which turned out to be a greater need than had come to mind. I found that I was bleeding down my pants leg. Checking to see why, I found that my shirt was slowly running red. I needed to put pressure on the surgery but I couldn't reach it. I could, as a last resort, lay on a rock on the ground until it stopped, but I wanted something portable.

I looked around in the small ditch along the side of the road. Maybe a small tree branch with a thick section that I could carry bent across my back would work. But better yet, there was a short length of rope. It was filthy, but so what. I had a bandage and a shirt between it. This was perfect.

I can't imagine its prior function, but here was a one fathom length of two inch diameter hemp. I put a knot in it, threw one end over my shoulder across my back, caught the other end in my free hand, adjusted the position of the knot over the bleeding spot, pulled it tight and walked on. It was exactly what was needed. By the time that I got to the boat building site the bleeding was controlled. Julie cleaned me up a bit and I helped John for a couple of hours.

I was now delighted to not be turning slowly into a candidate for bell ringer at a cathedral as was the hunchback of Notre Dame; and Robert never heard about the bleeding past the sutures and bandage. But in the fullness of time, the lab reported that they were somewhat uncertain about the growth identification which was passed to them. They thought that perhaps it had resulted from an insect bite. But then, we had walked in places where perhaps few Australians from the medical laboratory world may have trod. "Thanks for the job on the back Robert. The lump has never returned, and remains only in a memory of kindness, received from your mother's son."

Chapter 8 — Peggy is Back!!

***

Al and Ruth were a hoot. They were an American couple several years older than we. Peggy and Ruth especially enjoyed each other's company and often shopped together, etc. So it was a natural progression that we did other things together, such as our cassowary lunch. No, we were not going to eat them; we wanted to see them, as did Ruth and Al. So at church, when we learned that one of the local sugarcane farming members lived close to the Queensland State Forest Park where cassowaries were regularly seen, we excitedly accepted a mid week picnic lunch date with them. And rather than Ken and Ivy driving two hours from their home to Cairns to pick us up and return us afterward, Peggy arranged for Ruth and Al to drive us there for our mutual enjoyment and their meeting of Ivy and Ken.

When we arrived at the park, sure enough, several wild cassowaries were there! What a fabulous sight! We had however, been pre-warned of their unfortunate means of dispatching any creature smaller than the seven feet of their height, by a quick jump and simultaneously with both feet cut the stomach right out of its perceived human enemy. However, the solution is a very easy one. A person need only stand when an approach begins, and raise one arm straight up over your head, bend the wrist at a 45 % angle toward the cassowary, while bringing ones finger tips together by which the head of a cassowary or ostrich is presented at a height above that of the concerned Big Bird. You are thereby seen to be the biggest bird in the Park and therefore not to be messed with. It worked as advertised, but when our table was approached for scraps, we birds chose another spot to graze.

A few days later, a small typhoon was approaching and struck the coast about at Townsend just a ways south of Cairns. I was cavorting about in the dinghy watching the show and going aboard various boats chatting with friends. As one might expect, I am not lacking in at least the simple skill of rowing a small boat, feathering the oars in the process (especially with wind like this), and not at all shy of leaning into a pull on our nine foot oars when called on to do so. I was thoroughly enjoying myself as I watched with very great interest the wind "bullets" as they were breaking through the "wall." I think of the air as a large chunk and the wind as a separate chunk of air trying to push its way through. It gets large sections moving by virtue of its effort, and regularly pushes through the remaining resistance funneled as narrow slots by its force, like bullets through a wall. There surely are meteorological descriptions that can more properly portray the above, but let it just be said that I was having an enjoyable time.

As I approached the *Osprey*, which the wind was heeling over into the mangroves, I could see Peggy with her body part way out of the hatchway yelling something. The wind was just the slightest bit noisy at the time, so I couldn't actually hear her words, but the meaning was clear. And when I got there it was made even more clear by her nervous words of frustration, perhaps bordering ever so slightly toward misapplied beginnings of apprehension. Though I must also report that the *Osprey* was dragging her moorings and the boat was being ever so comfortably nestled into the mangroves beside us as the boat was shoved over on her side by the wind. We later learned that five miles south of us, seventy-five knot winds were recorded, which was in a gust much stronger than I know we were receiving here. The storm passed without any local damage.

I was still reading everything that I could get my hands on regarding making one's own sails, as Peggy brought the mail to the boat and excitingly announced, "The quote for new sails just arrived from Lee." Lee Sailmakers of Hong Kong were the ones who had supplied sails to a couple of cruisers of our acquaintance and they had found them excellent in every way. I might have given a slight tremble of anticipation to my hand had Peggy not already opened it.

"Wow! That's great" I said to Peggy's affirming head shake!

We had asked for a cost quote for a new mainsail (specifying number of reef point rows and cringle types and sizes) and four headsails, (specifying wind strengths for each, tack distance off the deck, as well as clew distance off the deck.) "Plate" effect is beneficial to a racer, but short-handed sailing with years passing before replacement instead of overnight replacement of a sail which a healthy wave has taken the lower section with it, is not to be risked. I prefer the foot of a jib well off the deck.

We ordered the sails with the required one-third deposit, the remainder due before shipment. Helping us with our local expenses was the fact that our income money was US dollars and the Aussie dollar at that moment cost us sixty-eight cents. So we were also able to order *Lexan*, a strong Plexiglas like product, for replacement of our canvas and isinglass roll ups as windows in the wheelhouse.

Oh how carefully I measured each window before marking the four by eight foot panel for cutting in Olgert's shop. When I brought the first one home and held it in place with its protective brown paper covering which keeps the "glass" from being scratched in transit and handling, I could none the less see it as though it were attached to its hinges, clear and beautiful with nothing but joyous exuberance which stretched from ear to ear; and as I stood there on that very narrowest section of deck and had taken the glass out to drill the holes for the now marked hinge bolts, a gust of wind grabbed it right out of my hands and threw it into the rushing tide of the river!

The river swallowed it instantly, as in total disbelief I could not for a moment grasp that what I had just seen could have actually happened! Yet simultaneously I also knew that I needed to get my scuba gear on my back and go down to get it!

By the time I was in the water I could detect almost no tidal flow, though the usual slow outflow was present. The water is the color of mud. I knew when I got to the bottom when my arm pushed half way into the muddy. The Lexan wasn't directly below the boat. I felt everywhere! I used up all of the scuba air and had to give up. I had the tank refilled, but had also begrudgingly accepted the fact that I needed to buy another sheet of Lexan, a very unscheduled expense. We guard vigorously against such events because of our budget's clarion announcements of pending doom were we to exceed its limits. Nonetheless, new Lexan was ordered, delivered, and the final touch of the wheelhouse completion now graced the *Osprey*'s smile. With the new windows, in rainy conditions we can prop the window partly open and still stay dry while airflow will keep us comfortable. And when in heavy weather, the window to weather is stronger than the amount of sea water which previously intended to slap us in the face for daring to be there. Lexan is reported to be bullet proof. I am happy!

***

Most of us now were in various stages of preparation for our approaching departure to Papua New Guinea. Al and Ruth were likewise scurrying about. They had sold the pickup truck with its camper to someone living in the Sidney area and agreed to deliver it to them. Peggy was invited to join them and did so, after which Al flew back, having work on the boat to do, and Peggy and Ruth took the train, the better by which to see the country.

Of course, one would expect to take a day to see the sights of Sidney, and Ruth and Peggy were no exception. There was reported pleasure taken in the notice of tempting displays as seen while "window shopping." After all, big city life is a far cry from sailboats cruising about in the Islands of the South Pacific. They had fun.

The next day, shortly after breakfast, they hurried to the big Sidney train station, picked their way through the throngs to their train's scheduled track and were among the early boarders. They chose their seats, delighted in their oversized proportion with individual arm rests and deep cushioning. The first class car was equipped with seats for two people on one side and one person on the other due to the width of the train not being able to accommodate more than that.

So with the traditional blast of the whistle to clear the track ahead, all occupants of all of the cars shuddered in unison to the accompaniment to the skidding of the engine's wheels on the steel tracks just before forward motion commenced. Steel wheels won the battle of inertia by the powerful effort of the engine. Sidney was left astern, as quickly its surrounding towns also gave way to *Australia!*

Chapter 8

Peggy is Back!!

The familiar, the habitat of mankind; vanished from sight and as though yet another venture of time travel had hurled them into another domain, the world outside morphed suddenly to a different planet. Here suddenly kangaroos were everywhere, on the train tracks or lopping along beside it amongst misshapen shrubs and trees and boulders looking as though some giant hand had strewn them about. Ostrich were equally busy ignoring the train and its space travelers from a future time. Ruth and Peggy were enthralled.

They slept the night away in these marvelous chairs rather than incur the expense of beds. When they arrived in Melbourne the next day, they were dismayed to learn that they were required to change trains, even though they had bought tickets through to Cairns. The problem was explained by the fact that the train tracks are of different space between them as those on which the present train had traveled. The tracks were narrower on the trains going farther north. It was further explained to them that their next train did not come to this station. It was at a station on the far opposite side of the city of Melbourne from this train station. "No there is no bus scheduled to transfer passengers, you just nab a cab! She'll be right mate!"

So Peggy and Ruth gathered their gear, and with bags in both hands and skirts flying they ran outside in the hope of finding a taxi cab to drive them across the city to a different train station which they hoped might still retain the presence of their sought after transport. All of which further spiced the overall adventure and fun of the varied taste of life just that little bit different from one's own home town.

The narrower gauge railway was no less pleasant than the other, with the possible difference of aesthetics, but in the fullness of time they returned to the century where Al and I were found to be, and we were both happy to see them. Ruth and Peggy had watched in wrapped fascination as a huge part of Australia had streamed past them as they had sat motionless and comfortably in their *theater in the train*. I will refrain from asking, "Which one was the reality," because although I have fun playing mind games, I do have a very firm grasp of reality, or were they really theatre tickets which Al had bought for them? Point of clarity, Peggy had paid her own way on that venture, regardless of what Al has been telling you! My editor will probably omit that silliness, so I won't worry about your incredulity.

One of the folks at church, upon hearing that we were going to PNG told us that her daughter was working as a nurse in the Sopas Hospital at Wabag, and would like to send some church-made blankets to her for the babies there. So of course we agreed to do so. (PNG is smaller than Australia but it isn't all that small as to think that we certainly will be at point X while there.) But the anticipation shining in her face was too happy to be rejected even as our agreement was taken as a matter of course. (A rejection would have been beyond understanding.) It was explained that her daughter was in the highlands and that it got very cold there, and that these infants could not in good health be thus exposed.

The women of the church, now including Peggy, had been crocheting baby blankets, an entire military type duffel bag full of these gifts were ready to be sent off to PNG. And here we were, to do it for free. The location of the hospital being somewhere in the *highlands* was not lost on my ear as an *ocean sailing* yachtsman. But if truth be known, there was a considerable anticipation of perhaps seeing unexpected areas mixed in with our tongue-in-cheek acceptance of the task. Subsequently, we have now become eternally grateful for the richness of memories treasured by us for all time, by virtue of the unique moments shared with those mountain people who are so remote from all of our prior experience. Thank you good ladies of the church, for granting us that simple task by which it is we, who are to become the ones most richly rewarded!

The sails arrived. Our work is done. And we are off for New Guinea.

CHAPTER 9

 New Guinea

I was excited as I raised the new mainsail! With the mainsail sheet cast free while at our mooring, I had my first look at the new mainsail! Up she went to the very masthead, two and a half significant feet above the old one aboard when we had bought the boat.

I next rigged the down and out haul reefing lines. These are the lines that place and retain the foot of the mainsail to the boom. The grommets at the two ends of the reef points were beautifully constructed and large, just as ordered to accommodate the reefing system of my preference which included the down haul of the main to each of the three reef points of the mainsail. These lines live forever as they are now attached to the sail. I also briefly raised each of the new jibs.

The *Osprey* tugged at her mooring restraints and seemed to be prepared to launch herself into flight as though from a high perch, as in my mind's eye I too prepared to soar! Finally, this grand ship seemed to shake her feathers from a long season of molting, to that of an even grander stature of maturity. Ah how magnificently she poised herself for flight!

With the clear knowledge of our impending departure needs, one would expect that prudence would not have permitted any distraction of attention or time for anything else. But alas, my perfection lays bare before you any claim to its existence. We were off on another day trip.

One of the church people told us about it. (See how much trouble these churches get us into!) There were ancient petroglyphs in the area, and someone knew someone who knew where they were.

The car accommodated the five of us comfortably. The church couple took us in their car and of greatest import to this was the presence of a retired Forestry Agent, whose accompaniment quarantined our personal propriety against any commitment of vandalism within the cave; and the obtaining of a permit to access the road toward our destination was likewise assured.

We came to a large steep hillside, not quite a mountain. There are layers of horizontal rock strata some distance up this face below which a great amount of ancient erosion has created a rather deep cave, unusual in the vastness of these surroundings. It took no effort to imagine, that due to the singularity of such a place as this and its stark aura that it be thought of by the ancients as a sacred place.

If the aboriginal holy men frequented this place, at least one of them had some artistic flare, because on the inner walls we found depicted a Man, an Emu, a Kangaroo, a Fish, a Turtle and many Spirits. Some would consider these as crude, viewing that the man depicted was rather no more than a stick figure, and that the animals drawn were not presented with an over abundance of detail. Though one need not expect art gallery approval for its nuance, its retention as historical insight is magnificence in its simplicity.

Over the centuries the aborigines have retained such findings of the ancients. And as the silent hand of time reached into this cave to wash away the color of their life, holy men with reverent care retraced those ancient colors where first they had so long ago been placed. Even so is this day that we, the present occupants of spaceship Earth, stand in this living museum's significance and with the awe felt appropriate in this an infrequent presence of time, a window has been opened through which we have journeyed back to the very day when a holy man stood before this wall of rock and lifted up his hand. Often such image presentations are coupled with secret knowledge held by the elders in stories relating to events held holy by them.

We feel honored to have been permitted to enter such a place of ancient memory, even though our personal history does not fully open the door through which we are able to see reverence, it does certainly grant us the opportunity to see and express honor to those of present and past lineage. I can only muse over the eons of time that these good people have walked upon this land. Their beginning was likely well before my fathers walked upon a place we now call Europe. Thank you again, good members of the church, for your kind adding of yet another time traveling experience. I love trips such as these.

I finished the preparations to get underway toward PNG, while Peggy finished some medical attention being cared for as an outpatient of the hospital, and with much fanfare of gracious friends of the yacht club and the church; we processed our documents with the Customs Office and were cleared for departure from this grand and giant land of Australia. We got under way in time enough to reach Fitzroy Island before dark.

With the anchor well set for the night, a familiar routine unbidden and unhurried took possession of those aboard the *Osprey*. A simple dinner, most relaxed and leisurely enjoyed, was mixed with conversation such as with any wife and husband after a routine day, secure in the knowledge that all was well with their world. Neither anxiety nor apprehension was present as we settled down to a pleasant nights rest. Tomorrow, another beginning would mark yet another new adventure. And though its anticipation was exciting, such as a new destination of a truly great vacation excites one with being kept awake for those few minutes after settling one's head on that comfortable pillow, this passage is only for a few days. Once entirely free from the Great Barrier Reef, our course is quite unencumbered. And maybe when we get some distance away, we might even find some wind for these brand new sails!

It was a great night. The water was protected and quiet, almost motionless. I didn't want to get under way early. We would be going through the pass too directly into the sun if we left much before about ten, prior to which the reflection of the sun on the water is the worst for being able to see through the water for coral hazards anyway; so we had a good excuse to proceed without any rush. Only on a one day sail, when you need to get to an anchorage before dark, do you need an early start. On a passage of a few days duration, obviously there is no such departure rush required. The other reason why I was in no hurry was the fact that here we are with a brand new sail inventory with no wind at all to which to present it!

The 16th: We left Fitzroy Island at 1 PM, having set the dials of the taffrail log to zero. There was still not a breath of wind. The *Osprey* endured the sound of our *iron mainsail*. Both she and we have oft times heard that sound so strange to the soul of an ocean sailing vessel. A few hours later, thanks to our diesel engine, the Great Barrier Reef of the mighty continental Island of Australia lay astern; having permitted yet another ocean cast vessel to be rejected by the jaws of its reefs and permitted to venture onward. Its jaws have grasped the ships of many who dared its reach.

Over the eons of time the reef has devoured both frail and mighty. As early as the ancient dug-out-log canoes whose sail power was that of palm tree fronds held up to the wind by people of the northern islands now called Indonesia, to the great Captain Cook's square rigged ships, all were playfully grasped by the reef, and upon being rejected, were spat out again. Even such great ships as these were dangerously mauled by their encounter with The Great Barrier Reef. Now having escaped its reach, I turn my attention northeastward; but as I do so, I give a respectful and silent salute to those many, who forever there remain.

Peggy volunteered to take a two hour watch as the autopilot was not functioning, and so it was that we began our intervals of two hour steering. At various intervals, the engine cooling water level and oil level quantity must be checked, so there are a few minutes of escape from the engine's noise. There is a love hate relationship with our *iron mainsail*. One hates the dominating loudness of the engine as compared to the pleasantness of voyaging under sail, but oh how sweet the sound when that engine's propulsion is needed!

The 17th: We motored across the quiet sea all day and all night. A star shot at dusk fixed our position as the taffrail log marked 262 nautical miles of travel. Shipboard life is always endowed by the presence of a smile, which was evident at the table with its breakfast eggs and toast, its cheese with tomato and lettuce sandwich at lunch time, and its dinner salad and hamburgers, at the appointed time whereby lights are not required in the galley at conclusion.

The 18th: With sextant in hand and Peggy carefully writing the exact time of the instant of my mid-morning sun shot, done just for the pleasure of it and without real need, the taffrail log read 313 miles. I never feel it needful to know any great precision of location early during a passage, though many cruisers feel that if they are unexpectedly encompassed by foul weather they want to be certain of their resent movements. The preference of my attention seems perhaps to be more focused on cloud formation as a weather hobby than what may be the interest of others.

The 19th: I found the oil leak problem and took care of it; changed the oil filter and tightened the alternator belt. We were still motoring, when during the night a little breeze picked up and at 2:30 this morning at long last I was able to raise those precious sails! At 3:30 the sails came down again. The breeze had disappeared. By 4:00 we were both in bed for some sleep till 8 o'clock when the breeze found its way back to us. We sailed from 8:30 to 10:30. The noon shot fixed our position at 12 degrees 03 minutes south & 148 degrees 54.9 minutes east. Peggy, uncharacteristically, wanted to see where our position was on the chart whereby she had a view of our progress.

The 20th: At dawn, a four star shot fix let me have the fun of telling Peggy the clock time at which she will first see land. And as though by the magic of my command for the land to then appear it was so, for how after all could it not – he says.

The log read 632 nautical miles since Australia, not very far at all, but we wanted some quiet restful sleep. Five days of wakeful motoring is much more demanding than dozens of days of sailing. Having passed through the doldrums toward the equator, one expects light to non existing wind. So motoring was an expected necessity. It was 7:30 PM when the anchor was finally secured in Dogadoga Bay. We were glad to be here. We ate a light supper, took showers, and before going to bed were treated to a sun set gloriously adorned with all of the regal splendor as befitting an occasion such as our arrival in these magnificent isles. Samurai is just beyond this small bay, and its officialdom will await the morrow.

Almost all of our wanderings among these forested islands are requiring the use of our engine. As we move about among these islands, it's easy to use the term "jungle" to refer to the primal unchanged shroud of verdant vines held high to the sun by ancient trees and timeless hills where no other foot has stood except the villager who hunts here with bow and with arrows. Maybe the absence of the great apes and frolicking monkeys as abide in the wilds of Africa seem to tame the place unjustly, but soon we will leave the boat and venture far into the highlands, and there we shall find — another world.

***

The *Osprey*'s documentation was completed the next morning, and her people were formally entered into the country by the officials in the town of Samurai. Little shops sleepily lined the small street where the customs office too was in difficulty retaining its wakefulness. So with proper quietness I raised the anchor and moved to another quiet spot where we were excitedly greeted by a group of children in their own individual miniaturized dugout canoes. When we were securely anchored, we talked with them and several came aboard, whereupon we were "formally" invited to come to see their school. We did so later in the day, firstly asking our way to the hut of the chief.

He introduced himself. His name is Papua, which he said means "Big Hair," and he announced the fact that he was the school teacher, so off we went to see the school. It was without walls. Some poles supported the thatched roof for shade. Chief Papua seemed pleased at being invited to join us for dinner aboard the *Osprey* and he regaled us with information of some of the customs of local tribesmen and their lives, and we in turn spoke of customs and lives of people of whom he may have only read in brief reference.

He told us of his anguish that the youngsters of his school have only heard of the place of their elders who walked in times long passed. There was a place where caves still show pictures on the walls of people and of animals and of birds drawn there by the ancestors of his students. This place is on the Island of Kawato, the immense distance of ten or twelve sea miles away. The problem was not the distance; it was the means of transport by which to get the school there. It was a great tongue in cheek wonderment as to how this problem might be resolved, when we all seemed to be overwhelmed by the thought, "Oh my! We could take the *Osprey*!"

Two days later, all forty five children and two other teachers were taken aboard for an all day outing to Kawato Island which is on the other side of Samurai and just off this island's shore. The chief had borrowed a motor boat. It was probably about twenty feet in length with a fifty horsepower engine. So the chief and principal of the school, was very impressively roaring about.

Everyone was well behaved and delighted as any child in the history of earth to be off on an outing and everybody absolutely tingled in their excitement. Only the local language was in use, but the excitement was contagious.

Somewhat of an event occurred on the way back. The good chief, not having left the shores of Kawato when all of our passengers had boarded the *Osprey*, could be seen making preparation for doing so. I got our anchor up, and starting back toward Samurai, while keeping watch that the good principal's engine gets started. It did, and I turned my attention back to the *Osprey*'s progress and the children aboard. Everyone was lined up sitting on the edge of the house with their feet on the side deck all facing outward from our boat and able to look both forward and aft, all chattering away happily. Everyone saw the chief start out toward us in a magnificent roar of speed and wake and spray.

He was about to fly past us on our port side with all of the speed that the fifty horsepower engine could possibly deliver. He was about forty feet from our side and had just caught up to our stern, when the towel tied around his neck was blown up and entirely covered his face. As he let go of the steering wheel with both hands to snatch the towel from his face so that he could see, his boat at full speed turned ninety degrees to the right and crashed into the side of the *Osprey*. The bow of his boat was up high due to the great speed and was launched up over the topsides, through the lifelines, over the deck where the children were sitting on the house and into the side of the cabin.

The children had all scattered, so no one was hurt except perhaps the pride of the chief.

The *Osprey* took the event in stride having sustained no serious damage. And the chief's borrowed boat appeared only scratched a bit and also continued under its own power. We made no further mention of the event and all carried on without showing that anything untoward had occurred.

Upon our return, the chief's expressions of concern were assuaged by our abundant assurance that there was no problem and he used his boat to ferry everyone ashore. Our air of joviality was sustained throughout as propriety required, and in fact circumstance afforded simple sincerity in doing so. It was an outing of import to the school, as the children had stood in reverent awe in the presence of their past.

I undertook no commencement of repairs in the presence of anyone here, and took our leave the next day making for Kanakona Harbor in Milne Bay where we had the pleasure of meeting an Australian couple who were living there. They invited us to dinner and Peggy brought a dish of lentils and a chocolate cake. We represented a diversion of events and conversation, and they graciously gave us insights into the area and its people. We enjoyed their warm hearted kindness and stories reaching back to the Second World War when the Corps of Engineers right here had found a stream bringing muddy water to this spot. They went up into the mountain, found its source, and piped the water of the stream for over a mile, which brings water still to this day, gloriously clear and delicious with which we filled our water jugs in several trips to the boat. We filled our tanks with this wonderful water never surpassed anywhere in our travels. Three cheers to the US Corps of Engineers!

***

As the *Osprey* left the protected waters of Kanakona astern, our friends took their place in our fond memories as we all waved our best wishes to each other. Several other beautiful starry night anchorages were enjoyed before reaching Normanby Island, named after an English explorer who was one of its early visitors. The island has both high mountain terrain and some flat lands. It looked as though the entire island had been a volcano with one side having fallen away into the sea, leaving this central area now filled by the ocean. It gave me a strange feeling to actually sail into the center of a volcano.

Our arrival appears to have been observed by the younger generation, for it gave hordes of kids a reason to run for their canoes and come churning their way to us as we got an anchor down. Youngsters are as much fun for us as we seemed to be to them. Because they come aboard not slowing their laughter through the candy that everybody was now joyously chewing. Awhile after they had gone (the candy must have run out) an adult fellow came up in his canoe. He too was invited aboard as everyone always is and we were able to understand each other's words quite clearly.

And soon, apparently upon feeling sufficiently comfortable to do so, he asked, "Do you have an apple?"

We were surprised at this and told him how sorry we were in not having one; whereupon he explained why he had asked. He told us that a long time ago he had visited aboard a sailing yacht, and that they had given him an apple. When he went home, he had described in detail to his wife how wonderful it was and he was just hoping that we might have one which he would take to his wife for her to experience. (Though his words were in Pigeon English the shine in his eyes was in English.)

We invited him to bring his wife for coffee later in the day. And after the usual balancing act of standing up in a dugout canoe in order to get way up onto our deck, a feat of which no one ever failed by falling backwards into the water, she too managed with some grace.

They sat on one side of the table on my bunk, and Peggy and I sat on her bunk on the other. His wife had not yet said anything. And though I took pains not to show that I was watching, I clearly saw that she was fidgeting ever so slightly. But as we talked on, she suddenly slid from her seat on my bunk and onto the floor where I saw her exhale an enormous expression of relief.

My words never missed a beat as we carried on, because we all understood her discomfort in this huge breach of etiquette which she was doing by having her head on the same level as ours which is not to be done in their custom.

***

We spent the night at this spot, but I was interested to have the full effect of being inside this volcano, so I motored us all the way in to the farthest end from the opening. Other folks came and went as the sun moved its way across where once lava poured red hot from the center of the earth. It was a very pleasant day as almost all are.

There were three in this canoe, two boys in their probable late teens and a lovely young woman was with them. I was surprised after quite a long stay that she told the boys to go – that she would come later. They left. She stayed. So as we talked while Peggy was on one side of the cockpit and this young woman and I were on the other, I was showing something with pictures of New York City in a magazine as I was trying to occupy time, our legs came in contact with each other and was instantly increased by her to my very great surprise.

Well, to make a long story short, I rowed her ashore, where she announced that she would go to quickly wash herself and return, for which I thanked her but indicated that I would return to the boat.

In many of the Pacific Islands, a white child is sought after which seems odd to me. I chose to leave the island early the next morning.

***

A minor nuisance happened on the 6th of October. I didn't notice, but I had cut my leg on something, perhaps as I was overhauling the sea pump. But at least I got the job done before Chris and his wife arrived for dinner with us. We had just met them yesterday where they were engaged as missionary teachers at the Gesida Island School of a church denomination other than ours, and it was great fun to hear more about his sailboat racing. Before coming here, he was a dentist in England. And to our great fascination we learned that he had sailed single handing in the "Around England Race" as well as other very prestigious racing events and had decided to take a giant leap from home to come to this school where they had found great enjoyment and pleasure.

He told us of a friend who was a frequent fellow competitor in some of those sailing races who took the weight aboard the boat with a serious enough concern that he never took more than one paperback book with him on a race. And as he would conclude the reading of a page, he would without exception, tear that page from the book and drop it overboard whereby the weight of the boat was lightened and therefore its speed increased. It was a fun evening as we all found ourselves consumed by our enjoyment which bounced about all over the globe.

Two days later, we sailed to Galaiva Bay on Goodenough Island where all of the women wore only grass skirts. These differ considerably from the grass skirts worn in the Hawaiian tourist shows, which are quite thick all about. All through New Guinea we found the skirts to be quite thin by comparison and longer in the back than in the front. And very logically, when a woman chooses to sit down, she will reach behind her and gather the skirt in her arm and bring it all in front of her so as not to break the straw by sitting on it; a very practical habit indeed.

The attire of the men varies widely by area and by the tribe to which he is member. Some of the tribes tattoo the faces of their young girls with blue colored patterns of markings which identify the various tribes from each other. Thus the adult women are also identifiable accordingly.

I have never shamed the title of mechanic by so much as even having thought that such an honor of distinction was within my possible reach much less my grasp, but alas, the fervent silent urging of my gentle repetitions of turning the starter key of the engine, persisted in perfectly matching the silence of my urgings. The breeze had chosen to join the general silence and was almost undetectable as I continued to be aware that we really need to get a few hundred yards further to anchor with any security at all. With no detectable wind, we sailed. Having gained that few hundred yards a couple of hours later, I lowered the anchor with immense relief.

We were being watched. He watched us from his small house on the island beyond the coral area between the shore and the boat. And after quite some time, he rowed out to the boat and introduced himself. He was an Australian. He had surmised our problem and had come to commiserate with us and brought something with him which he did not disclose for two days as we talked together while I carried on a conversation with our esteemed engine. I had solved the engine problem quite readily this time actually. Maybe my conversations with it had helped. There was air in the injectors. We were ready to go again, but we stayed for the conversations with this man!

This good man had for many years been the captain of the trading schooner that had plied the waters of these islands and was not only filled to overflowing with wondrous tales of those times, but was willing to talk about them! He was especially interested to tell me about one specific island which shall remain unnamed. It was an island on which a truly vast copra plantation was operated. And the point of interest was that it was run by a king who was proclaimed to be king by all of the people of the island. The man was an Australian. When he came to the island the people were, to say the least, not well off. He organized the collection and processing of copra from the existing trees and had more planted. He organized the scheduling of the trading schooner to buy the copra and to acquire the Australian subsidy for the crop. He arbitrated disputes of the people, disbursed income to the workers and started a store with part of the money from the copra sales whereby everyone could buy what they needed, etc.

The trading schooner often stayed the night for the enjoyment of a great dinner prepared by a number of the young women who were among the varying number of the King's attendants. Pleasant conversations over a game of cards always followed these dinners. The good captain, being an honored guest of the King, was always offered his choice of an after hours companion, but as the Captain told us that he was married and therefore, of course, declined that particular pleasantry.

The general life of the island was described to us in detail. Also the unusual manner in which the store is operated was described. The store was on the second floor of the King's house. In the morning, after sick call, the King would go up stairs and from a window call out in Pigeon English, "Does anyone want something from the store?" He didn't have to call loudly because people were already gathered outside, if not to buy; they were there to see who bought what.

If the desired item is in stock, the price is announced and a bucket is lowered to receive the cash which is counted upon arrival on the second floor. Then the item is lowered to the purchaser. This system has the advantage of preventing the temptation of theft, etc.

The good captain seemed unusually interested in my personal life and habits and with some skill in conversation had learned some considerable information. His skill was such that I never once realized that I was being interviewed. He then went on to say that he was at this very time recipient of a group of four men from the island we had been talking about. And that these men were a committee of four, charged with the commission of his returning with them to be their King because the old King had died. He did not want to go. And he told me that if I would be willing to be the King, that he would arrange it with the "committee."

Well, how often is one offered the Kingdom of an island in a tropic paradise of the South Pacific? In spite of that vision, all of my rushing thoughts were negative. I had visions of rusted inoperative and obsolete equipment, but most of all, I was aware of the current price of copra. The value was so low that Australia was still subsidizing the price so that the plantations might have a chance to survive.

I also knew that PNG had forced the Australians out of the country and were no longer the protectorate of PNG, so what happens if the copra in no longer subsidized? It took me all of perhaps six seconds to decline his offer of introduction and recommendation to the group and my ranking among the Kings of the earth faded forever away well before my coronation. But then, I don't wear the title of mechanic very well either.

It was pleasing to see that the good captain still holds the needs of the islanders in great sincerity. And that man's inclination to recommend this simple sailor to such a responsibility is an honor which though most graciously offered had no triumphal or elevating effect.

And though humbling would be a better description of my reaction, the event remains treasured amongst the list of astonishments in the memories of my mind. I also remember Peggy's reaction to all of this, which had something akin to "Don't you dare" masked within it.

And this from the woman for whom I gave up a kingdom! – Tsk tsk.

***

The next day we anchored in Tawanaguna Bay on Goodenough Island. No village was on this shore. It always gives me pleasure to walk upon a beach where no footprints are found upon its sand. The edge of its world, with rich greenery enhanced by the ever present cocoa palms swayed romantically as though moved by the silent sound of music heard only by the wind, knows only itself; while a completely different sea world of turquoise blueness is very real but never known by the land, though divided from it only by the whiteness of the sand which my toes are feeling. Though beautiful as it was, we stayed just one day, as I was increasingly interested to enter our first fjord.

The course of our voyage was somewhat wandering, but the ultimate intent was to reach the point where our promised delivery of the infant's blankets, made by the hands of the ladies of the church at Cairns, was to be presented for dispersal by the Sopas Hospital in the highlands. But even such pressing responsibilities as these, aboard the *Osprey* must look patently toward the fullness of time for achievement. We sailed on.

Chapter 9 — New Guinea

A small sailboat was on the same general course as we, and though it was several miles behind us we could occasionally see it well enough with the binoculars to not recognize it as one that we had seen before. Each day we would spot it still maybe half a day away.

If it had been a prior friend of ours we might have waited to share an anchorage just to hear the news of each other's travels. We never try sailing together, but evenings with friends are great fun. We sailed on.

The infection in my leg was doing remarkably well. It was more swollen today than even yesterday, so we opted for a course of penicillin to reverse this progression. After all, this is the reason why we carry this supply of medical stuff around with us.

The mainland of New Guinea was close on our port side as we had watchfully skirted the coral reefs which occasionally reached out toward us. Our course continued close to the shore for yet another turn to port as we followed around this point of land.

But at long last, here it is! "It looks like a fjord to me!"

The chart shows a rock hazard in the center of the entrance into the narrow fjord like bay which is easily avoided. And the almost towering grey cliff faces on both sides of this bay have an acceptable reason to claim status as a mini fjord. Such steepness above water also speaks as clearly to the fact that these cliffs plunge downward as steeply as that which is visible, wherefore difficulty in anchoring securely was a forgone conclusion.

We found a small spot before getting all the way in to the cliffs where an anchor could work and secured our position. What a fabulous place this is! And a village stood just off our port side where we came in. To our usual pleasure, our guests began to arrive. We recognize that generally we are the only show in town. Village days routinely pass without change, and to have a yacht arrive as though from another world is exciting to see.

The first reaction has to be, "What have I got that these people might buy?" The interest is seldom for money. However, we are thought of as possessing an inexhaustible supply of great stuff, and that we most likely need fruits and vegetables because we can't bring our land with us, so it's likely that we will pay enormously with clothing or pans or dishes.

The fact is that we take pains to never make a trade of goods in which someone could feel that we under paid them. Although we are on a very close budget as seen by our country's standards, by comparison we are wealthy beyond imagination.

The first canoe arrived. He had been paddling quite fast to be the first which we took care not to notice. He was invited aboard and in the fullness of time he asked if we had a hair comb for which we might accept his fruit in trade. He said that his wife wanted to be able to comb the hair of their child. Peggy had such a comb and another item or two which were added, because the fruit looked great and was abundant.

Others were still aboard several hours later, when I called out, "Peggy, look– the boat that was behind us just came into the bay to anchor!"

It was smaller, probably about thirty feet over all, with a singlehander from Australia aboard as indicated by his flag. He was busily trying to get securely anchored before dark and was quite some distance away from us so we would talk to him later.

A time does come when we have all that the two of us can eat and the day's trading comes to an end. This is always understood, and tomorrow is another day. But everyone comes aboard anyway, even if the trading is finished.

Often the trading is just an excuse to come aboard and look at the boat and at us, but other times it is very serious even to the point of specific food orders being placed with one of the people for a couple days hence. This is especially true when we have been at a place for several days, as mutual trust is then established. Special orders may well require a distant trek through rough terrain to select the perfect item in fullest ripeness, for it has almost always been perfection.

As our last visitors were leaving, they told us something about a ceremony and something about people coming from other villages and something that sounded maybe like a party tonight in their village and that only men would come. I was immediately intrigued and said that I would come. I asked if gifts were to be brought and yes this would be good, so next I needed to find out what sort of gift was appropriate but got nowhere at all with that question.

At the appointed time, I rowed ashore with all manner of interesting possibilities dancing in my head. There were a lot of people attending whatever *this is*, and inside the first hut which had large openings in the walls apparently as a general meeting area, seven or eight men sat talking, and outside the hut was standing the other yachtsman. We greeted each other cordially and immediately began talking about where we were from, and places where we both might have sailed, and of possible mutual friends but clearly we had not crossed paths before. One of the men inside the house had moved close to where we were talking, so I figured that he was the one most likely to understand what we were talking about and would report back to the group. It's a natural thing to want to know something more about the strangers who were here, beyond the fact that they are from the boats.

Everyone was dressed in their finery for the occasion. In this area, tapa cloth is worn by both the men and the women. Tapa is a very practical "cloth" made from the thin bark of trees such as the Mulberry. The sections of bark are enlarged by overlapping sections being pounded to force the water soaked bark fibers of each piece into each other progressively until a large piece is formed. When the tapa cloth is dry it is decorated with the local patterns and colors which have been used over the eons of time in its village. This cloth is quite soft, pliable, and strong.

The tapa is worn as a skirt. The women's skirts reach to just above the knee. The men's skirts are just a little shorter. Arm decorations are also worn at any festive event. These cover the upper arm. These arm bands have a matt rolled into them; and necklaces of shells are worn as well as feathers to decorate the head and face. Large feathers are worn about the head, while small ones surround the face during major festivals and enormous time is required for this. The event of the evening was festive but did not require "tuxedos." Upper body covering was not worn by either the men or the women during this special event nor as a daily necessity.

Our fellow yachtsman and I must have talked there for close to two hours as we both waited in ignorance to see what was going to happen. And what happened is that nothing happened–nothing at least of which we were aware. There was some foot shuffling done in a circle by some of the women in what appeared to be dance, but this didn't last long. Clearly the "no women communique" was garbled somewhat by the pigeons in my head. We spoke our respects to the men whom we thought might be the elders of the tribe and went back to our boats.

The next morning, before the children's canoe trip to school began; the boy arrived again who had seemed especially to have enjoyed his time aboard. We invited him aboard and he had some breakfast with us, since that is what was happening at the time. He was more than absolutely delighted and stopped at the boat again after school. The school is in the next village

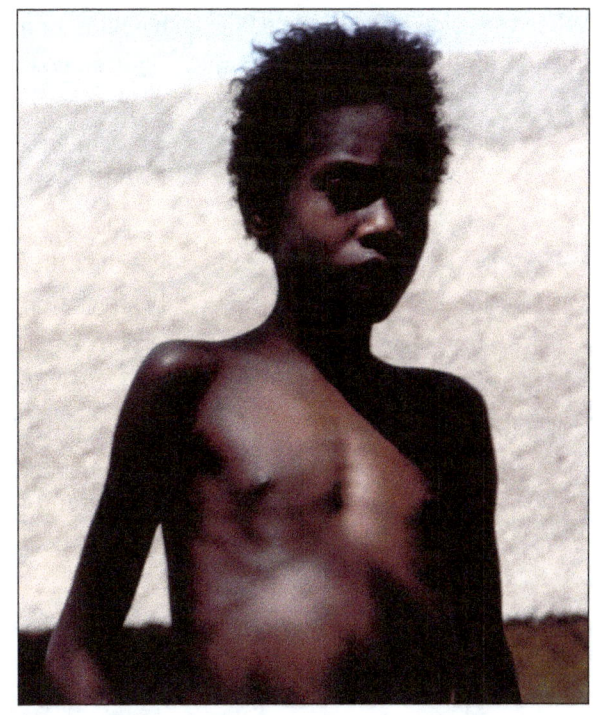

from here. And all of the children had their own canoes which they would paddle out from their harbor, out into the huge bay to school and back. The sea is almost always quiet here at the equator.

We learned a great deal from this boy. He was about nine years old. And we told him stories of life in far off places and he wanted to reciprocate by telling us anything that we might want to know about life here. We talked about his school and his family and I wanted to know about last night's event.

He said that it was part of the ceremony of the red hair. A girl is put in a special house for a certain length of time. Then she is taken into the sea and washed and red dye is put in her hair; which means that she is recognized as a woman that a man can have if he wants her as wife. So last night, the men could come to see her and if one of them wants her for wife, then he must send people to talk to her father about what is wanted for the bride price and about what the boy is willing to pay.

When the bride price is settled through negotiation, he then must get back to his home village and get as many friends as he can. When they are ready,

maybe several days later, all of these young men will come to the house of the woman. Her uncles will be there to fight them. Sometimes some are killed during this fight. If the boys stop fighting and run away, the boy cannot have the bride. If the uncles, who are chosen at the birth of the now bride-to-be give up, then the boy must do the next thing required by custom. He must kill a wild boar.

These pigs are wild. They are tusked boar, very fast strong and vicious. We had seen a man sitting on the porch of a hut in this village who was recently crippled by the tusks of a pig. His legs were savagely gored.

The pigs are hunted with bow and arrows and spear. So I said, "What if he cannot kill one?"

And the expression on the lad's face was incredulous that I would ask this as he said, "Then he must keep trying until he does!"

When he kills the wild boar he cuts out the fat and brings the fat to her family, and they sit around chewing the fat, (which are the exact words the lad used as translated from Pigeon to English). Upon this conclusion they are thereupon married. Payment of the bride price is often delayed to a specific future time.

I can grasp the concept of a staged and ceremonial "fight" to say that this young woman is of too great a treasure for her to leave my household, but if that was the original intent it has long been forgotten. These events are mini-war battles of which I was truly amazed to hear. I also learned that these chosen "uncles" wield immense influence during the early life of a female child, much more so than her actual related uncles who apparently are not involved at all. But customs, though very long standing, are very local and vary widely even within relatively short distances.

Along the coast, in most areas, the bride price may consist of only a few pigs (not the wild boar type); while in the highlands we were to find that the price is much more expensive. A perpetual system of borrowing pigs from family members is done everywhere in PNG. These debts are never forgotten. And if you have loaned two pigs five years ago and now need three pigs, you can rely of your prior debtor to get three pigs somewhere if he has to borrow them, and so the cycle continues.

The other boat had spent just one night and we again had become the only show in town. So the pleasure of visitors was on an unorchestrated arrival schedule with two to four people in attendance with us most of the time and canoes strung out behind us rather like little ducklings on a pond. It was wonderfully interesting to meet everyone and to try to glean a little information here and there. One of the women who spent time with Peggy turned out to be the witch doctor's wife. In PNG, and elsewhere in the South Pacific, these men carry the title of "Magic Man," and very quickly, these two women became the very best of friends.

One of the biggest problems that she shared with Peggy was the fact that after a few years of marriage they still remained childless. Learning that the Magic Man was prohibited by the fact of losing his power were he to engage in the process of procreation during specific times of the lunar cycle. Peggy inquired about her friend's cycle; and was able to enlighten her friend concerning these mutually occurring events and the resultant consequence. Whereby, the feeling of guilt and inadequacy was removed, and replaced with enormous relief.

Relating only to the astonishment of hearing about Peggy's very old age, all of the women who came to the boat now wanted to feel the skin of her face and to feel her hair. The word spread through the entire village that she was fifty-six years old! After each experience of this close up inspection, each of these women proclaimed absolute amazement!

"Oh oh! Good pela face," as they would touch her face. "You pela wrinkles no gotim," they would say in amazement and they would feel her hair between their fingers as they all inevitably told her, "Oldest ever our people forty-seven."

A few days after the evening "event" at the village, a young woman came aboard who seemed to be about the same age as the "Debutante" of the red hair, so after awhile I asked if she too had the ceremony of the red hair. Her expression instantly changed as she said, "No." She said it not in anger, but it sounded rather more like a mixture of resignation and sadness.

I said nothing. I didn't move. I didn't look at her expectantly. I just sat quietly. We had been here several days and were likely well spoken of by the villagers, enough so that she finally explained with sadness in her voice, "The uncles must say for the ceremony of the red hair. *And the uncles do no wish to die."*

I said, "Ah—so," as I slowly shook my head sadly in the affirmative.

In a few minutes she unburdened her sorrow to me about how she and her boyfriend wanted to marry each other and that since the uncles refused to allow the ceremony all they could do is run away maybe to a city and be married there. But to do that, she would be giving up her land. In PNG the ownership of land passes through the women exclusively.

This would impoverish both of them, because obviously the food comes from the land as a result of the labor in the garden which also happens to be the exclusive domain of the women. Men do things such as the "slash and burn" technique of making a new garden space. But their other duty is not to be ignored, for as the women work in the gardens, the men are there to protect them from being stolen by neighboring tribes. So although they may be sitting in the shade, they must remain ever vigilant! And if exhaustion and sleep were to overcome them, they could rely on the call for help from the women. More frequently though, in a given spot only one woman and her husband may be in hearing distance. This beautiful young woman and her boyfriend were bound within the iron grasp of a tradition entirely beyond their control.

* * *

A man came to the boat. He was welcomed aboard and secured his canoe which drifted slowly aft until reaching the end of its cord. He had brought nothing with him. And I could see that he appeared to have something on his mind, because he seemed to be arranging some thoughts before presentation. I waited. Finally, he presented his question.

He said that over the years he had seen yachts come into his water, and every one of them always go around the rocks at the entrance even though they cannot be seen. He wanted to know by what magic these captains from far away places know about a shallow danger in his little waters. He was in awe of this.

It took some time, but I believe I was able to convey the concept of minimization of actual space onto a paper called a navigation chart which I showed to him, for he went away with apparent satisfaction.

This is the day the committee of one arrived. "Do you have a gun?" is the question he presented with no preamble of any kind.

"Yes I do," I answered without shyness or hesitation.

"Problem we pela kasim," he said and went on to explain that the village problem was in their failure to have been able to prevent their main garden from being destroyed by a monstrous wild boar. No matter what they tried by way of barrier he always broke through and would root up and destroy the place.

"Supos you pela kill dis one pela pig?"

I said that I would and asked when we should go. I asked using the word "we" because I was not agreeing to just go out on a hunt without a guide to some location. Tomorrow morning was the scheduled event.

At about nine the next morning a young man arrived with his canoe. He was probably in his early thirties, and greeted us with the announcement that he was to take me to the place where the pig will come.

Well, not knowing how this was planned, I went with him in his outrigger canoe up toward the head of the little bay where we beached the canoe. The boy who was our most regular visitor was at the spot of our arrival as well as a friend of his a year or so younger. The four of us were soon on our way to the appointed place.

I had of course brought the rifle, its ammunition, and a canteen of water; none of which the boys wanted me to carry. So it was that my guide carried his bow and arrows, I let the boy carry my unloaded rifle, I carried the ammunition, and the boy's friend carried my water canteen. In addition to the boys carrying my stuff which was to their great apparent pride, they also both carried their own smaller version of my guide's hunting equipment.

The trek was not an arduous one and when concluded, the boys presented their treasured burdens. The guide had chosen the spot where there was a large clearing, possibly where gardens had once grown. Garden clearings are used until the harvests decline, after which a new forest area is cleared by the "slash and burn" technique.

A small tree stood about a hundred feet (about thirty-five meters) up a gentle hill from a small valley and the clearing went another two hundred feet beyond it. The boys immediately began hunting through the brush and bushes of the clearing for small animals of any kind in the hope of finding meat for the family table. It was fun to watch their very serious effort.

My guide and I took our leisure in the shade of a small tree as we talked and watched the boys. A well worn trail passed through the little valley area of this clearing. It was a pig trail. And this is where the great boar was expected.

While we had yet slept this morning, at first light, the village had been marshaled to spread out through the jungle area and in the same manner as African "beaters" thrashed about with branches and shouts to drive the boar not only away from the noise but ultimately down the trail directly in front of me, so group planning was precise and carefully orchestrated.

My guide must have been chosen for his possession of the best Pigeon English for my benefit, and indeed our conversation was easy. The boy's hunt continued as the hours passed, and discovering that I had gotten thirsty, I reached for my water canteen first offering some water to my guide. He declined my offer by saying "No" which was expressed as though there was something else other than lack of thirst.

I drank. I closed the canteen and said nothing. And in a few minutes he explained why he took no water. The pause I suspect was caused by the natural concern of my being from a different place and culture and therefore concluding that his belief might belittle him in my eyes regardless of the fact that his belief is based on certainty of fact. But fortunately, perhaps by the word of others regarding our reputation, he felt that he could explain why he did not take the offered drink.

He told me of the fact that the Magic Man had put magic in his bow and in his arrows. If he shoots an arrow into a pig which does not have magic, it will not kill the pig. The pig will just break the arrow off. But if he shoots a pig with a magic arrow the pig, "Imy kil im tru" [He kill him true].

He asked if I believe this and I said, "I do." I did not say that I believe that the added confidence of the hunter is the true "magic" in this.

He went on to explain that if after he picks up his bow and arrows in his house and goes to hunt, were he to drink before he returns the bow and arrows to his house the magic will leave his bow and arrows. And he would need to bring another gift to the Magic Man to have magic again put into his bow and arrows.

I had the guide move the boys out of the directions of possible danger from my line of fire and before long a magnificent creature burst at full run from the forest into the clearing exactly on the trail predicted!

He was huge majestic as he ran, not as a rabbit with darting fearful eye, he moved in regal splendor. His head was not bobbing up and down as I watched mesmerized as he ran from my left toward my right. His hooves hurled him onward at a speed without variance. I watched him. And I marveled at his beauty and the poetry of motion almost forgetting that I watched him over the barrel of a rifle. I had absolutely no wish to kill this thing except that I know the problem here. Who has the greater right of possession of the garden's food?

I say again, I am not a hunter. All of my targets have been made of paper at a firing range for practice regarding self defense from approaching attack. But the boar was now opposite me on the trail. I fired a shot and saw a small cloud of dust spring up behind the pig. I had aimed but stopped following the motion as my mind instructed fingers to pull the trigger.

The pig never broke stride, even as I later learned that the bullet had passed right through part of his hind quarter. I watched him run. He ran onward unfazed. I tried a second time and saw no change in stride whatsoever. The trail turned leftward and he was now going directly away from me which resulted in a non-moving target except for a growing distance which now was indeed a long way off. But alas, the boar's fate was set when the hunt had begun, even with my limited expertise.

Before long, the village arrived. I was asked which part of the prize I wanted for our table, but declined in favor of a village feast. Lavish thanks were expressed for the garden safety as well as the gift to the village. In the midst of all of this merriment, a very old slender rather wizened man came up to me saying that he wanted to shake my hand and proceeded to do so saying, "Gun bilong you pela, imy kasum long pela mout!" [Your gun has a really long mouth] by which he has killed this pig!

The boys had been less successful in their hunt but were as eager to carry my stuff back as they had been this morning. The village clearly felt that it had been a great day.

Our favorite daily visitor continued to interest us with his tales of local customs of which I was able to conversationally confirm from others with slight variations plus additional information. It was his introductions to me of these matters which enabled me to acquire added depth from others without which I would not have even become aware of a particular custom at all.

We talked about how magic is brought from the Magic Man and about what all is involved. "Would the Magic Man be willing to put magic in my rifle?"

"There is a Magic Man in my family, and I will ask him for you!" And so it was that a very old man came with his canoe to the *Osprey* at an appointed time.

He came with great dignity and great solemnity. He paddled slowly. Before boarding the *Osprey*, he lifted some things out of the canoe and carefully placed them on the deck. They were leather sacks, one a little smaller than the other. He handled one sack at a time. The gentle slow motion by which his hands eased these sacks onto the deck conveyed the utmost of reverence for their content in the knowing eye of this man, esteemed above all other by his title of Magic Man.

This was not the husband of Peggy's friend and either had been superseded by him due to stronger magic or he may have been from a close village, I didn't ask. I only knew that this Magic Man was somehow related to our young friend to whom the boy was undoubtedly obligated. I rather expect that everything that transpired aboard had been proudly discussed at home.

I took the Magic Man's cord which he used to secure his canoe and I tied the canoe off the back of the *Osprey*. He and I sat down in the cockpit where *magic was about to occur!*

Peggy handed the rifle out to us–something that she would never again be able to do, because once magic is put on an object such as a spear or hunting knife and left at home in the hut and the man's wife were to pick it up, her arm would shrivel up immediately and never be usable again. Thus has it been declared over the ages by the Magic Men of New Guinea. The concept does appear to have a rather convenient protection against irate wives.

After confirming that the rifle was not loaded and showing him how to see that this was the case, I handed the Winchester 30/30 Rifle to the Magic Man who held it at arms length in both hands. His expression reflected the immensity of the grave event which was about to occur.

He brought the rifle ever so slowly toward his staring gaze as with all of his strength his mind inhaled all of the soul of the trigger mechanism, and in like manner he transfixed all of the detail of the butt of the rifle, and then the breach, and the sighting mount, and the side of the end of the rifle before finally exhausting his strength by peering down, down, down into the very opening of the barrel itself. And now, after taking a couple of deep breaths of revival, he solemnly slowly returned the rifle to my hands. I laid it in my lap and watched the preparation of the next giant step, for Magic was about to begin.

He had brought two bags which had been transported in a larger one. He opened one of these bags and took from it a piece of wood and ceremonially cut two small slivers from it no more than an inch long and an eighth inch in other dimensions. He took one piece and placed it into his mouth and began to slowly chew on it, giving me the other to do likewise. I was astonished! It was Sandalwood and released an aromatic perfume that burst free and filled my mouth with a wonderful aroma that was way beyond my expectation!

He took the rifle again, and solemnly exhaled small puffs of this scented breath upon each of the parts which he had studied so carefully a few moments ago, and then placed the rifle into my hands and indicated that I should do likewise. I tried to do so with my very best attempt to emulate exactly what had been done and the manner in which it had been done, but I omitted the hidden quick glances at him that the Magic Man had tried to surreptitiously direct to me for the purpose of gauging my reaction to his presentation of the magic.

One does not ask for something to be done and then belittle the doer by gesture of any kind. This was serious in the extreme, and all honor and respect is appropriate without the impulse to interject one's own culture, a sin which has never been committed aboard the *Osprey*.

I was impressed! Another bag was opened. Out of it came a crustacean bug of some kind. I could not recognize its habitat as land or sea. It was a couple of inches long and its body was covered by a thin shell-like protection.

Holding it between his fingers without releasing it, he bit the shell just to the point of breaking it and then removed it from his mouth; and handed a fresh one to me. I repeated his procedure and likewise removed mine and returned it to him. These creatures were returned to the bag and again we took turns blowing our breath with full ceremony upon the rifle's assorted parts and locations and thusly the ceremony continued and was finally complete.

The necessity to validate and retain this magic is to present a gift to the Magic Man. I had asked the boy who had arranged this event what such a gift should be and was each time instructed by his saying, "Whatever you want to give," which didn't help me at all. So I settled on the option of giving him a choice.

I carefully explained in Pigeon English, that we were greatly honored by his time and ceremony by which he had brought magic to be placed in my rifle and that we did not know what gift would properly convey our gratitude and appreciation (not using these words but rather their meaning) and therefore wanted him to choose one group of gifts out of three groups which we would show to him from which to select.

Peggy handed the first group out to me which I arranged on the cockpit seat for him to see. She next handed out to me the second group which I also arranged. But as she was handing out the third of the groups which I had so carefully explained that he could choose one of, he said, "No—no—Is enough" – referring to the two groups and proceeded to gather up the two that were displayed. Well, we of course did not wrestle choice-number-two from him! But viewing the fact that we are painfully careful to be generous, this haul that the Magic Man received for the event was even double the amount of our usual generosity and had to be his best deal ever, which must also have gone a long way toward his satisfaction of having really impressed us with his magic. Actually, other than the first shock of the "price," the show was worth every bit of it. A tiny question remains. Was my Pigeon English all that bad, or were we *snookered*? Here again, we really don't care. Besides, it was also fun telling you about it!

That duffel bag which we had carried around with us from Australia was not invisible to us. Nor was the required delivery of those crocheted baby blankets by the church ladies of Cairns ever far from our minds. We needed to begin to prepare for our departure from this place, the news of which sped though the village, and crowds of lovely folks came to wish us well. Many brought little gifts pressed affectionately into our hand.

CHAPTER 10

THE HIGHLANDS

"Well Peggy, we're finally going to get those baby blankets out of here," I said. But she knew that time schedules and the *Osprey* have never been on more than a nodding acquaintance. So although she knew that eventually this promise would be fulfilled, she knew better than I that our course toward a destination has on occasions failed to be a perfectly straight line.

Years ago, when we had been in the Island Kingdom of Tonga, we had met Peter and Rose Begol. They are the missionary school teachers who had witnessed that twelve-passenger commercial airplane in the process of being loaded with so much passenger cargo into the back storage compartment that the plane had her nose wheel lift off the ground and her tail section drop down to the ground due to the overloading – *oops*.

They had told us many wonderful things of Tonga when we were there and had kept in touch with us over the years as we exchanged letters which had just a few months ago told us of their transfer to the school at Wabag, PNG to the hospital compound at the village of Sopas. Their fascination of this new location was infectious, and yes we wanted to go there, but time was becoming limited – and such places as the Sepik River area where the masks were made was also calling us (well, calling me). How can we just willingly choose to miss adventures like either of these very different places—life is tough—but maybe there is a solution!

We were anchored at a village where we found that a mission school of our church was run by a young couple from Canada with whom we became instantly acquainted. It was fun for us as always, and they could hear the language of their country, even though our being "Yanks" required their forgiveness for our gross accents and mispronunciations. They told us that the big dock which jutted out from this village was there to service the regular schedule of the local trading schooner; and a thought was born.

"We would be happy to have someone watch over your boat while you're gone!" And the next morning we locked the boat securely, having moored the boat with a line to the shore trees and two anchors from the stern in deep water.

Although it was by no means a sailing vessel as the reference of "schooner" implies, the term *trading schooner* has become known as a category of service rather than one which designates the type of the vessel's rigging. She was much bigger than I had expected. She was steel hulled with a couple of decks and was of very considerable tonnage. Cabins were even available, but we chose to sleep on deck as apparently everyone else of the crowd of locals was doing. This was not a tourist ship and few accommodations were offered. I was surprised to see such a large number of locals using transportation like this and wondered why so many were doing so.

About all that can be said of the night is that we survived it. The noise of the huge diesel engines was not a particular inducement for romance and the entire rusting ship vibrated by the thrust of the pistons within her engines whose copious smoke emission was beyond our ability to entirely ignore. When the smoke was present, the soot was there to supply confirmation if required. We docked at midday at the town of Lae and a taxi took us to the church headquarters. We were introduced all around, and "our Sopas mission" was heralded with instant excited happy echoing saying, "And the truck is here!"

Well we soon learned that the Sopas Hospital truck was right here at this very moment picking up supplies, which meant that rather than these good folks giving us complex instructions about how we might get ourselves way up there in the highlands on our own, they were going to supply us with transportation and a driver as well. We were absolutely astonished at our good fortune and everybody at the Headquarters of this Mission was ecstatic for us.

We were enthusiastically welcomed by Harry. He seemed to be delighted for the company on the two-day trip to the village of Sopas beyond the small town of Wabag. He had a regular place to stay for the night and assured us that we would be no bother for them either.

In just a few hours we three jolly band of truckers waved a hardy farewell to a crowd of well-wishers on the loading dock, who moments ago had prayed to God for our safety. Going to Sopas is just not taken frivolously. It is deep into the heart of New Guinea to which we so blithely intend to leap.

But it started out in great nonchalance.

Harry was talkative. He was keeping up a steady banter of worthy information. Firstly, about the great pride of which he was justly possessed in all of the countless attributes of this particular vehicle, which he conveyed in tones near rapture. Its manufacture had, of course, occurred in the country of his own origin, a fact not at all lost on us. He knew the size of the six tires which bore us so majestically along, as well as its tonnage which, had we been more proper truckers, would not have been lost on us. But all of these vital statistics and specifics were shared with us with such warmth and charm in the best tradition of a first class tour guide that we were having a merry time indeed. And he would invariably spot exotic birds to point out to us. Even the occasional cluster of the truly huge butterflies that grace this land were caught by his quick eye. And we learned wonderful things of the daily life of these unique butterflies. Harry was a hoot!

We had left Lae behind us and still the road was paved. We were constantly climbing ever higher in elevation. And we had seen a gasoline station a few minutes ago. We knew it was a gasoline station because Harry said that it was. Or more precisely, I should not have said that "it" was a gasoline station–I should have said that "he" was a gasoline station. We had seen a man sitting comfortably in the shade along the edge of the road. He had a large can beside him. The can contained gasoline which this enterprising young man had bought probably in Lae or Goroka and ridden the bus to where he sat. His village would be somewhere not too far away, to where his "gasoline station" would disappear each night.

We saw a couple of other such "stations" on our trip, but others may have been "closed" for the day. I was impressed. We saw just one other entrepreneur of a different sort on this trip. He must have been known far and wide for either the quality of his product or perhaps for the perfect wood which he may have gone a great distance to find which the men in this area didn't have or did not know where to find. He sold war bows.

The road was excellent. The paving was remarkably clear of large pot holes, and we had been truly zooming along for about four hours. I wondered if Harry talked to invisible passengers if no one was riding with him, or if we could claim some credit for his keeping up with such a steady flow of mostly one sided conversation. We would have been able to join more freely in this discourse were it not that it required such an enormous volume of speech to enable one to be heard over the shaking rattle of each part of the truck and the roar of her engine and the voice of its muffler, long since rusted away.

The roadway was quite clear from any obstruction on either side, even though we were climbing all the time. It was not as though we were climbing mountains. The banks along the roadway had climbed or descended on the opposite side quite gently. Most of the area through which we traveled was lightly wooded with sizable patches of an almost brownish growth of grass about three feet tall.

At this spot the banks were a bit steeper and the curves a little sharper and Harry suddenly shouted, "Okay – I want you to close the window before we get to this curve!" Mystified, I complied. I was the one sitting by the door.

We zipped around the corner with Harry appearing to be leaning forward just a little, and when we could see beyond the curve, Harry said, "Okay – open up again."

"Ya see right there" as he pointed. "That's where they stopped the bus." He was chuckling at this point. "They had drug a small tree across the road, just too big for the bus to get over. And they couldn't go around it due to the banks. So when they got stopped, the *scoundrels* (as they are locally called) jumped aboard. There was no door to keep them out, and they robbed everybody of anything of value, including everybody's clothes! So here they were, including the bus driver, totally naked!"

The bus was almost full. It only ran a couple of times a week and these were sizable cities at each end of their trip. More than half were locals who were in business dress as their station required. But even if they were in village attire, in most areas to be entirely uncovered is embarrassing.

But firstly the tree was drug to the side of the road after the robbers left, and then the bus driver drove his unusual group into Goroka, down the main street to the largest church in town, stopped in front of the building, and went inside successfully finding assistance and some semblance of modesty was returned. The closing of the windows was in an attempt to keep the rascals out if any were here.

"Here's our lodging," Harry hollered as he took a sudden right turn from the road. He had volunteered nothing of where we would be staying.

We had thought it was to be at the house of an acquaintance. We had continued to wonder if this was to be a village house or one of western style and we instantly could see that this was apparently a local area church headquarters with accommodations for people in transit such as we; because we could see a small motel-like building having perhaps six or eight rooms as indicated by the equidistant spacing of the doors and the size and shape of the building.

Dinner was to be ready in about forty-five minutes and about twenty of us ate together cafeteria-style amidst much talk and laughter, which after a quiet night's sleep began again as though no time had passed, as we all joined in a cafeteria style breakfast. Shortly, however, off we went; tucking away another group of friends in that comfort zone of our memory.

Chapter 10 *The Highlands*

Today we would be in Wabag and beyond, to that highlands hospital at the village of Sopas. When we left Goroka behind, we also left the pavement. But the unadorned earth will serve as well for the truck, and though our teeth may chatter as the dust adds some grit to them, we only have about eight hours to go. Eight hours of bone jarring full speed roar of the truck's engine, and by some mystery the dust-cloud kept pace with us.

"We just passed Wabag," Harry triumphantly yelled. "It won't be long now," he promised.

The truck rumbled to a halt! We had arrived with a truck loaded with required provisions and medical supplies, plus that parcel from Cairns, Australia.

There was a small hospital housed in this one story building which stood with one end facing us. A compound was beyond it and several separate one story houses fanned out from it; each with one end toward the compound.

Everyone not otherwise buried beneath a blur of duty, rushed to unload the truck, which meant that there were five. Upon seeing us, each of them froze momentarily in shock followed just as quickly by grinning hand shakes and welcoming words. Not many visitors have been experienced way up here! Tomorrow, when there is more time, we will reveal our mission of delivery and formally meet the daughter of the good church member in Cairns for whom we had ventured so far from the sea.

Charles and Rose Begol and their son Pete, were at the house when we were brought to it! These were the friends whom we had met years ago in the Island Kingdom of Tonga. And stories of their travels and school adventures filled the dining room table as heavily as the bounty which crowded our plates; when suddenly a loud sound of chanting was heard. "What's that?"

The quick explanation was that there had been a war. One of the men of the Sopas Village had been killed in that bow and arrow battle and the sound which we were hearing was our Sopas people telling the other village that they were being given safe passage to come here on a certain day.

The Highlands   Chapter 10

I rushed out of the house. There they were, less than a hundred paces from our windows. Approximately thirty men stood in a formation of five men shoulder to shoulder, with six such rows as a military formation might march.

It was a march, not to gain movement, but rather to gain unison. They took tiny steps forward. They were in close formation and in perfect step with each other as they shouted at each man's maximum vocal capacity. This is the highly efficient telegraph system of New Guinea.

I could not understand the words, but I had no doubt that they could be heard across the valley. I was impressed! The message was short and was repeated four times. It was dark when they had begun, which was timed to coincide with the people of the other village being together. The first call was to get someone's attention who would then shout to their own villagers that a message was being sent; the second was to reinforce the first; the third was assumed to be heard; and the fourth to repeat it to make sure nothing was misunderstood.

On this announced day, these two tribes are to come together so that it can be determined how much the Sopas Village was to be paid for one of their warriors having been killed in the last war. His family members had lost a father, husband, or uncle or cousin. By tradition everybody needed to be reimbursed for their loss. Yes, the winner pays. But this is not an adequate deterrent to the battles. These wars rage constantly throughout the highlands.

We were told that no bows and arrows were allowed by either side in these meetings. Strict tradition forbade it. So although we were told that tempers may flare, negotiations usually proceed with bloodless decorum. The event was to occur in just a few days, and Peggy and I were not going to miss it.

* * *

It was more than delightful to see these friends again. We had talked well into the night. And it was impressive to realize that we were now at the very end of the road system in Papua New Guinea. Beyond here, seldom ventures the visitor. Beyond here, the highlands have glimpsed few sights differing from any other than what it has known for thousands of years.

We were up early the next morning and after breakfast pleasantries we went outside in front of the hospital where patients were arriving. Perhaps twenty paces down the slop of ground from the entrance doors a folding card table had been placed in its daily spot as a triage desk. A nurse sat on a folding chair and a line of people awaited her instruction. This nurse separated the people into groups dependent upon the urgency of their condition and or its type, instructing them to sit with others of similar condition to be escorted to the appropriate area of the hospital for treatment.

There were no other chairs and the folks sprawled about just sitting on the ground talking. She told us that a few days earlier a man had come to the desk, was asked what his problem was and was told to, "Please sit over there by the man with the arrow in his side." The man to whom she was speaking had an arrow sticking out of his leg.

She said that these folks are amazingly patient and will sit for hours awaiting treatment. Everyone on the hospital staff, as with all such facilities around the world, is in perpetual fast motion of effort. Everyone is seen as quickly as possible. Wonderful things are done in even these most primitive circumstances.

An astonishing medical feat was performed right here at this hospital not long ago. A man had been brought to them with an arrow actually piercing part way into his heart. They had to open his chest, clamp the opening when removing the arrow, and then stitch the heart closed. The person who told us this was not the surgeon, and for all I know the event may have been somewhat embellished during repetitive telling of the event, but I am certain that fantastic accomplishments are achieved even in such primitive environments as these. I salute the skillful dedications of those who venture around the world to help care for those *beyond the end of the roads*.

The sight of a couple of fellows sitting on the ground talking to each other, one with an arrow sticking out of him in one direction and the other with an arrow sticking out of him from another direction, is a picture which differs somewhat from our past experience of the view from the front door of our homeland hospitals. And to be told that this is a regular type of event here at Sopas confirms what we had been previously told, that these local wars rage constantly throughout the vastness of New Guinea.

There are over 800 distinct languages in Papua New Guinea. This is due to the fact that the free mix of people, and hence the merging of languages over time, has not occurred here. One does not stroll about in these circumstances where arrows speak louder than words. Yet a complex system of accepted movement does exist in places, though these too are subject to change without warning.

Even government roadways are sometimes blocked by a village demanding payment for passage. And even a government coastal navigation light to warn seamen of a hazard projecting outward from the shore could not have its light to shine due to the village there having removed the battery from the light and having demanded payment from the government of some outlandish amount (like a million Kena) for having the aid to navigation in "their area." We were told that this light had not functioned for years.

Local visitors to this hospital are treated to a unique experience as viewed through my eyes. They are checked for weapons, due to the zeal of the opposing village in any particular war. Men occasionally seek to come into the hospital for the purpose of killing the merely wounded opponent right here in his bed!

* * *

At the appointed day, the victors began to arrive; and shortly thereafter so did Peggy and I. The men of both tribes came in traditional attire which here consisted of a loin cloth held up by a vine belt wrapped around the waist several times, in which a small hatchet was also being carried. These were steel-headed hatchets, very business like, not the stone headed hatchets which we were to see in some areas. The head hair of the men was decorated with sundry things and devises such as feathers and paint. The faces too were painted with various colors of strips and blotched and a few had painted the upper body but to no great degree.

A large open field, about the size of 100 x 50 feet was the designated area. The opponents stood in a single line along each long length of the field, facing each other on opposite sides of the field. We chose an area to sit which was perhaps twenty-five feet beyond where one of the lines of warriors were, but we were quickly urged by the nearer of the warriors to move right up to where they were. We did so.

This invitation seemed to be offered due to our camera being in plain evidence and they seemed to feel that we would have a better view of the proceedings. (We were later to discover that we were on the side of the victors, not of our host village the Sopas tribe. At the time, we had no idea of this, and had chosen the spot because it had the most shade.

However, this was not a problem due to the fact that we were known to be neutral observers. We had not wanted to interject our presence. After all, we had no idea exactly what was going to happen. We had been told that usually no fighting occurs, but that this is not always the case. And although one man stood alone with a bow, no one had arrows.

We later learned that the lone warrior was the man who had shot the arrow which brought about this event. He stood alone. He never spoke, nor was ever spoken to during the entire event. He was the man of honor and his bow was held in one hand with its end resting upon the ground. He made little movement and no gesture during all of the time of these proceedings.

We could not understand the language, which was local. A spokesman on our side of the field would address his apparent equal on the other side and clearly an argument would begin. The heat of the argument was matched and surpassed by the shouts between them with indignations clearly occurring as fists were shaken and the rage went up higher with each exchange until begrudging consensus was finally reached; to be immediately followed by the next set of protagonists in like manner, followed by the next. The day passed. Agreement was reached. The payback day was agreed upon, and we shall be there for that event as well.

While all of this bristling hostility was going on, the warriors close to us were perpetually checking to be certain that our view was not being hindered by their jumping a step or two forward as the shouting and fist threatening was going on.

As the event was concluded and a short time of milling about by the separate groups occurred, I let it be known that I was interested in buying a bow. It was to be an old bow with wrappings to prevent splitting, if it was to be representative of reality.

One of the men came to me saying that he had such a bow which his father had made, so I told him to come the next day to the hospital and that he only need ask where the house of the visitor was, to be directed to me. But as soon as I started telling him to come, he was already backing away; for I had forgotten that there was no safe passage for him tomorrow. Were he to have come, he knew that he would likely be killed. He did say that I could come to his village, but that too may have presented risks, though unknown.

We came back to our house with three dimensional moving pictures in vivid color upon the sparkling mirror of our minds. And it seemed as unreal as a theater show as we recounted the day to our hosts. But this was reality. This is where the war had raged just days before. This is the village where a man had been killed by the shot of an arrow. This is where the consequence still swirled about these hills.

We again talked well into the night.

* * *

The next day we were invited for a ride. It was to be with the hospital's four-wheel-drive Land Rover. This is a large SUV or light truck type vehicle. A *baby weighing* had been scheduled for several villages throughout a large area of this road-less terrain. This machine can go anywhere. A driver-mechanic, one nurse with her gear, and the two of us were off early.

There is significant difference between the types of house design in New Guinea, as would be expected in so huge an area. In some places, houses are elevated on stilts with a log leaning up to the door with notches cut in it for steps, but in most places the house is built on the ground. In the remote areas of the Highlands where we are now, the houses were generally built with thick thatch walls attached to the frame poles of the house, as is the roof likewise. The thickness serves as a needed barrier to ward off the cold up here in these elevations.

One enters the house in a drastically stooped posture, forced by the extremely low and very narrow doorway. It is always the only opening into the house. The houses are oblong in shape with a thin fiber-weaved wall separating an internal back area. It crosses the width of the house and is eight or ten feet from the back wall. A door less opening is in this wall for entry to the women's and children's sleeping area. The highly prized pigs also spend the night there. The pigs are tied with a vine to a stake driven into the ground to prevent their roaming.

In the first room, a fire pit for cooking and warmth is dug starting about four feet from the door and extends in a shallow straight line toward the back. It is approximately one foot wide and perhaps six or eight feet long. A small fire is kept burning day and night. The fire is enlarged along this pit as cooking quantity requires.

Due to this burning with no chimney, the entire roof of the house smokes as it snakes its way through the overlapping thatch. It was always an interesting sight to us, to see the houses of a village all emitting smoke from various areas of their roofs on these cold days. It somehow lent a comfortable feeling to the scene. I was amazed the first time I entered one of these houses to see how shiny black the underside of the roof was from the accumulation of tar residue from the fires. And I rightly or wrongly ascribed the short lives of these people to the visual picture of this shiny tar blackness residing in their lungs.

When a man enters a house in which he resides or visits, he proceeds only to the right of the fire pit, while women always go to the left. And whereas the women sleep in the area beyond this room, he sleeps to the right of the fire pit where his spears and bow and arrows are also kept.

He guards the house against invasion and has the great advantage over his enemy by virtue of the intruder being stooped over and partially off balance when entering. The spear is the weapon of choice whereby the intruder is killed.

Today, as we arrived in a village, everyone there immediately rushed about with shouting and glee, gathering up the babies. A few worried mothers came with concern in their face and in their gesture. Fortunately most came away smiling.

Our nurse had a folding tripod from which her scale was attached. It had a cloth containment from which a baby could not squirm out, and one after another of these loudly objecting infants had their weight recorded for this date, this named village, and this child's name. The record would shortly reside at the hospital.

This nurse was the daughter of the Cairns, Australia church member who, at this nurses urging, had organized the baby blanket project in which Peggy had participated. This nurse had cared for the mothers, as much as possible, and now ran the program of teaching them better child care. On occasions she had needed to transport mother and child to the hospital when life itself was endangered. Such things are not done without the permission of the Village Chief.

It was to Peggy's extreme pleasure to see the little girl who was given the blanket which she had made when we were in Cairns. This small gift, which conceivably could keep the warmth of life around this little girl—in this far off village, in this far off land, in the cold winters of this mountain's high elevation of 14,800 feet above the sea– still warms her memory. And even today, it can grace her face with a smile.

The sun was settling down past the peaks of the mountains as we were returning to the Sopas hospital and the loveliest of all aromas greeted us. The table was set, we were invited to sit, and the aromas burst into visual reality as promised. Our hostess had outdone herself again!

* * *

Neither Charles nor Rose had heard when the payback was scheduled. They each had their daily work duties which called fully on their time. Likewise, the entire staff of the hospital with its pressing demands seemed not to focus on the constant drama surrounding them.

They were, of course, aware of the events but this was not a world of which they were participants. And the world about them also considered them as the outsiders that they were. The forward thinking Chief of the Sopas Tribe had granted permission for the hospital within its area but its function was as a totally separate entity from itself.

Later that day at lunch, Rose told us that payback was to occur tomorrow, and we told them about being turned back from our morning wanderings. It had been a gorgeous morning and we had walked down the path to the small river at the very bottom of the valley where we had found a swinging bridge crossing a small river. This was the typical one person wide swinging bridge suspended by two multi-vine cables which become the hand rails. Single vines are tied to these cables every meter or so and looped vertically to the other cable forming the support on which one walks.

This was not to be our first swinging bridge, but it is of sufficient novelty to put grins on our faces, only to be stopped by calls of concern from someone rushing toward us on our side of the river. He came up to us with urgency mixed with reticence to approach. But in Pigeon English he anxiously conveyed that not very far beyond the river a hostel tribe's territory began.

We had no idea how far *not very far* was, but we did not argue. We did not cross this swinging bridge. We contritely returned toward the house, thanking our self proclaimed rescuer for his greatly appreciated assistance.

The next morning we chose to return to our established spot from which to watch the proceedings of "payback." We heard them coming a long time before their arrival! Apparently most of the Sopas village and certainly all of the relatives of the killed warrior were in the same large clearing where we had seen them a couple of days ago. But the atmosphere was totally changed to that of happy anticipation. Everyone was either laughing or at least had a smile in broadest delight upon their painted faces. Sopas was lined up as before. The family of the slain warrior was present in the line in declining rank as indicated by the quantity of payment which had been agreed upon.

The first ones to arrive from the victor's tribe were carrying sharpened stakes a little less than a meter long. The person to receive payback had a stake driven in the ground about two meters behind him, followed by several other stakes driven in a straight line behind that one—also each about two meters apart. This went on for some time as some recipients had six or eight stakes driven and others two or three, or one or none.

The arriving victors were dressed in similar formality. Each group was in full formal and festive attire with elaborate head dress and artfully painted faces. Even the women wore some face paint and many necklaces.

The payback arrived with its one note orchestra in full screech and its flags at full mast! The screeching was from fifty or so unwilling pigs being prodded by sticks and each being "led" by a vine tied to a front leg. A pig was brought to a person and tied to the stake behind him or her. Some of the older women receiving a pig would shriek her delight, patting the pig all over as she would literally jump up and down in her ecstasy. Everyone was excited. And the money was arriving all the time as well.

Bamboo poles about twenty feet long had short slits cut through the bamboo every foot or so from the top downward, each with a one kena note stuck through it. A kina is close in value to a US dollar. The poles were carried straight up and as high as possible. There would be an average of fifteen kena notes carried onto the field with each bamboo pole waved high for all to see the amount of money being brought to the Sopas Tribe and to each relative.

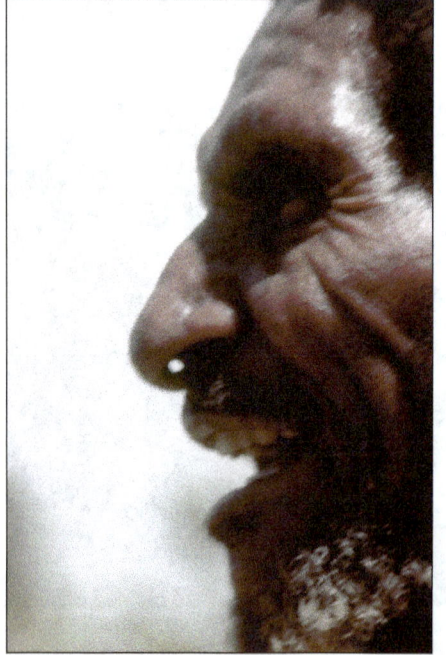

There were fifty or sixty bamboo poles of money and fifty or sixty pigs. It was as festive as any carnival I have ever attended. The recipients cavorted in their glee, and just as loudly the pigs shrieked their displeasure.

The victors who had brought this wealth of payback displayed neither reticence nor show of ill will. They went about the business as agreed upon, and having received the word of compliance to the agreement, they peaceably withdrew from the field and returned to their own territory.

The Sopasians reveled in their gain, with no visible display over the loss of one of their own. However, I'm sure that their grief was felt every bit the same as our own would have been. But perhaps, having grieved, they may be more readily able than we to step so quickly into the next reality–that of acceptance, then pride, and then into this ecstatic delight which we are watching.

Again our camera's film had looked and recorded, as had the better camera of our mind. I noted the absence of that solitary figure who had stood separate from the tribes; the warrior who had been approached by no one; the warrior—with the bow.

* * *

Just before dinner at our friend's house, a knock sounded at the door. It was the nurse with whom we had traveled for the baby weighing. She was quite excited! She told us that word had just arrived from Port Moresby that the government had asked the Sopas Hospital to bring a communiqué to the Chief of a village at the extreme limits of the distance over which they travel, and she wanted to know if we would care to go along.

Now this may surprise you to hear, but before the sound of the last letter of her last word, both Peggy and I were already simultaneously saying yes with enough enthusiasm to leave no doubt as to our sincerity! We were told that the trip would take all day, and that the driver with whom we were already acquainted, had been to that place before and clearly knew the way. What good fortune for us that we are here for such a great opportunity to see the farther reaches of the Highlands so far above the tropic jungles below.

Needless to say, we were ready at the early appointed time and with a wave from several of our friends both new and old, and with grins plastered on our faces from which we were unable to escape for hours, onward we crashed over rocks and into small hidden jaw rattling ravines. The Land Rover seemed to choose its own pathway over these rolling foot hills. There was no semblance of a roadway. We drove through the brush, with as much grace as any four-wheel-drive vehicle can hope to curtsy her presence.

Chapter 10 — The Highlands

We were in the Highlands, way above sea level, and *mountains stood* before us. They seemed to be playing a game with clouds who were saying, "Catch me if you can!" as they dodged about.

Peggy and I were hanging on as best we could. Hours passed. The driver was working every minute to turn one way just before suddenly turning in the opposite direction.

His efforts were entirely for the survival of the Land Rover in his charge, but his occasional yell of, "Hang on!" was unnecessary. We certainly were hanging on, when suddenly all of our good-humored smiles vanished instantly.

We had basically been following the upward curving valleys of the ascending foot hills, and as we came around one small hill, we drove right into a war! Arrows were flying from the right and from the left; and we were going directly into their path. "Quick! Get the windows up," yelled the driver.

We were closest to the warriors on our right. And to our shock and amazement, a warrior close to our right side jumped out from behind his concealment, shot his arrow at the enemy, and immediately looked as us (ten feet away) with the unquestionable expression on his face and gesture of, "Did ya see me – did ya – did ya?" which seemed incongruous to the savagery of his painted face and body as he carried a narrow shield strapped to one arm while carrying a long war bow in that same hand. Hollywood could not create so frightening a visage — somewhat undone by his grinning pride.

We proceeded slowly onward; right through the entire field of battle, and were not the target of even one arrow! Closing the windows to keep the arrows out of one's car is the sort of thing that will certainly get your attention! On the left and on the right, warriors were scurrying about, shooting as they went, and jumping back again behind rocks or trees or anything to conceal themselves. At any given moment a dozen arrows were in the air.

We had been climbing ever more steeply not long after the war event. And the driver has now surely chosen the way wrongly. Maybe he had been more unnerved by the encounter than we had realized, because the face of a mountain was now clearly blocking our way. But no, he knew exactly where we were. We could now make out a rather wide pathway that snaked its way upward. It was steep in the extreme. And some of the tight turns of the switchbacks could not be made by the vehicle without backing a few feet followed by full turns of the steering wheel with a few feet forward again, followed by a few more such maneuvers. This was serious driving with never a hint of hesitation. He knew where we were going!

I was sitting on the mountain side of the trail. Peggy was on the side that dropped down over the edge. She looked only once.

At the top of this mountain was our destination. And as we came to a stop, we were instantly surrounded by a crowd of villagers. The car had been heard approaching. The crowd must have been four deep around the car, with everybody talking excitedly at the same time. Some seemed to be trying to open the doors for us but the door handles may have been a small mystery.

We opened the doors, and as we were getting out, many others had been coming. In a moment or two, the crowd opened to allow the approach of a delegation. There were about five men in this group, whom we took to be the elders of the village. The Chief stepped toward me.

"I am so sorry that you are here," he said in halting Pigeon English.

That would normally take one aback somewhat, but I instantly knew what he meant, which was confirmed by the great sincerity with which it had been said. We had arrived without his opportunity to have prepared appropriately to receive us. Presumably there would have been some ceremony perhaps with festive food and drink.

But before I could make response he immediately followed it by saying, "Everything is so bad here," which instantaneously put me on stage.

"Oh Chief! Me pela look look ground blongum you pela! Imi good pela true!"

Chapter 10 — The Highlands

And went on to say how abundantly the gardens have supplied good food by the work of the people for I see how happy and healthy they are, and how beautiful are his mountains up here in the sky and how good is the taste of the breath of his clouds. All of these things were true in my eye, and I said so with enthusiasm and much gesture of arms and pitch of voice.

We are always viewed as being wealthy beyond imagination. And perhaps as compared to some circumstance such a conclusion is forgivable. So it is natural to want to protect oneself from being belittled, which is often the reason for such deprecations as his saying that everything is so bad here.

And once assured that we are not here to look down on them, as I was busy trying to praise everything in sight, I was watching the Chief and his elders progressively ease, and by the time I had finished everyone was smiling happily.

About this time a young fellow presented himself first to the Chief and then to me, wanting to serve as translator. He told me that he was a student in a mission school where he had learned English. He was perhaps ten years old and spoke reasonable English and his Pigeon most assuredly was wonderfully superior to mine. Both the Chief and I were delighted, and the boy fairly glowed in his pride.

The Chief and the boy talked briefly, and when he returned the few steps back to me I said, "I see that man."

"Oh yes, he is an ancient man, but a good worker." The man of whom I spoke had always stood at the close outside edge of the crowds as we moved about. He was never a part of the group. I judged his age to be perhaps thirty. And I understood by what the boy had said that he was not as bright as most. In many communities with whom we have become acquainted, such folks are thought to be so because of having been visited by the gods and are not looked down upon therefore. How fortunate is such a perception.

The boy had returned from the Chief apparently with an invitation to us to walk through the village if we wished, but I would not put it past the boy's boldness to have come up with the idea on his own. The village was in fact just to the right of the vehicle where it stood, and it formed a semi-circle on the ever so slightly downward slope of the ground at that point. There were perhaps thirty thatch-roofed houses. All of the roofs were exhaling smoke from their entire surface.

The "ancient man" caught my attention again a couple of times and he always stood with his arms folded in front of him in a manner of one trying thereby to stay warm. I was trying to see if there was something about the fellow that may have ostracized him from acceptance other than the boy's description of his being an ancient man. But I could see nothing different about him–no disfiguring scars or facial difference, etc.

When I saw him standing in front of one the houses, I noted that he was dressed like the other men with a sort of loin cloth and no shirt, but I now saw a difference between his appearance and absolutely everybody else. None of the other guys had chest hair. He did.

It wasn't greatly abundant, but there it was. Is it possible that the fellow was judged different enough from everybody else because of this? Now it so happens that I am entirely covered by this manliness, and since I am held in such unworthy elevation of high esteem, if this was his problem I thought that I might help the fellow out.

Every place we moved, the whole crowd moved with us. So when I approached the fellow the crowd was in a semicircle enclosing him as well as he stood in front of this house. I took off my shirt and he and I stood face to face grinning at each other, as the women were yelling their delight (not due to my glorious personage I can assure you) but to their delight of seeing my display of similarity to this fellow. And with all of this loudly voiced approval in a language beyond my understanding, I could feel the gentle pulling of my back hair by the crowd who could reach me—until finally I put my shirt back on.

I can never know if I helped his social status or not, but I figured that it couldn't have hurt.

We returned to the delegation and the driver indicated that he had spoken to the chief, who proceeded to speak to me in general conversation as translated by the boy. We spoke thusly for a few minutes and he told me about his having five wives, which meant that he was a man of means, because wives are bought from their fathers throughout all of New Guinea. My response showed that I was impressed with his status as reflected by this prosperity. He then told me that one of his wives had died and I expressed my regrets accordingly. Whereupon, he offered to buy Peggy from me. I thanked him in a manner by which he understood that the honor which he had just extended to me was intended to convey that my wife was a person of much value and that his offer granted expression by him of the fact, and that I was being complimented by his offer, round-about though it may have been, and that the entire matter was one of social grace on his part and was taken as such by me accordingly. I thanked him for honoring me in so gracious a manner.

He now offered us the hospitality of sleeping the night in the village, for which I thanked him profusely but indicated that unfortunately we needed to return. After this there was some discussion amongst the Elders, and abruptly the Chief and the boy without so much as a word–just walked away! Well, I was astonished at the apparent insult, and determined not to move one step from the spot and simply watched them. The two of them were talking together as they walked away. They spoke in their language so I could not know what this was about. They had walked over to the front of the vehicle as they talked and after a few minutes of this the boy came back to me and the Chief went back to the Elders and was speaking animatedly to them.

The boy ventured not a word of explanation, so after a few minutes I said, "I saw you talking to the Chief."

"Oh yes," he said as though nothing unusual had occurred. "I was explaining to the Chief that the machine makes his own light."

It was dusk now, and the Chief knew that we could not safely get down the dangerously narrow path along the cliff, hence his invitation to sleep the night. There was no concept of head lights on a vehicle.

I could conceive of no more eloquently phrased description of the fact of our being *beyond the roads and into another time* than the words of this boy to his Chief, on this distant mountain top, in this far off land called Papua New Guinea, than when he explained that, *"The machine makes his own light."*

Everyone was crowded around the Land Rover. The driver was ready. Peggy and I took our seats behind him. He started the engine, and turned on the headlights. We were looking out of the closed windows at the crowd of these lovely men and women and children all speaking their farewell in their own language when I spotted the ancient man. He was closer. He stood grinning with his arms folded over his chest. It was colder now. Quite some time ago, I had put my sweater on to keep warm. And I said to the driver, "Wait a minute!"

I got out of the car, walked around the back of it to where the fellow was standing at the other side. I took off the light brown cashmere cardigan sweater and was in the process of giving it to him when the women with shouts with ecstatic frenzy took over. About six of them were all trying to put it on him at the same time. I heard the name Jesus loudly called in prayer amongst all manner of actual raptured glee with oohs and ahhs in an absolute mêlée as they got the sweater on him. It was beyond any experience of our lives. They had burst forth with singing as the vehicle was turned around for our decent, and the children ran behind us waving and laughing until we had gone too far away.

I sat there, numb from the experience. I did not look back. For in the eye of my mind, so great was the chasm which stretched between us, that surely I could not see across a distance so vast.

The gift of the sweater was in itself of no great consequence. But I found myself pensive, for I thought of my father. He was a man of some personal dignity who wore that sweater often in the informal setting of home and hearth. It came to my hand at his death. But I would like to think that had he seen this unusual event, I would have seen a small smile and slight nod as he turned back to his book. And having seen that slight smile, I followed it with my own—from which I took some small pleasure.

The driver again had to carefully negotiate the trail down the mountain, especially where we could not make the turns with just one try. All went without incident until we had returned to where the war had been. Several warriors jumped out in front of us with arrows at the ready.

There was no jolly "Look at me" this time. We were savagely stopped. We couldn't just drive through them. Maybe there were wounded needing transport. But this was not the case.

The driver was told to get out of the car. He was taken to the back of the vehicle. They wanted to see all about inside. We soon found out that they were not after us in any way. They simply wanted to kill any of those of the other side whom we might have picked up to bring away with us.

Several hours later, we arrived back at Sopas without incident, and we dropped into bed for a short sleep. Tomorrow we would be leaving. We had one other destination in mind before seeing the *Osprey* again.

***

Though our sleep was gentle here at Sopas, the wonderment continued. But somehow our minds in sleep must have been released from the restraints of wakefulness. Such must have been the last few days, for how else can we explain an otherwise impossible travel into a time prehistoric.

Perhaps when we awake, we might understand. But for now, let there be a pleasant folding of the hands, and then perhaps to dream. And having been so instructed by that unknown entity called the sandman of our sleep, we are no longer aware of *any* time or *any* space.

We awakened to a mini-hubbub. Rose was rushing around creating a magnificent breakfast for our send-off, and when it was known that we were awake, everyone was talking at once. Peter was telling us about the cheese biscuits his mom had made for breakfast which was one of his favorites; as Rose was asking Peggy about our preferences regarding the many mysteries of sundry ways to cook eggs; as Charley was explaining the bus schedule and who was going to get us to it.

Peggy and I looked at each other and could not resist laughing. "What's the matter?" asked Charles with a baffled look of his face. "The bus bandits thing! You know about the bandits at Goroka don't you?"

"No–what did you hear?" asked Rose who stopped short in her tracks.

So we told them that the driver who had brought us up here had told us that not far from the place where we spent the night at the local church headquarters, bandits had stopped a north bound bus and taken everything of value from everyone, including all of their clothes. And knowing that we would be going back by bus, every time that we had talked about it, we couldn't help grinning over such an event occurring to us, even though we have a firm grasp of the reality of real potential danger.

They hadn't heard about the killing of the two doctors either, so we told them of the two Fijian doctors touring on the same road about a month ago. It is the only road coming up here after all! These men were darker skinned than the locals, so this was not a race related matter.

They had been driving a long time and there are no such things as "rest stops" or even gasoline stations, etc. where one might relieve one's bladder. So they stopped at the road side to do so. The area where they stopped had no people about. There was just a vast area of tall brown grass covering the place. The grass was perhaps a meter high.

The sound of the car and its stopping and the sound of the doors slamming awakened some men who had chosen this spot to sleep away the heat of the day. And as the two tourists were concluding their necessity, these men had risen from their rest in this high grass and immediately came toward them to see what this unusual happening was all about. As the tourists saw the men coming, they started walking away, and as the men starting shouting excitedly they walked more briskly, and when the men came to the road and the car the yelling was loader and the tourists now in terror started running, the men now in mob frenzy ran after them!

Days later, the pastor of the church of our membership, asked one of these men who was a deacon in his congregation what happened. "Well, they were running! So we ran after them! And we caught them! And somebody said kill them! So we did!"

Such things are beyond our comprehension. And we try (even though in this instance we are at a loss), we try to remember that we have entered a world other than our own, but we come away without ability to understand.

Charles and Rose told us about the Australian couple who were conducting business of some kind in Goroka. The wife, being startled upon returning home to find someone in the house burglarizing the place, screamed in her fright; whereupon the young man fled from the house. And because he was running, the people of the town ran after him; and being totally given over to mob like loss-of-mind frenzy, they killed him.

The parents of the boy, perhaps in his late teens, came to the couple of the house and demanded payback from them because it was her fault that the boy was killed. If she had not screamed, he would not have run; and if he had not run, they would not have run after him and therefore would not have killed him.

Of course, we could not ask Rose and Charles for an explanation of such an event. The tendency toward mob behavior is a subject beyond my pay grade as well.

"Breakfast is ready!" Rose announced with a certain note of triumph in her voice, and just was her pride. What a send-off! And as we brought our supplies, now including three war bows and ten arrows (which we had wrapped in a blanket to disguise our *warrior like appearance)*, others came to say their farewells. There is an immensity of goodness within the hearts of those such as these. "Good folks, please know that this humble sailor salutes you."

We were brought to the bus at Wabag a few minutes early, and the hospital driver of the Land Rover helped us aboard and made certain that the driver knew where we wanted to go and the bus to which we wanted to transfer. We paid our fare and joined everybody else in happy-sounding conversations. We couldn't understand their language, nor they ours, but we all recognized each other's pleasure in being off on a trip. We were on the way back to the boat, but were to be interrupted by our intent to see the birds!

***

New Guinea is home to many exotic birds! And we have seen many of them, but the magnificent *Bird of Paradise* we had not yet seen. Peggy, however, has been investigation how best we may go about finding them and has found that there is a place, hidden well away in the valleys close to Mount Hagan; a small resort has been built.

A number of female Birds of Paradise are enclosed within an aviary visible to the free flying males. These guys are adorned in all of the magnificence by their glorious plumage, and they come to present their individual charms to these females – apparently unaware of the barrier preventing the females from joining them. Another case of us poor males and our perpetual state of blindness to all things of our surroundings other than to the presence of that one special person. Such is the effect, *that wonderful effect,* which you ladies have upon us mere men.

Off we went! The road, instantly proclaimed its objection to such abuse as being pounded upon by yet another set of treadless tires on yet another loud rickety bus thingy, that it threw a cloud of dust at it, but the thing was always almost past before the dust hit. Those of us inside the thing however, were very aware of the dust, especially when our teeth happened to come together. But none of us really minded at all. Everyone was in holiday mood. It was fun.

About four hours later, we arrived at the fair city of Mount Hagan where a gathering of half a dozen buses were found reasonably together, in not exactly military precision of parking proximity perfection. It was a more natural grouping as perhaps that of an elderly gaggle of geese. But our efficient driver knew exactly which man drove the bus the 50 kilometers to the Baiyer River Sanctuary, where the *Resort* of our destination and its bird preserve is located. Our driver loudly called him over by name, and this good man seemed pleased to escort us to his van.

He chose to honor us by our sitting on the front seat with him so that we could see the roadway at its scenic best advantage, and we enjoyed talking with him. We awaited the arrival of others and the appointed time of departure. We shared our lunch equally with him and he subsequently seemed to take pleasure in his solicitude toward us throughout our journey's joggings.

The roadway was unpaved, of course, and we found that its dust was about of the same taste as the other road. The driver was in great form. He drove with a flourish of release of his hand after its having so marvelously achieved the turn of the steering wheel that its motion continued on through the air as that of a conductor grandly directing a great symphony. And though the music was unheard, the poetry of motion was distinctive.

The scenery was magnificent as well. After what had seemed like a downward plunging full speed dash over this twisting road, the van came lumbering to a sudden stop in a huge cloud of dust. The driver said that this was where we were to leave him. It did not look promising! There was nothing here! Yet the driver knew where we wanted to go, and we had enjoyed a camaraderie that made me feel that we were not being put out here for some nefarious reason. He had stopped the van where a rather wide path lead off the roadway and smilingly had waved us in its direction.

The van left. We started to walk. We did so with some slight trepidation. But in fifteen or so minutes, there it was! Oh how we were looking forward to a good dinner! We were down to three candy bars and some peanuts! The driver had been hungry.

It was a rather small structure of unpainted wood but the simple fact of its very existence still held visions of resort-style luxury of accommodation and elegance of food service within, even though its exterior appearance fell somewhat short of the usual ambiance with which the designation of "resort" is usually associated.

No one was at the meager reception desk, but we heard voices. Going in their direction we managed to startle the folks by our presence. "How did you get here?" said the first one, followed immediately by the other's saying, "We are not open!"

However, we were hearing other people. "Yes, there are some people here, but they have special arrangements."

We explained that we had come by bus and we needed a room and asked what time dinner was served. We were given a room. There was no bedding available and there was no food and no one to prepare it if there had been any. The people who were in the group staying here had brought their own food and were leaving tomorrow.

We asked about the birds, and yes they could be seen at daybreak and we were told which trail to take to find them. We looked at each other, grinned over the great difference of what we had found from our expectations, but the birds are here and we are here; the rest will unfold before our eyes – we hoped.

We found the others. Our presence was again met with, "How did you get here?" Our simple explanation was met with what we could only interpret as amazement, which did nothing other than amaze us by its reaction!

These folks virtually bristled with super camera equipment which shouted professionalism; which did not surprise us when they told us that they were with the National Geographic Society Magazine. There were four of them and they had been flown in here by helicopter. This is not the first time that we have been upstaged by our associates, though it was puzzling to us that such affluence of travel would be chosen by a camera crew for a magazine. However, we were more than compensated for the small inconvenience of our accommodation disappointments, by the fact that the austere organization of the National Geographic Society had also chosen this spot to find the elusive Birds of Paradise! As always, "Well done Peggy!"

At first light, we started silently down the pathway indicated to us. The camera crew had concluded their work yesterday, so the entire area was ours. We saw that the females were beginning to move about, and twenty minutes later, there was a blaze of color not far away. Nonchalantly at first, looking constantly in any direction other than at the females, he moved ever closer until he could stand the closeness to these wonderful creatures no longer; and as he moved himself slowly this way and that, showing each part of his plumage to its very best angle and reflective sun lit colors, he now looked intently for the first possible slight indication that his presence was being observed. Wow! Wow, *we* certainly had seen him, and seen his breathtaking colors and contrasts which only New Guinea's male Bird of Paradise can boast! We were awe struck by the magnificence of such a creature. Wow! What a display! What a courtship invitation! Gentlemen, how fortunate our opposite gender is, to be graced by all of our grandeur! (Oops – does something not sound quite real here…?)

Other males came flaunting themselves before their captive audience who mostly ignored their presence entirely; which may be an experience shared by most of us males, and with similar frustration. Oh the anguish of despair! However, the remainder of our time was spent in whispered words such as, "Here comes another one! Wow! What a sight! And to be this close to them is fantastic!"

We were still whispering to each other when we got back to the resort; how grand an experience this has been! And that's when the police burst in to our vision!

They had rounded up the film crew and were herding them toward the outside doorways with all of their camera gear! Our presence had been told to them by the film personnel so we were known to be there, but none-the-less, upon seeing us they demanded to know how we had gotten here! The police were clearly excited, and apparently agitated at discovering us here. They didn't really listen to our explanation—just said that we need to quickly get in the car! Well, with such a clear invitation as this, we proceeded accordingly and the reason for the film crew's helicopter choice of arrival was now made clear to us. The road used by us to get here had been taken over by bandits not long ago. The police escort for the film crew's evacuation was clearly evidenced by the policeman beside the driver with his shotgun and the two men in the back seat of this open vehicle as they each moved their rifles in the ever changing directions of their eye movement as the driver maintained his concentrated forward leaning over the steering wheel with his foot never easing from a full thrust of the gas peddle.

Where we had enjoyed what seemed a somewhat hasty ride down into this valley, we now roared over the road at full speed with a gigantic dust cloud; slowing for nothing as our guards, bristling with guns, nervously looked in all directions, apparently as much for their own protection as for ours.

We came skidding to a stop in front of the police station in town, where Peggy and I were escorted politely to the presence of an official who with great politeness most earnestly suggested that prior to any future movement about the country we might inquire of the police regarding their knowledge of any unrest in our intended direction. We were most sincerely appreciative of this kindness and expressed our gratefulness with appropriate expressions couched in words of humility. At the conclusion of our brief education, the camera crew having already been taken to their departure point which remains unknown to us; we were taken to the appropriate bus, bound for an uneventful trip back down to the city of Lay and hence to the schooner, which brought us happily back to the *Osprey*.

CHAPTER 11

 AND THEN...

We could see the *Osprey* from the deck of this ship which nestled to a stop at the deeper "T" end of this commercial wharf, miniaturizing the *Osprey*'s proportions. That little yacht has so often been the entirety of our world, and has always sailed upon the boundless affection of our minds. It is perhaps true that we were possessed by the happiness of our returning as we awkwardly carried our stuff down the gangplank, for we were laughing merrily as we were boarding the *Osprey* . . . when I saw it.

It stopped my laugh in mid-breath! The forward deck hatch had been pried open! The hatch was closed now, but the boat had been entered!

I opened the padlock on the entry hatch to the cabin, and we rushed in having unceremoniously dropped our baggage in the cockpit. From here nothing seemed disturbed. The galley was next. All of Peggy's copper pots still hung securely attached to the bulkhead. But beyond here, and under the foreword deck hatch, here thieves apparently had grabbed whatever came to hand and shoved it through the hatch to someone on the deck. Clearly they had been interrupted or feared that they would be, for so much more could have been taken. Tomorrow we will see if our boat watchers might be able to put the word out for a buy-back reward in hope of some return.

Of course, anyone watching over a boat can only let their presence be known occasionally. It is we who are the ones having taken the risk for her safety and well being.

The drawers had been emptied of all clothing as well as all shoes which were stored below the dresser. But the hanging locker (closet) had not been opened, due perhaps by virtue of the elegant closure system from the hand of Ralph Wiley, the boat's designer.

The most unfortunate of losses was the taking of Robert Lewis Stevenson's pocket watch, given to us by one of his heirs. It was not functioning at the time, and it saddens me that a gift of such a treasured item, given from the heart of his descendant to our hand, was likely just chucked into a hole in the ground so as not to be traceable to the thieves to whom it was worthless.

We are so fortunate that our loss was not greater than we found it to have been. And even though we regained nothing from the police, nor resultant from the large sign propped on the boat saying that a reward would be given for the return of the stolen items; we temper our anger by accepting the fact that such events must be taken in stride. Perhaps our recollection of the old adage regarding the uselessness of crying over spilled milk may have helped the processes. We stayed for about a week during which time we took great pains to assure our friends that we harbored no ill feelings toward them due to the event.

We felt called upon to once again take our departure. We had heard that sound again—that call of horizons hidden beyond the curving of our Spaceship-Earth's shapely form; and we bid farewell to our friends the evening before we got underway for a revisit to some special places as we were turning again toward Australia.

* * *

One of those places was in the mini-fjord where we had met so many who had become friends, as spoken of in Chapter 9 regarding the uncles who do not wish to die, and of the pig hunt with the village, and so much more.

Upon arrival, we were remembered happily. For folks came in chattering groups, calling back and forth to each other as the dug-out canoes greeted the *Osprey* while she was still anchoring; circling her as they awaited a spot to have their tie-off line attached to our boat. Their owners clamored aboard. There is no more lovely a reward than to be joyously remembered. To be thus welcomed can moisten the eye of even a very salty old sailor.

Our travels tend to recognize few schedules, but we knew that our coming time in Australia was to include preparations for our Indian Ocean crossing and around the southern tip of Africa. Much needed to be done, and we bid our last goodbyes to these lovely people who granted us the awesome privilege of their acquaintance. One is permanently enriched by so fathomless a gift as this, which has been granted to us by so many people over the years. We have sat together. We have talked together. We have eaten food together. Is it true that we are the sum of our experiences in life? Such questions are beyond the pay grade of a simple seaman such as I.

We had been sailing happily along the lush verdant coastline of beautiful Papua New Guinea, stopping each afternoon for a one or two nights stay. And far too soon we were back in the little town of Samurai to process our papers for departure from this country for our sail toward Australia. The formalities are simple and as usual were without complications. We would spend the night at anchor and planned an early morning departure. Peggy gave me a hand getting the dinghy aboard. I lash the oars to the dinghy's seat as well as the canvas sack that holds the rowlocks. That way, once launched, the dinghy is ready for duty without the need to find her necessities stored elsewhere. The mainsail halyard is attached to the dinghy's painter and by use of our electric winch, the dinghy is raised out of the water bow first, straight into the air, swung over the cabin and lowered into position stern first close to the mast and the bow is lowered onto a brace just forward of the main hatchway where she travels securely out of the way in this upside down manner. Four super strong diamond-shaped pad eyes are bolted to the cabin top, and I'll take a moment to describe what has been an immensely satisfying system which secured the dinghy there on the cabin roof.

A ½ inch line is permanently attached to the pad eyes close to each side of the dinghy fore and aft. These lines are lifted over the side of the dingy toward each other at their centers and come to within approx a foot of each other. By tightly lashing these lines together at only this one place, the dinghy is secured. Even the lashing line is permanently attached so this item comes immediately to hand, not needing to be located for duty. The placement of the pad eyes also aides this simple yet elegant solution. No sea motion of the *Osprey* nor seriously heavy storm has ever threatened to move her; not even the conditions encountered in the Southern Ocean toward New Zealand.

We had a lovely dinner there at Samurai, Papua New Guinea, and we slept contentedly. Tomorrow I hoped to introduce our new sails to their true reason for being aboard. Our "sail" from Australia with these lovely new sails aboard had been mostly a motoring event due to the shameful absence of any worthy wind. I hope that this will not be the case on our return! However, that hope had not forced me to turn over in my sleep too often, because upon waking, I have recollection of nothing but the pleasantness of breakfast interest by which I was greeted the next morning. Peggy smiled.

As always, breakfast was a delight. And though I was anxious to get underway, we both saw the other moving and even speaking more slowly than usual in our purposeful accomplishment of wishing to not hurry the other.

Probably more swiftly than either of us realized, breakfast had been completed, dishes and pans cared for and returned to their places, charts had been reviewed, taffrail log readied, mainsail cover removed and stowed. But when the anchor was raised and secured, I could no longer hide my smile.

***

We were going sailing! And though it was not to be a very long voyage, and thought it was a passage which we had done before, beyond Australia lay the great Indian Ocean and the passage around the southerly most point of Africa to Cape Town, with visions of safaris and wild new experiences while there!

So many horizons yet to look beyond! Such indeed are justifiable reasons to have caused this very broad smile of mine.

I had started the engine before bringing the anchor aboard, and I now raised the mainsail in the hope that the wind might get the idea and join the fun. We started motoring. Five minutes passed and the wind had not noticed. Five hours passed and the wind slept on. And then–I felt it.

It brushed my left cheek, and that feeling rushed down my spine and up again. It shuddered my entire back once more; not with the fright of dread and fear, but with that very same physical feeling of an actual tremor and tingling— but of anticipation! And the *Osprey* felt it too, because she simultaneously leaned to starboard in her excitement.

I trimmed her sails to match her movement. And then — then, with an unmasked grin, my right hand moved forward unbidden and silenced the coarse song of our diesel engine. And then — then I heard that sweet swish of sound as a bow wave pressed itself against the hull. There was no other sound. And now, having taken your seat in the audience–watch with us, for the dance has begun.

The deep-voiced ocean breathed his pleasure. The wind began oh so gently to sing her ancient anthem as it now seemed that an entire choir of voices stand at the call of the conductor; and at the movement of his baton, it breathed full an enchanted sound accompanied with the wondrous gusto of a full symphonic orchestra! This shall be a glorious ballet!

And then – then the next curtain thrust open and for just one second the dancers were motionless – when with a flashing thrust of the Maestro's baton, life was endowed to this event of magnificent.

To the *Osprey*, now dressed in the gowned grandeur of her new sails, I presented my hand. No dancer on any stage was ever offered a more genteel touch. And my hand simultaneously embraced the perfect smoothness of this lustrously varnished teak wheel which guides the rudder directing our dance. I knew that this was a premiere performance. Such perfection of beauty has never before possessed the entirety of this ocean. Even the stars twinkled to the sway of the dancers.

And then — then the music of the dance filled this monumental auditorium with its momentous sound. The dome of this ballet theater arched above us from horizon to horizon — the stars, as chandeliers, blazed to the drama. And then — then the *Osprey*, as though with a leap of sheer ecstasy, joined the company entering from stage left for her premiere performance as a fully matured creation of beauty, thus gowned for the dance. She seemed not to touch the sea as with breath taking flight and whirling beauty she was born across the stage with gloriously astonishing speed and grace. For thus the *Osprey* flew across the sea to magnificently shatter all of the previously recorded speed of any prior passage.

The highest rating of designation to which a ballerina may ascend is to the title of Principal, achievable only after years of arduous effort. It has been so with the *Osprey*. Now, after having crossed the entire great South Pacific Ocean, to at last have new and more powerful sails, she has earned the new grace which is the presence of her being. For beyond here, she now soars with the heart of eagles. Her name is *Osprey*–and she now flies across the surface of the sea.

Never prior to this voyage has the good *Osprey* been fully clothed in the glory of such sails. Wherefore now, the ocean herself has called forth a jubilance of sight and sound with which to present her crowning as a Queen of the South Pacific Ocean.

The dance had begun with a breathing of gentle breeze as though spoken by the now awakened violin section as just one single clarinet whispered an answer. The mainsail, looking from the masthead, surveys the motion of the sea and the readiness of the *Osprey* below. The new genoa sail embraces the entire foredeck and stretched aftward way beyond the mast as it sought to press out those alien shipping wrinkles from its fabric. All sheets were poised to the baton of the Maestro as he conducts this glorious music upon this the greatest stage on earth; for here is true vastness. Here is the Coral Sea of the Ocean of the South Pacific. And then — then the Maestro with the fullness of his command, awakened a joyous excitement of the entire company of the ballet as crescendos followed each other, as the full ecstasy of the dance begins!

"Okay crewman, Peggy and I are going below. Sail her full and by."

So, you take the perfectly varnished teak wheel in your hand. You feel the welcoming smoothness of it and you feel the press of the passing wave against the rudder. Your orders are to keep her sails full and sail her by the slight changes in direction of the wind as it alters between the gusts and the otherwise steady direction.

You are not sailing by a compass course, but rather as how she prefers to sail as best for speed. But none the less, you want to keep a mental running note of the possibility of an overall direction change of wind which would require sail adjustment to return to the course of intent. You are checking the compass every once in awhile, but it's getting more difficult. The sea spray is beginning to cover your glasses with too much salt for you to see a compass card.

"I'll try what Dan does. He licks his glasses with his tongue to get the salt off. Hey, it works! It's not perfect, but I can see the compass numbers again."

No, we have never had a crewman aboard on any blue water passage, but I wanted to force you to think of yourself aboard if you have not already been sailing with us vicariously. And yes, I want you to taste the salt on your lips and to feel the living motion of this sailing yacht at sea. And as you look about and no longer see that place called land, you suddenly realize that as far as you can see, you are entirely alone in an alien water-covered planet and as that penetrates the very depth of your mind, you also become aware that you and this little ship are in fact completely up to the task to which you are called! And then — then is when you too—will smile.

Oh how she sails! Gone are those soft sounds of the wind so gently whispered yesterday which breathed the beginning of our dance. Now with full voice this symphonic orchestra gloriously thrills our senses as our ballerina's slender grace is born across the stage by the boundless might of her cavalier. She dances—with the sea.

"Well done crewman."

Now, the tireless hand of the windvane steering system has effortlessly taken over the perpetual requirement of helmsmanship. Each wave pushes the bow to starboard on this course, so a little more left rudder is required to return her to the needed direction. Without that rudder change, each following waves would set her farther off course, until she would be so far from a safe presentation of her sails to the wind that real disaster could occur.

To watch the wind slam the upright plywood blade of our windvane steering unit over sideways due to the boat having gone slightly off course and hence result in the presentation of the wind coming from a slightly different direction, and thereby to see the gears of its axis turn the rudder of its system, is mesmerizing. This powers the entire process, because its small rudder is also on an axis. It rides effortlessly straight down in the water flow which rushes past the hull until the wind blows the wind blade over and thereby slightly turns the water-blade rudder. When that happens, that rudder powerfully skates upward by virtue of being turned slightly against the water flow passing the hull.

Having a nylon line attached to it on one end and to the ship's steering wheel at the other, the helm is turned until the *Osprey* is once again on course, at which point all parts of the system are once again in equilibrium. What a wonderful boon this is to short-handed sailing. This crewman never tires, never sleeps, never even eats or drinks.

Just for the fun of experiment and personal education, I have toyed with self-steering methods which employ a line to pull a kink in a jib sheet which is then led to the tiller, off set by the tension of elastic bands such as surgical tubing. But having used this infrequently, and though fun with which to experiment, it certainly is not to be thought of as a satisfactory choice for the serious long distance sailor regardless of how tempting this may sound whereby the cost of purchasing a windvane steering system can be avoided. Years ago, I bought a little book entitled, *Self-Steering for Sailing Crafts* and found it to be great fun. As the kink in a sheet is decreased by wind strength as a boat's course changes, this pull of the line to the tiller is increased and the course is changed back accordingly. If the wind force is decreased by the boat heading farther into the wind, the pull on the tiller is decreased and elastic cords pull the tiller in the opposite direction. Trim tabs on outboard rudders are also a very versatile control to alter the power needed for tiller steering.

The *Osprey*'s rudder is controlled by wheel steering, not by a tiller. And for our system, I made a teak drum for the self steering system which rides directly on the steering wheel's shaft just aft of the *Osprey*'s steering wheel, to which the windvane's steering lines are attached. A simple copper rod is inserted through a hole drilled through the hub of the steering wheel and into the windvane control drum which connects the power of it to the boat's steering wheel, whereby a course is maintained relative to the wind. That copper rod sounds dangerous sticking out of the steering wheel's hub, but it had a loop bent in the end into which two fingers can enter, giving a good pulling grasp for removal under pressure.

The gears of the windvane gave me many hours of grief requiring my getting completely out of the boat and onto that little aft platform, occasionally using both arms and legs to keep myself out of the sea while underway, but I would never go long distance sailing without one.

We were still roaring along through all of the night and the next day. Oh how she sailed!

I had been recording the daily reading of the taffrail log. Wow what speed we have been maintaining on this entire crossing! This is fantastic! It's only the fifth day of this voyage and we will be arriving today! Oh how I wanted just a few more days of this and told Peggy so! She lowered her eye brows in a threat that said, "You wouldn't dare!"

It is befitting to such a very august occasion as this, during which the *Osprey*'s maiden voyage with all new sails, that she be granted such perfect wind and sea conditions as these have been. With these sails which are bigger than the *Osprey* has ever had, due to the heightening of her mast and tacking her fore-stay farther forward, gave her much more power than ever before. This accounts for the speed with which she has made this crossing to Australia. It

Chapter 11   And Then...

was memorably fantastic! Good Ed Cutts, the great naval architect, was right. She did not need anymore mast height than this two and a half foot addition.

I was to later learn of the wondrously generous gift which Peggy had given to me during this voyage. Having seen the enormous joy that I was having during this sail, she succeeded in totally hiding from me the fear that she was experiencing from our sailing speed, as a "rooster-tail" followed in our wake. There is no greater monument, in tribute to her love and affection for this simple sailor, as is this selfless gift. It stands forever enshrined within my personal Sailing Hall of Fame, where she is eternally enthroned within my heart.

Were you to have been sitting comfortably in the Ballet Theatre watching the dance of our passage—about which I have been having the fun of mixing my metaphors—you would have been totally unaware that a ballerina had needed to pack her feet in ice during the intermission, and that the carpenter of the back-stage crew was frantically repairing the central brace that holds the next scene's screen from toppling over backwards. If the screen had fallen during the performance, it would have completely destroyed the evening's illusions.

Likewise, there are many "back stage" happenings as part of this voyage. I wanted you to enjoy the sail without being interrupted with everything that was going on because I was concerned that you might have gotten swamped with all of the other small things which were happening which thereby might have robbed from you the pure pleasure of our passage. It was an absolutely glorious sail! Yet as "crewman aboard" I don't want you to miss this part of our voyage either, so let's go back and take a look "back-stage" aboard the *Osprey* during this passage.

Peggy had kept some notes of this reality. And I shall be specific as to how you would go about doing some of these things were you to have been aboard. Only for the sake of my metaphors, have I written of events other than in the order of actual occurrence, but stay with the fun as you now will see "back-stage" as well. Those who are less interested in the minutia of detail shall not be criticized for failing to read the rest of this chapter, nor failing to refer to some glossary to learn some old English terms that are part of the lexicon of today's sailor.

Peggy said, "Dan, I think we're taking on water!" It wasn't news to me. The automatic bilge pump, which is activated by a float which is lifted when the bilge water gets to a certain level, activates the bilge pump until the float on the switch is closed when the water is low enough to no longer lift it. It wasn't working. I had already checked the float and confirmed that it wasn't jammed closed. I had checked the wiring and all connections were fine and checked that the battery retained its charge. Ocean sailing has a distinct motion about it, which moves the bilge water about in all directions. Being able to locate a leak by seeing water passing over a dry section of the hull is impossible. No area of the hull within reach of the bilge water is ever dry.

Bilge water is almost always oily to some extent, which is reason enough to want it not to surge up the sides of the hull to soak the mattress and bed sheets which are hard against it. This bilge water seemed to be more oily than expected.

I had tried the Whale Gusher hand pump which is mounted in the cockpit inside the starboard lazaret. This is a powerful hand pump which I mounted so that it can be pumped while sitting, thus requiring reduced manual effort and hence supplying longer pumping endurance. But alas, it too had abandoned its ability, so now I have been forced to option three, the unmounted hand pump. Were the arrival of more significant quantity of the ocean to start joining us, I would firstly carefully check all through hull fittings including the propeller shaft stuffing box, etc., and next repair the electric bilge pump and others. But let's try this first. There is very little water to be cared for, and would not even be noticed in a deeper bilged vessel with less roundness than ours.

The unmounted hand operated pump is stored in its place in the forecastle and now put to work for the first time ever. The deepest point in our bilge is just forward of the engine room and directly below the entrance hatch to the cabin. A foot stirrup holds the pump down opposing the upward pull of the handle which thereby draws the water into the pump and when pushed downward it thrusts the water into the 2 inch diameter exhaust hose which by early planning is long enough to reach the cockpit which is self draining overboard. It is a comfortable spot to be braced while standing to perform this duty.

I was required to do this every few hours, but only about ten or so minutes were needed to empty the bilge each time. No concern of danger accompanied this event, and as time passed no significant increase of water presented to require further investigation of its source. Only by virtue of its being a slight nuisance interruption to pleasantries is it included in Peggy's list of what I have named our back-stage activity.

The wind has been picking up since yesterday and continues to be slowly backing, which refers to its compass direction moving to lower numbers. So "crewman," come out with me to see exactly how I put a reef in the mainsail.

When the wind is abaft-the-beam I usually choose to reef the mainsail in a way which requires no steering assistance from Peggy while the windvane is up to the job, and I do so in a way which keeps the mainsail from flailing about in the wind. For you to comprehend the process, I must first introduce you to the mainsail's arrangements: There are three rows of reef points, and the following discussion will explain how this sail is reduced in size by one person with ease, under progressively deteriorating weather conditions of wind speed increases.

Step 1. The boom has a topping lift. I raise the outboard end of the boom with the topping lift to the level of the reef chosen, and simply haul that outboard clew to the boom by the line which always lives there, and belay it to its cleat on the boom. I can frequently do this without even using the winch on the boom which can give more power than one person. The boom is now way upward from horizontal.

Step 2. The mainsail halyard is eased enough for the downward travel of the mainsail and belayed there temporarily, as the down haul of the mainsail at the mast is used to haul the sail down the mast to the same line of reef points as selected in step one, and it is belayed in place. This can be done with one hand as the other retains the halyard. The height of the top of the sail is obviously lowered thereby and the boom has returned to horizontal. Now the mainsail halyard can be used to tighten the luff of the sail at its reduced limit, by using the mainsail halyard winch on the mast, as tension loss has resulted.

Step 3. The topping lift which handles the outboard end of the boom is now eased which brings the weight of the boom back onto the trailing edge of the sail,

Step 4. We now have a pocket of loose sail cloth hanging from the bottom of the boom. At this point it may or may not require immediate attention. If it is raining as it now is, that pocket may quickly fill with water and hence this weight may even cause sail cloth deformation over time and therefore must be closed. To care for this, a series of reef point ties made up of small stuff (perhaps ¼ inch line), extend along the length of the reef and are at about two feet apart. These ties also are permanently attached to the sail and are used to hold this pocket in a roll which you thusly provide. By standing on the windward side of the boom, about mid way between the mast and the boom's end, reach down into the pocket, grab the deepest point of the pocket with one hand [sometimes requiring you to reach under the boom to press some sail cloth upward to your grasping hand] and with a firm quick motion, lift that sail cloth upward. The wind will often cause the sail cloth to slam together, accompanied with a snapping sound, which brings most of the entire length of the pocket together like a piece of folded paper. Now if you roll this gathering under itself, instead of on top of itself, there will be no water held there which comes running off the sail sometimes in great quantity. So with a reasonably tight roll at this point, grasp the sail-tie from the other side, bring it under the sail (not under the boom), and tie it to the sail-tie at your side of the sail. The ties are generally not long enough to pass under the boom anyway, and tradition says that sail damage can occur by doing so, due to possible tearing of the sail cloth at the tie attachment point. The clew cringles of the foot are, however, to be secured directly to the boom and also to the mast at the inboard end.

My habit is to now go midway forward from the first tie and do the same role of the foot pocket and tie as described, followed by midway from the center to the end of the boom. The remainder can be tied in any order of preference.

As other sail reductions of size are needed, I simply remove the turns on the winch drum of the prior cringle line and secure that line to its cleat. The other ties along the reef may stay in place, as the mainsail may be unreefed in stages as the wind decrees over time. If in the process, I have lost some of the tension needed for the foot of the sail; this reefing will be taken care of by the tension of the new cringle line's effort. Under usual conditions, the gathering of this excess sail cloth need not be cared for immediately. One may prefer to go below for a rest or for lunch, with no ill effect to sail or conscience, assuming that there is no major rain at the time.

No significant difference in mainsail reefing procedure is called for whether the wind is aft or abeam or forward.

So you have seen that all of these lines required for handling the reefing of the mainsail live with the sail at all times; which might shock the skipper of a racing yacht. However, that good fellow may have a dozen crewmen at his call and may even have various weight mainsails to use as conditions change, rather than ever having a reefing requirement. However, the single-handed skipper of a yacht entered in an around the world race, is one in whose presence all seamen will grant respect; for we too have glimpsed the sea. Yet, such seamen as these, may, however, even have electronic self-furling systems by which manpower is replaced by motors and may even roll the luff of a mainsail into a pocket inside the aluminum mast itself, or roll the boom to receive a reef.

But back to our world, the proper securing of the clew cringles at each end of the reefed mainsail foot is critical for proper sail shape at the foot and must therefore have the ability to be pulled outward along the boom to establish a proper tightness. To accomplish this, the cringle at the mast end of the boom is to be firstly secured to the boom by a strong hook or simply tied to the boom and mast.

The bitter end of the out-haul line is attached to a pad eye on one side of the boom about 10 inches aft of where the leach cringle needs to be drawn above the boom, and on the opposite of the boom from that pad eye, a cheek block is bolted through which the ½ inch reef line is passed and then brought to its own belaying cleat.

I take a certain pleasure from these cleats, perhaps because I designed them, drew them onto blocks of wood, cut them out, sanded them smooth, varnished them with many coats of varnish and bolted them to the boom.

These clew lines also live permanently attached to the boom at its end to the pad eye, and hence through the sail cringle, then through the cheek block, and then to a cleat on the boom after turns on the winch drum can be taken to supply as much power as needed to get the mainsail foot stretched tight. With this arrangement the reefed foot of the mainsail is drawn outboard and downward to the boom at the same time. When unreefed, these lines travel upward with the sail while their bitter end remains attached to the boom.

Jibs must also be changed underway. But even this can often be done quickly enough to not require steering assistance beyond the windvane's ability. However, an imbalance of sail power distribution may require unusual rudder changes greater than the norm, which can be beyond the self steering's capability, whereupon, I call for Peggy's steering assistance.

Our jibs are kept below in the forecastle, each in its own marked bag. Anytime a bagged sail is brought on deck the possibility of its going overboard exists, a drama which is vigorously guarded against. The sailbag is immediately lashed to the life line by its draw strings and has thus far never gotten away from me. Without fail, when bagging a sail as it is being stuffed into the bag, the tack, head, and sheet clew are always entered into the bag last and hence are immediately available before removing the sail for use. Thereby the new sail to be used is already attached before the wind can grab the bag and all of its sailcloth.

Also, in heavy weather, I will secure the quick release type of belay at the end of its tack wire, to the tack ring on deck where the present jib is attached before taking down the currant jib. No matter the size of a wave boarding over the bow in an attempt to slurp this sail away, this replacement jib is going nowhere.

Using a tack wire lifts the foot of the sail farther off the deck and out of the reach of a boarding wave while underway. Under heavy conditions, people have also been known to be washed overboard. So as previously described, in such conditions I wear a harness attached to a jackline as a precaution which reality has never been called upon to fully test. (May I be forgiven for claiming a moderate degree of footing acumen—oops, have I coined a phrase?) But viewing the fact that Peggy is neither a real sailor nor navigator, to lose the skipper overboard is guarded against. And in heavy weather, I have always heeded her request for this precaution.

Ladies, please permit my having a private word with the gentlemen aboard. The records of the fishing fleet in Alaska record the loss of crew overboard. On the occasions of subsequently finding them, which is unfortunately sometimes after their demise, the fly of their pants is very often reportedly found to be open.

I recommend, that you consider the use of a container while in the cockpit, rather than a direct overboard procedure. The container can be emptied overboard and if of a disposable construction can also be dropped overboard after several uses. Even in open ocean, the disintegration life of any such thing is to be considered.

"It's time to pump the bilge again. You need to start an every other hour pumping schedule, and your watch starts now. I'm going to get some sleep. Call me if she starts having trouble holding course. If the windvane has to be helped, awaken me and we'll change to the number 4 jib since we're down to two reefs in the main now." Or that's what I might have told you if you were actually aboard with us. Sailing at night while you're roaring along at these speeds is exhilarating and beautiful. Even with these drenching rain squalls it's comfortable and dry in this wheelhouse. What a great addition to the boat and to our lives this wheelhouse has been!

That woke me up. It was just a little bigger wave than most, just enough for me to feel a change. I don't know how long I was asleep, but as usual, even small changes in motion get one's attention, not from being startled or apprehensive, but simply as the normalcy of life at sea.

We are really just roaring along, even with our reduced sails. And the *Osprey* is perfectly in her element. We are on course. Her sail power and trim are just right for our conditions for maximum speed. But after breakfast I may try the number four jib to ease us just a little for Peggy, and also that we not arrive before dawn the day after tomorrow. We need to see where to enter through the Great Barrier Reef.

We are absolutely roaring along. And of course, we cannot see any evidence of the Great Barrier Reef somewhere to starboard of us. But we know that it would certainly be snarling in these conditions of rain squalls and wind. But I am content that the course chosen is a secure one and we slept well.

I awakened every few hours to pump the bilge and to check that all was well in this black and blustery night. The course remained as chosen, which meant that the wind had not changed in direction nor for awhile in average strength. The compass, which swings above my pillow is read only on its underside, and is by habit checked by me each time I turn over in my "sleep." It is not at all as though the *Osprey* is just let free to take us where the wind wishes when we are not in areas of hazardless horizons.

This night is black with torrential rain. The coarse voice of the wind howls at the *Osprey*, who ignores this boisterousness in her delight of showing us how wonderfully she can dance as though with actual wings she were now gowned. Oh how she sails!

Chapter 11 — And Then...

The sun could no longer be held back. He shoved the clouds aside to see the dance of the *Osprey* and I have never seen him smile so broadly in his approval. I made breakfast for us and would have gotten a sextant shot to determine our position on the chart, but the sun went back to sleep, so breakfast is next.

The windvane continues to hold our course and we continue to roar along gloriously. It's about mid day. Wind is slowing again, and I made another jib change and also shook out another reef in the mainsail. The sun is seen intermittently but indistinct through the clouds. I just pumped the bilge again and have definitely determined that the oil is coming from a seal in the transmission.

Checking the oil level has shown that we still have above the minimum required fluid. So if an emergency engine use were to present, we can still use the engine and its transmission. A little oil goes a long way when sloshed around with a little bilge water.

Not long after Peggy's lunch, I saw an opening in the Great Barrier Reef. I wasn't absolutely certain, but I thought that it was the Fitzroy Pass. In any event, it was broad and clear, so I called Peggy up to steer for me as I eased the mainsail and jib halyards to sail the *Osprey* with wind abeam as we entered Australian waters in majestic style.

It turned out to be Trinity Pass, not Fitzroy, which meant that we were not quite far enough southward. And now that the wind had gotten tired and passed the job over to his cousin the breeze who had in turn reawakened the sun; we found ourselves in the quiet broad waters between the reef and the land, quite some long distance away. And due to the declining strength of the breeze, it was becoming apparent that it was likely that our iron mainsail was to be called for, and with it our leaking transmission.

So I checked the level of the transmission fluid again and found that it would need more oil pretty soon, so "Okay crewman, please take care of that" is what you might have heard me say had you been actually aboard, for this too was part of the "back stage" happening.

The transmission, of course, is aft of the engine and requires one to climb over top of the engine on one's stomach with various iron parts poking into various parts of one's body. Such climbing about most certainly would get grime all over one's clothing. So rather than soil my limited clothing supply which Peggy always volunteers to clean, even though we have no washing machine, I always choose to enter this dark domain, unattired.

I chose to crawl into this space beside the engine; twist myself around into a 90 degree angle, and reach around to the other side of the engine where my body could not fit, to recheck the oil level with its dip stick. Oil can be put into the transmission through the dip stick tub but I did not have a funnel with a small enough spout to fit the tub, so I will need to remove the eight bolts that secure a six inch square plate on the transmission to enable me to pour the fluid as I have so often done.

A proper-sized wrench was gotten from the tool box and the awkward but simple procedure commenced. The bolts with their lock washers were carefully held in my hand, the oil was added. I held the plat with the fingers of my left hand and the back of my right hand which was holding the bolts, and as the plat was about to be replaced—oh my—I dropped a bolt into the transmission.

The boat was rolling a bit, but how could such an amateurish thing happen? I am certainly no mechanic, but this is ridiculous! Well, I'll never know. Had I bumped my arm on something at that crucial instant? I do remember that I gasped! I got my magnet which is at the end of an extendable rod, and probed in all conceivable angles for what seemed hours and finally got the bolt out. I thankfully replaced the cover plate.

I might have been able to just slide out of the engine "room" on the accumulation of grease and drenching perspiration with which I was covered. But with Peggy's help for areas beyond my reach, some of which I had not known even existed, the clean-up job was done much easier than the cleaning of clothes would have been.

The breeze died completely and we motored into Cairn's Harbor. It took six hours of motoring to get there, whereupon, the engine started overheating and a new problem presented itself "back stage" in our ballet.

Only one small additional problem occurred here at the end of our dance. We had anchored in a designated area to await the Customs Officials entry formalities for Australia. One notifies Customs of your arrival by calling them on a specific VHF radio frequency. However, I could not awaken the radio and for the briefest of moments, I was tempted to speak loudly to it which would have been of no avail anyway. Instead, I asked a passing yacht to call for us, and in two days they arrived to welcome us back to Australia.

When the breeze built up again, we sailed up the broad creek beyond town to the Cairn's Cruising Yacht Squadron and old friends.

Had I originally included all of our small events as you now have seen them, I think that you might have lost the true joy and excitement of this little voyage. It was a wonderful joy! And I ask that you remember the spectacle of it as you sailed with us as in the earlier part of the chapter without all of our interruptions, even though these too are occasionally part of cruising under sail.

Peggy and I enjoyed your company aboard, vicarious though it was. Please join us on our next adventure. Peggy is a great cook! And fun is on the *Osprey*'s menu!

CHAPTER 12

Australia, The Third Time

Our passage from New Guinea had its mechanical problems—such as the fact that our transmission will no longer function to move the boat forward or backward. However, we have a breeze and we have sails, and we have full knowledge of Smith's Creek and The Cairns Cruising Yacht Squadron and its mooring system along the mangrove side of the waterway. So having checked the *Osprey* into Australia with Customs, I prepared the boat to sail, took up the anchor, and off we went.

The tidal current was with us, and the process was without incident. The dropping of the anchor well prior to the unoccupied mooring spot and close to the boats ahead of it, allowed the *Osprey* to fetch-up on her anchor line perfectly to swing the boat beside her new mooring spot, needing me only to row the dinghy twenty feet beside us to the mangrove bank to secure our first line. By easing the anchor line the boat swung gently to her proper place and the remaining procedure of securing was swiftly completed.

I studiously prevented myself from looking about to see who may have been watching the event of which I was (in my view) justifiably proud, simple as it was. The smooth handling of a boat in any close quarters is considered a display of good seamanship. I am proud of my humility! (Another oxymoron?) The anchor was retrieved by use of the dinghy.

I had a mechanic inspect the transmission. He was unable to repair it but knew of a good service center in Brisbane that could do the repair. Brisbane is 1700 kilometers south of Cairns. I will just mention that our transmission took three train trips to Brisbane but upon its third return it was indeed restored to its glorious function. We did have to pay twice for the repairs because one of the return problems was blamed on the Cairns mechanic, but in the meantime, an enormous amount of our visa time had been consumed.

During this time, I rebuilt each of the bilge pumps. The Whale-Gusher pump needed a gasket kit so more time passed while it was on route to us from the US. The other pumps had parts locally available.

Peggy had taken the opportunity of our delay to spend a couple of months back home with her family while I carried on with maintenance needs. I rewired several of the running lights; replaced some of the rusting steel of our down-wind running poles; recaulked the teak decks [an enormous task]; installed new belts and filters on the engine and changed the oil; made a larger front door in the unused coal bin for Peggy's use for added canned food storage; painted the hull and bottom; bought a new motor for the dinghy; replaced the engine mounts and realigned the engine with the final return of the transmission. Peggy returned in the midst of all of this.

During our third visit to Australia, there was a wonderful non-stop social life which brought fun to our experience. Even at church we were astonished one day to see as visitors, our retired pastor and his wife from our church outside of Washington DC.

They had no idea that we were even sailing, much less to find us in this little church in far off Australia. Over 2000 of us were members of that church which sometimes had a full orchestra joining the huge choir. It was great fun talking together.

***

We were ready for our departure and we checked out for Indonesia. The wind was at twenty-five to thirty knots which is more than comfortable as we started north inside the reef. We were able to anchor each night, but invariably with considerable discomfort due to the boat rolling in the exposed waterway for the first few evenings. It got progressively better after a few days.

While in Smith's Creek for a time, a grass like seaweed had grown along our water line which I wanted to scrub off. I wanted clearer and warmer water to do this and Peggy and I were talking about my getting into the water today when a local commercial fishing boat motored up and asked if we would like a fish.

We thanked them heartily and we talked to the two of them for quite awhile. They had seen our US flag which probably caused their curiosity.

Peggy had been ill-at-ease about my going in the water in this area and brought up the subject with the fishermen whose response was, "I wouldn't even put a finger in these waters."

The next morning, as we were preparing to get under way, Peggy pointed to the next little atoll and said, "Look at the size of that crocodile!"

Knowingly I said, "That's not a crocodile—that's a huge log," as I too looked at it with the binoculars that she handed me.

"Well, if that's a log, it's got legs!"

I looked at it again. It was gigantic! It would take two people my size to reach around its midsection and maybe touch fingers. It was enormous!

I could not believe it was a crocodile. It had to be at least twenty feet long! When we looked it up in our Australia book, indeed we found that they do grow to this size and often migrate between Australia and New Guinea. If perhaps some sailors on an ancient square rigged ship had seen one of these, no wonder they spoke of sea monsters.

A couple of hours later, my "log" moved himself off the beach. I did not get into the water that day – I felt that the water was just a little too chilly.

Chapter 12 — Australia, Our Third Time

A few days after this, as we were walking northward on the mainland beach, we saw a very small sailboat at anchor and walking toward us was a young couple with their two children way behind them picking up sea shells. We greeted each other with mutual surprise and were soon in pleasant conversation with these folks from Australia's northwest coast when they told us about the kids a few days prior, running down the beach to them, both screaming in abject terror. It was raining! Never in their lives had they experienced rain! The girl was five and the boy was six years old.

***

We will be leaving the Great Barrier Reef this morning. It happens to be Thursday, and Thursday Island (yes that's its name) will be abeam shortly, from where we shall continue making toward Sumatra. The wind has piped up terribly. I've taken the deep reefed mainsail down and we're sailing with just the #4 jib as this will certainly be one boisterous departure from Australia. We are taking our final departure from this fine and varied country. The official in the Thursday Island Customs Office had bid us safe sailing, as he beckoned his head toward the window and the howling wind outside.

This now is our second day of making toward Sumatra after having officially taken our leave from Australia. The wind still spat spume off the wave crests. The Arafura Sea has managed to make our conditions worse than when we left Thursday Island. We would normally have waited for this stuff to ease before actually shoving off, but our visa time had expired some time ago, and the anchorage was somewhat untenable anyway, so we had chosen to go. After all, eight or ten foot seas are not really a big deal. No serious weather was forecast, and most weather like this seldom lasts for more than three or four days. This blow had started a couple of days ago.

It was a couple of days later, as the boat dropped down from a crest to the point of the next troth when BOOM, we hit the ground with our keel! The entire boat shuttered from this truly fierce impact! It shuttered us to our very teeth! My mind immediately leaped from one possibility to the next searching for answers. How can the sea be this shallow here? Or had we dropped down on a whale? No—there was not a fraction of an inch of absorption in the strike. It was one jarring slamming hit, and we were just as suddenly lifted by the next wave.

If we are about to ground on some newly formed open water reef instant action must be taken to save the ship! I threw the helm to port as I asked myself where I was taking us. My answer was just as instantaneous as the grounding had occurred milliseconds ago. We're making for the Bay of Carpentaria. Right now we are blind. I've got to get us away from this unidentified danger. I've got to get us to a sheltered anchorage to figure this out. I need more information.

But there's a problem here as well! We have no charts for Carpentaria. But most of our sailing over the past years has been by watching the color of the water for hazards, so I really was not unduly concerned about this. We did have approach charts for the area. These are charts which cover large areas and would be like using a map of Europe if you were looking for a street address in Amsterdam. There are no depth soundings on these charts, so I was not surprised hours later that we very suddenly had very shallow water as I had put our bow in between a couple of small islands which had offered a protective lagoon beyond them as an anchorage. The *Osprey* could not pass between them. We spun around and sailed on.

We knew that the mining town of Gove was in this area, but its location was not shown either. We sailed farther into this huge bay with thoughts of finding Gove and possibly gleaning some information, and checking the boat for damage. The grounding had felt as though the boat were to have been hoisted by a crane and dropped on concrete. It was beyond any experience of our lives!

We sailed on southward along the western shore. The bay is about 300 miles east, and west by approximately 400 miles north to south and is at the NE corner of Australia. Nothing was looking promising for an anchorage. We hove-to for the night. The *Osprey* had taken no water into the bilge so the old girl was holding her own. We slept. With a back-winded jib and the mainsail in deepest reef, the boat was comfortable in her snug dance of this age old two-step which kept her forward motion interrupted with an almost equal backward-slide in this zigzag manner of beginning a sail forward, only to be back-winded into a stall.

Morning came. The wind continued. The bay opens toward the north rather like a huge irregular "u" shape, with islands forming the upper reaches. I sailed us directly toward the west shore for a really close look. There wasn't much to see. The land stretched nearly flat from the shore toward a horizon with only a few silent cacti refusing to give a hint of Gove's location. The shoreline appeared to have bays leading inward, but the desert beyond offered no clues either. Shall I turn to the right, assuming that we had passed it, or turn left and more deeply into the bay? We could see smoke rising from the area to the left. I turned toward the smoke. But, when we at long last got to that area, the smoke was not from chimneys of Gove's ore processing, it was a desert brush fire that covered several miles.

I had sailed us into a small cul-de-sac bay which was shallowing but offered an anchorage protection from the main wave motion of the Arafura Sea. I chose a spot for the anchor that would let us swing in any wind direction change that would still give the *Osprey* a comfortable depth of about fifteen feet of water. In the years of our sailing the South Pacific, the tidal range had seldom passed two feet.

There was an opening to the sea not far from us, and I had decided to sail out in the morning and get a sun shot with the sextant for a good latitude line, even though I was quite certain that we had come too far southward into the Bay of Carpentaria. The latitude line will be usable on the charts which we have. Gove must be NW of here. And it must be well hidden from the bay or we would have seen it. It must be farther inland, we'll find it in the morning and figure out what damage we have and hopefully I can get a usable chart of these waters. I am totally baffled by our grounding. It was too weird. To have slammed down hard as we came off that wave, and be just as quickly lifted off without touching a second time was mighty good fortune. Or something weird happened here, which being beyond any past experience, has baffled me. I need more information.

We were later to learn that a shift in the earth's plates, along the Indonesian islands where we were, had caused an underwater earthquake which jabbed the ocean above it upward with an enormous punch which had hit the *Osprey* as well. Air is compressible, such as in scuba tanks for divers, but water does not compress. We had been hit with no less than the force of movement in plate tectonics itself which was the source of this explosive concussion. That memory will never dim.

* * *

We were still asleep when the next horror began.

BAM! We hit bottom again, from dropping off of a small wave. I've never had a nightmare before. The hit was not jarring. It was nothing remotely similar to the hit we took at sea. BAM! We hit again. We were going aground in our anchorage? Were the waves lifting us and then dropping us on the keel in their troth? No!

There was only a shallow covering of sand over the rock bottom below the boat. BAM! We hit again. I was on deck before the next shuttering of the *Osprey*'s hit. But it did hit, and again I felt the hit in the pit of my stomach. I exhaled a gushing silent groan as though I had taken a full strength punch to the gut from a powerful professional boxer. This is a nightmare! But as I ran to the foredeck and the anchor line, I suddenly felt a true sickness in the pit of my stomach. I realized that this was my fault. Yes this is an area that we had not been in before. But this never excuses bad seamanship.

I felt anger at myself for not having realized the obvious! That huge quantity of ocean water, bulged up by the force of the gravitational pull by the sun and moon, brings that elevation of water across the South Pacific rushing westward until it is stopped by huge Australia. We had apparently come in here at a high tide which has now rushed out. And we are hard aground!

By the time I got to the anchor line to take up any slack before engaging the engine on the up-lift of the next small wave, we were not being lifted anymore.

At least the boat wasn't being abused by the bashing now, and there was nothing left to do until the next tide lifts us off – but even that was not to be. Another five feet of water left us. The *Osprey*, with her keel hard aground, now was way over on her side. The keel was on the hard bottom, but the rest of the hull was lifting and falling with each wave as the weaker portion of the side of the hull came closer and closer to hard bottom. The waves continued. The hull lifted and dropped still with water under her side but it was getting close—

BAM — we hit hard on the side of the hull. And that's where the tide stopped. With each passing crest of each wave she was lifted and then pounded in her side. I too took each blow with increasing anguish. For hours she was being tortured like this. More hours passed and I finally said, "Peggy, get our passports and money and ship's papers together in a waterproof carrier. We'll take food and water in the dinghy. The boat may break-up."

I had gotten no response from my distress call on the radio earlier. I had hoped to get a local boat in here to help drag us off this spot when the tide comes in and or get us to Gove if we failed to save her, but no one answered the call. So if the boat is destroyed, we've got to get to Gove by sailing the dinghy. It has sails and a mast for the job. I'll leave a letter attached here to state that the boat is not abandoned and that we are returning shortly. I had thoughts of offloading some things to the shore which we might be able to hide. But for now, we can only wait to see if she can possibly survive this horror.

Peggy had immediately set to the task of preparing to leave the *Osprey*. She had not said a word. She had not gasped at the realization of what I had asked her to do. Her movements were without hesitation and totally efficient in every way. This had been her home for many years, but she had been given a job to do and she went about it as proficiently as I knew she would.

With each sound of each hit as the side of her hull struck bottom again, the entire boat from stem to stern and keel to mast head trembled as each plank in her hull seemed to shudder from the horror that was taking place. But every nightmare comes to an end eventually, and this one finally did too. For at last, the side of the hull had water between it and the bottom without a hit! The tide was coming in! She slowly started righting herself!

The keel was still aground, but the *Osprey* was coming more upright all the time. I got the dinghy launched and rowed two additional anchors out toward deeper water. When I got back to the boat I winched all three anchor lines to maximum stretch so that when the first slight lift of the keel off the bottom by a crest of one of these small waves, the stretched tension on the lines would move the boat its first few inches toward possible salvation.

Each tiny movement needed my re-stretching of the lines. The main line went to the anchor's hand powered windlass which could not put the stretch on the line that I needed, so I took it to the mast halyard winch. The structure of the mast could withstand the forward pull as the winch is only about a meter above deck level where the mast is solid timber. For the other two anchor lines I took one to the port sheet winch and the other to the starboard winch. None of this is at all reminiscent of usual anchor line handling. These lines were carried all the way back to the cockpit. But it all worked! The ½ inch, three lay nylon anchor line stretched wonderfully. And with each little lift, hundreds of pounds of tension moved us forward.

I was putting all of my strength into each of the three anchor line re-stretchings to the point of my exhaustion. But after hours of this, the good *Osprey* was afloat in this deeper water where the anchors now held her. And when noon was approaching, we sailed out through the opening whose waves had tortured us so relentlessly and I got a good latitude line with a sextant shot of the sun, enabled by the clear horizon over the sea needed for the sextant. And still, she took on no water into the bilge. We started retracing our course back along the dissolute Outback coast of north eastern Australia.

This time, where I had chosen to turn south eastward toward where we could see rising smoke, we turned north westward, south of those lead islands, and not long afterward we saw a paved road along the shore. Can Gove be far beyond? Of course, let's not forget that this is the Island *Continent* named Australia. A short distance here in the Outback may be a four day walk. But as the road approached a bend in the shore line what a great surprise greeted our eyes! Boats! Quite a few boats! Mostly they were sailing yachts like ours! With people on the decks and on the shore! And that building that looked as though it could be a yacht club building, indeed turned out to be just that.

The anchorage and the depth of water in all directions to which the *Osprey* could swing will be meticulously verified before I put down the anchor. There was no town to be seen, but what a sight this was after our tribulations.

I sailed us past a couple of anchored yachts to call out greetings and confirmed that we were free to choose a spot to anchor without club preapproval. This was true, and tomorrow we shall row ashore to begin the search for information. I will be inspecting the boat by careening her on the shore. We are not expecting to be here long at all. But perhaps Peggy can include her log of daily accounting so that it may be known that we were not just arbitrarily extending our time in Australia, a time which had already expired.

See Appendix B to find Peggy's Log III.

I finally raised someone in the Philippines on our two-watt powered amateur radio; and after a brief discussion of various things including his inquiry as to my intended route of travel approaching the Philippines, he asked what guns we had aboard. After telling him, he said, "Well, if you don't have automatic weapons aboard you might consider not approaching from the south," which we would be doing.

In some of the wanderings of my mind in dream, had enjoyed thoughts of hiring an entire village to go up into the mountains of an island of the Philippines to cut appropriate teak trees to bring back to their saw mill for planks to replace our hull planking from the waterline to the keel. This would involve air drying the planks before use and would mean that we would spend at least a year or two there. The local annual wage, plus a monetary rate of exchange which favored the US dollar, made these thoughts a potential viability but requiring confirmation. Had we been able to do this, the life of the good ship *Osprey* would have been immensely extended.

However, not having automatic weapons aboard, and actually not seeking to engage in outright combat for the purpose of gentlemanly visitation, coupled with the requirement of possible work to be done on the boat, I chose rather quickly to cast an eye in another direction, and just that quickly a solution was presented and the course to gain it was instantaneous.

We would sail to the US territory of Guam where we would not have any problems regarding the length of time for the boat to be there and hence, work on the boat would not be interrupted. So the intent was to sail through New Guinea to Kapingamarangi Island and then northward through The Federated States of Micronesia, and then northward to Guam. This would take only a few months of leisure sailing. We arrived there about four years later.

***

Between our present area in the northeastern corner of Australia and New Guinea is a very interesting area called the Torres Strait. It is entirely encumbered by a maze of coral with wandering narrow passes between bristling hazards designed to destroy any hapless yacht within its reach. All of this area is made torturous by virtue of a five-knot tidal current that rushes through there, as it plunges over the north of Australia trying to get its gigantic mass of water into and across the Indian Ocean making for Africa as it is pulled by the tail of the moon.

We checked out again with the Customs Office on Thursday Island. Again, the wind howled from the north. We were roaring along, when **BOOM!**

The jib sheet block, whose position can be moved on a track for jib adjustment, through which the sheet block rides on the track screwed tightly through the top of the toe-rail gave way, where the pull of the sheet was resisting the power of the wind.

This huge force pulled the track screws right out of the toe-rail bulwarks and bent the bronze track to a U shape, leaving nothing to control the jib. I came about and again returned to Customs at Thursday Island.

The Customs officer grimaced and asked how long the repairs would take. I told him that rot had gotten into the wood, and that I needed to cut away that part of the toe-rail bulwarks and replace it, and then would immediately be underway. His second grimace was smaller.

Neither of his reactions had been delivered with malice and I set to work cutting away a lot of the five inch high toe-rail; located wood to replace it, formed it, epoxied and screwed it in place with very long screws, applied some paint, reattached to track, bade farewell to our Customs officer and after those few days we were off again.

The wind still blew strongly, not quite matching the strength of our determination, however, nor that of the *Osprey's*. She took another look at the wind and at our somewhat treacherous and intricate course and shook her feathers, lowered her head and took flight.

We roared along as I watched carefully our water depth. After a number of hours of this intense sailing, we fetched the lee of one of the only islands in the Straits. Here we will anchor for the night. The trick was, not to drag anchor in a trap such as this.

I had chosen our arrival time at this island to coincide with the time just prior to the onslaught of tide. This gave the best time for passage, but the worst conditions for the anchorage. There is a hymn entitled "Will your anchor hold?" If she were to give way, an immediate powering of the engine would be needed. I slept little. The anchor held.

I was glad to see the first glimmer of beginning dawn starting to erase the black of the sky. Quickly the ancient climb of the sun shown light all about us to once again revel what a snarled maze of coral surrounded us. As far as we could see, the ocean appeared in dulled hues of color.

Below the surface of the sea, the glorious colors as seen by a scuba diver were there, but looking out from the deck of the *Osprey*, there was only darkest danger with brownish hue. The end of slack tide had occurred during the night and tidal rush had followed. The sea still boiled with the rushing water pouring through these snaking narrow valleys.

We could not begin northward very early anyway. The sun needs to have some elevation to give me an angle of vision into the water ahead to be able to detect any coral blocking the way as we negotiate the safe canals and also to see their coral walls. So there was time for a hardy breakfast. There will be no chance for leisure once we're underway. I will need Peggy's help steering when I need to run up the ratlines for better visibility angles in close quarters.

We're off and motoring. I had checked engine oil levels, engine belts, fresh water quantity in the heat exchanger, secured the anchor on its bowsprit with a tie-down, and today especially, I enjoyed the plastered grin on my face. To negotiate the coral passages through the Torres Straits from Australia to New Guinea, may in the eye of some be an achievement of some small note.

With the anchor aboard, we dropped back from this little island, back into the deep waters of the opening between steep banks of coral on each side. The passage way leads northward toward New Guinea. The heart of every sailor wants to raise sail, but I resisted doing so. The problem of a dropping wind strength made me choose the engine power as an assurance of clearing the coral before dark.

I put her to full power when possible. There is no place to anchor anywhere today, and we must have light to get us through this maze of the Torres Straits.

First the jagged coral wall to port of us is getting too close and needs a bit of turning to starboard of the *Osprey*'s steering wheel to return us to safety, only moments later needing to gently turn to port as our wake churns our way along. The channel passage narrows and widens as it wends its way.

Our speed is reduced proportionally to the increase of hazards which present. After a day of careful and concentrated effort, the *Osprey* won the race with the sun. Before the first dimming of the light which had made the choosing of our way possible, our course brought us safely passed the last of our hazards. We were clear of the infamous coral encumbered maze called the Torres Straits.

Even as there were several miles of open water on the Australian side of the Straits before coming into the coral, likewise this is the case on the New Guinea side.

Daru is our nearest port of entry and turned out to be a very small community actually on a little island just off shore. It is the closest entry port in PNG from the country Irian Jaya, New Guinea. We arrived without incident and anchored for the night. Tomorrow we shall formally be entered into Papua New Guinea in an area of the country where the *Osprey* has not sailed before.

I gave a mental salute to Australia for their accommodation of our time with them due to delays in the repairing of our boat and our unusual event in the Arafura Sea.

I remember a slightly tired lowering of the head onto my pillow that night. But I also remember the slight smile which accompanied it. To pass through the Torres Straits, in the mind of some few, may be immodestly thought of, as the Mount Everest of coral survival.

"Good night love."

CHAPTER 13

 New Guinea Again

We are anchored at Daru, and just across the bay, the mysterious Fly River swims far upward into the jungles of New Guinea. I remember reading that the famous sailing yacht *Wanderer* had gone up the Fly River and I read about the experiences encountered by its illustrious owners, Eric and Susan Hiscock. Blowguns are used by the tribesmen in this area, and they spoke of the amazing accuracy of this device.

I had traveled vicariously with the Hiscocks aboard *Wanderer* in the many books which the name of their yachts presented to those of us whose sailing days were yet on a distant horizon. Their wonderful "how-to" books were my eager classroom. And when I read that the *Wanderer* was marooned up the Fly River with no hope of getting off its grounding until the next super high Spring Tide, I wanted desperately to find a way to go there and help them get off. They were my heroes. If they were to fail her refloating on that coming tide they could be marooned there for months awaiting a super high tide, especially complicated as the rainy season was coming to an end which would further lower the water level in the river. But alas, I also realized that my mentor was possessed of greater expertise than I, and that they had local brute strength available were it to be called for. The Wanderer was freed on her next super tide, and sailed onward upon many more seas and within their many books.

Should we go up the Fly River?

Our first morning at Daru was an enjoyment. Firstly, our entry duties with the Customs Office were required and next came our usual strolling about ashore to capture a sense of the place.

Here is a very small community. But there are huge wide paved boulevards, with each side lined by giant mango trees. This is an astonishment. Thoughts of the origin of such planning brought our minds to the army engineers of the Second World War who might have been the ones to have focused on such a huge scale. After all this is where the airport was built as well. The mangos were perhaps half grown and completely green, but the teenage boys were busy throwing rocks to try to dislodge them with surprising success. I suppose that the coming ripeness of such a huge harvest was not likely to be consumable, so the loss of these green ones would not be noted. How grandly picturesque this setting presented itself to us. It is marvelous!

We were soon captured by our church membership and lovely times ensued.

The Fly River, with its many mouthed openings into this general area, brings much mud and silt with it, so eye navigation is an impossibility. Remembering the Hiscocks going aground up this river with *Wanderer*, gave me thought to inquire if the church pastor could recommend a river pilot to us. Our charts went only as far as the limits of this small bay, not into the rivers themselves. A day or two later, he brought a man to us for the job, which was granted. His English was surprisingly good and he could understand most of what we said without my need to use pidgin-English. This was looking great!

From Daru, the mouth of the nearest of the river mouths was visible just across the small bay where we were. This section was named the Oriomo River. The Fly River breaks up into numerous tributaries just prior to its entry into the sea. Most of these carry differing local names while some, as this one, have their names also shown on our charts.

In the exact direction toward the mouth of the Oriomo River from Daru, there is a reef shown on our chart with insufficient water over it to keep us from harm. As we started across the bay I had told him the draft of the boat.

I made certain with hand gestures that he understood what draft meant and I waited to hear his warning. None came. I asked him if any dangers lay in the bay and was told to carry on directly to the river. I went around the danger. I showed the problem to him on the chart. It was all news to him. So much for our river pilot's knowledge. Rather than bring embarrassment to him and to the good pastor by putting him ashore, we took him up the river with us even though it would have been more enjoyable to not have had him aboard.

On our planet with 70% water, the land is the small place. But when in a river, the water world is the small area and the land is vast! Here, the jungle reaches away in an immense and impenetrable maze. Only the occasional low narrow pathway of jungle cat is crossed by smaller prey. Yet man too has hewn paths out from his village, even to this river where he carries with him a very formidable weapon—a blowgun with poison tipped arrows. And the monkey way up high in his tree is not safe from this hunter. The hunter is skilled with his weapon and the monkey is brought back to the village for food. As we travel upriver, we are seen by many such hunters. Few are seen by us.

What we see here in Papua New Guinea, especially in places such as this, have not changed in millennia. Before an ancient tree falls in the fullness of its time, twenty young ones already reach upward for the sun. So the shadow never ceases. Only dimness lights the jungle by the unseen sky. Only mystery shrouds the scene from the deck of the *Osprey*.

The denseness of this magnificence spins the imagination. The fringe of untouched grandeur is within reach from our deck. Time and storm, wind and vine, tree and fern have bent and twisted and thrust ever upward this ceaseless power of unbridled growth into the marvel that stretches beyond the edge of this water. Here is defined beauty! Here is defined magnificence! Here is jungle!

A few days have passed. There has only been the occasional village with a few huts. We haven't seen many people at all until this moment. Here on the west bank is a school. It's a boarding school of some church group with probably forty or fifty students perhaps about nine years old. We were curious to know which of the churches was doing this and found that our people had started this school a long time ago and that another church had been running it for several years now. The buildings did not disguise the fact that a very long time had gone by since first they stood here.

Lots of children were welcomed aboard, all delightedly peeking into the windows and down the entry hatch to see the wonders of a boat like this. Everyone giggled through each moment aboard which was to our great delight. We invited a husband and wife team of teachers to come aboard tomorrow morning for a pancake breakfast which they seemed pleased to accept.

The next morning they arrived at the appointed time. We could not fail to notice that the two of them were now four. They had invited a second couple to join them for our breakfast, which suited us just fine. Peggy's breakfasts are always great and this was no exception. That afternoon we started back down river.

Our depth sounder did not work at all in the river. The sediment in the water must have been so thick that the echo sound of the device must have been completely diffused by it. Our titled river pilot was of no assistance, nor was he asked for any. We had learned that he had gotten to Daru as employee on a ship, which must have inferred professionalism in the mind of the pastor who recommended him. But a deck hand does not a pilot make.

We also have a very firm grasp of the reality that, whereas our heroes the Hiscocks had been aground here for a prolonged time and we were not, it is the simplest fact of luck and happenstance and most assuredly not seamanship capabilities, that has enabled our avoidance. I shall always doff my cap to this voyaging couple whose experience and passages far exceed our own. They remain my ideal of voyaging under sail.

We learned more about our passenger (crew he was not). He had arrived here with little money and now had none. Wherefore he had been marooned in Daru for some time without the cost of passage back to Port Moresby where his wife and children live. He was desperate to get to Port Moresby. We were going to Port Moresby next. Would we take him with us was the question. His offer was phrase with hope in his voice, "I could help you steer."

Well, it's about a six-day passage. And yes, it would be nice to have him take a four-hour night watch to steer for us so why not take him. It will help the fellow and make the passage easier for us. He was ecstatic.

We gave him a full day to extract himself from friends and to gather his things, which thankfully were not of an undue abundance, viewing the limit of our space. Tomorrow we would clear customs with three aboard. This will be our first time having a crewman aboard to share some of the duties of a passage. If the wind drops so that motoring will be needed, the windvane cannot steer for us, and if we have a lot of that it can become drudgery.

The three of us waved our goodbyes to the folks of Daru whom Peggy and I had only briefly known. And another lovely place of peace was left in our wake.

Clearing the Customs Office of Daru, PNG had been without complication, and we are making toward Port Moresby. The wind chose to mostly abandon us just a few hours later, and I had our crewman with me at the helm to show him the compass which will show him the course to steer. Not surprisingly, the compass was a new and strange device to him. My explanation of what causes the compass to function as it does, turned out to further the mystery of it rather than to understand the concept.

We were motor sailing now, with very little aid from the sails. But I wanted as much aid as we could get with this little wind, to reduce our fuel consumption. I had filled our two tanks of fifty gallons each, plus our usual ten five-gallon plastic carrying jugs with diesel fuel before leaving, but especially at the beginning of a passage fuel usage is to be considered.

Andrew's eyes had not grown large as land left our view, so I thought that fear was not what was prohibiting him from concentration on what the connection was regarding the compass and our course.

I kept trying intermittently to have him steer while he was also watching the compass. And it didn't matter whether he fell off course to port or to starboard as I would reshow him the numbers on the compass card that I wanted him to stay on, he would have us 35 or 40 degrees off course and not understand the requirement of turning the wheel toward the numbers on the compass Having shown him on the chart our direction and hence our course to steer, had made no evidence of imprint. I checked his vision for possibly being the problem, but he was able to tell me the numbers on the compass card to which I pointed.

I absolutely hid my disappointment from him. I showed no frustration by voice or by manner. And I finally told Peggy that the steering was going to be done by the two of us. Her written comments of this passage have 3 or 4 comments saying, "I can't believe that he can't steer!" I am equally certain, however, that he was also disappointed that he was not able to do for us that which he had said that he would do even though he never said so.

With a kiss on her hand, I suggested that she take the next deck watch and steering duty. She was fully awake and could do it without discomfort. I told Andrew to go below to his quarters in the forecastle and I took a nap in my bed. Thus Peggy and I alternated the steering duties as we made for Port Moresby some 5 or 6 days away.

The days passed pleasantly enough, except for the constant steering requirement. Food was in its customary abundance of quantity and variety, and its cooking delivered sights and aromas seldom ever known by this quiet stretch of ancient sea. Our passenger too, was recipient of that royal treatment of which Peggy is so wondrously endowed. Such marvels do not occur full blown without planning and talent and time, so if for no other reason than this, I spend more time at the less artistic functions of the passage such as steering and managing the boat than I ask her to share.

There is a beauty at sea as the *Osprey* makes her way. She is always accepted by the other sea creatures as one of their own, be they sea birds in flight or porpoises who join us in their play. And as the sun washes himself when he ducks down into the water for his evening cleansing, the other world presets itself with that gentle but darker side, until the stage lights dimly turn on, firstly with a few dozen, and then a few hundred, and suddenly all of the multiple billions of stars suddenly look quietly about until that instant when the last candle of sunlight is blown out; and then with unutterable majesty the night is ablaze in all of its glory while yet seemingly to actually deign to watch with apparent glee as the *Osprey* cavorts upon the sea.

The wee small souls aboard have never thought themselves as more than mere and brief visitors upon this world. But oh how grateful we are to be among those few, those fortunate few, whose soul has been touched by such grandeur. One is never again the same.

Our passenger slept on.

It was a dark night when we fetched the Port Moresby bay. We had not been here before, and I have not often entered such waters at night, but for this area we had new charts. And range lights showed the safe passages to point "A" where another range of lights brought us to point "B," etc. So we were able to come right to the yacht club anchorage without concern of any kind. It was fun and we had arrived!

Andrew certainly was a nice enough fellow, and I'm glad at least that we got him to Port Moresby. He also was good enough to help me scrub away the sea growth from the bottom of the boat before we bade him farewell, of course, with sufficient funds to get home. However, we have never been very inclined to seek another crewman. Maybe I should not use the term "crewman" in reference to this good man. But we have not taken passengers on ocean passages either before or after this one. The boat is not really intended for such accommodation.

* * *

Some time ago, we had told friends and family to address mail in care of the American Express Office at Port Moresby, PNG. And we were beginning to feel that we were abusing this wonderful service that this company offers to its traveling customers. So they were our very first destination.

We were escorted to the appropriate desk by the receptionist where a large ruddy fellow sat. It was encouraging to see that his greeting smile extended nearly from one ear to the other as he said, "So you've finally arrived! We've been looking for you for years!" And with genuine enjoyment this Australian brought us to the company safe where our stack of envelopes were very safely kept indeed, all very neatly bound in a ten-inch-high bundle which he displayed with jovial pride.

He carried this treasure for us as we returned toward his desk, lifting it when he would catch the eye of a fellow employee which brought ever echoing smiles as our parade continued. Everyone seemed to take pride in having retained this mail for these wayward people. We were their customers. They were proud. And we were grateful for their endurance.

Reading mail with old dates is always filled with fresh delight! And it's always fun to report to the sender when it was found and the events which had prevented its finding us sooner. To be spoken to vicariously in letters from family and friends can bring with it a warmth and closeness with them beyond even that of chatting in the drawing room or across a dining table.

We were not intending to spend much time here. But we did certainly enjoy meeting the folks at church and we were interested to hear that a different church group was to hold a "Miracle Healing Campaign." I had skeptically heard of these mass gatherings and, of course, at the appointed time and place I was toward the back of the crowd. Before me milling about were perhaps 50,000 people [obviously an estimate.] There was a huge stage perhaps 60 feet long. At the forward center was a podium, perhaps ten feet from the edge. The man who stood behind it had the only other white face in the area other than mine. He had eight assistants whom I assumed were pastors of local churches of the same denomination. Four were positioned to his right and four to his left, all standing a few paces back from the podium.

The event got started with lively singing followed by a brief sermon. Then came "the call" for those who wanted to be healed and huge numbers pressed forward. The man who stood beside me, with whom I had exchange conversation, told me that he always comes to these. That he had gone up there once, but it didn't work. However, he said that he keeps coming each time because maybe sometime it will work. He had told me of his illness.

There was a line of folks directed to the speaker and other lines to all eight of the assistants, as stairs covered the front of the platform. At the podium the speaker intoned the Spirit to heal this soul, whereupon he would suddenly, and sharply push back the person's forehead, and what appeared to be as on queue, the individual would fall backwards to be caught by the two men in position to do so. Then in reasonable unison the eight other men did likewise. On one such occasion, one of these fellows started to proceed, but saw that the speaker was not at that instant looking at him, wherefore he stopped in mid form until he was being seen and then rapidly performed the remainder of the sequence.

I realize that my report of this event sounds disrespectful, but this most assuredly is not the purpose of my intent. Yet there was a concerned sorrow in the back of my mind as I could imagine hearing from untold numbers of devoutly sincere Christian pastors to their equally sincere congregations that miracles are occurring in New Guinea as 50,000 people are healed.

The fervor with which I seek to avoid all reference to things of religion clearly in this case was beyond my ability to refrain. But permit me to simply say that in this, the one such event of which I was in attendance, I personally did not come away with a positive point of conclusion.

As required, we again presented our papers to Customs and Immigration and recorded Andrew's departure from the boat and our departure toward Samuri where indeed we have been before. The *Osprey* was ready; Peggy had bought supplies and was ready; and I had already been looking forward to getting underway.

***

It was about mid day when the outer marker in the Port Moresby bay was left astern, as our thoughts paused to wonder what unexpected adventures may await us.

We were to sail southward to the cape and then eastward toward Samuri. There was not a breath of breeze much less wind so our faithful engine will be moving us pleasantly along. But no drudgery is expected in this area. I should be able to find anchorages each night. And we had no sooner secured the anchorage for this first night, when ten boys came racing out to see a sailing yacht that had come so close to their village.

They had all seen ships and yachts pass by but we were the first ones whom the youngest boy could remember, much less come aboard. It was fun for us too.

Conditions were the same for our second day and we anchored close to Eboma Island. We were stretched toward our hosting limitations today, because an entire school group was here. Fortunately the canoes limited the number of young people that they could carry, so we had a few minutes between groups to prepare for the next onslaught of giggles and laughter as they too were happily shown about.

I have often mentioned these hosting occasions because of our perception of their importance. Our presence is within their domain. The very least that we should do is to be gracious with our presence and remember that we are the strange ones.

On our fifth day of motoring our engine gave forth with a terrible clanging noise such as has never been heard before! I turned the engine off instantly, raised sail and made our way as best we could with this light breeze until I could get an anchor down in water shallow enough to reach the bottom.

As suspected, the trouble was with the clutch, which is in the bell-housing, which has two of the four engine mounts attached to it. In order to take the bell-housing off the engine, the engine will need to somehow be propped up on something other than on the hull planking.

Suffice it to say that the support was accomplished, the housing removed, and there it was. One of the thick springs that hold the separation of the clutch had broken. I thought that there was no likelihood of finding such a unique piece of equipment, but I looked carefully anyway through our store of parts. But there was one! Exactly the right size and made exactly for this clutch plate, found here in the South Pacific so many years from our home port of Oxford, Maryland where she was built! Reassembly was as straight forward as had been the disassembly, and tomorrow we shall be off again.

The next day there was no clanging, but was I getting paranoid? There is no way that I could have made up an engine hesitation! But it's fine now. I don't go around looking for things to bother my sleep. The wind had still not returned and we motored on.

There was not even a ripple on the surface of the sea, as we moved nearer to the cape. What a gorgeous day it was for watching the life beneath us. But a sailor prefers to sail. It is the primal want for those such as I. Yet even that deep but unspoken brooding vanished at the speed of light which brought it to my eyes as I yelled, "Peggy! A chambered Nautilus!" She was sitting in the cockpit where I stood, so she saw it almost as soon as I. I spun the boat around and it was still there! We could hardly believe our eyes! It was no more than three or four feet from the surface. We could see its fins propelling it along, We have seen live Chambered Nautilus in a tank at the New Caledonia zoo, but we never expected to see one like this.

They spend their days in one or two thousand foot depths and come to the shallows at night to hunt their prey. But to these guys, 300 to 800 feet is their "shallows." This one was three feet under water! It was amazing. Having no facts to make sense of this, I ventured the thought that perhaps it was dying even though those fins seemed to be going at full speed. We watched it for awhile longer before returning to our course. And a few hours later, we saw a second one, also in water of about thirty feet of depth and again about

Chapter 13

New Guinea Again

a meter from the surface. They swim with the large opening of the shell at their underside and facing forward with the fins moving beyond those edges. What a day! [That "opening" retains the main body of this creature, and is not empty at all, nor open. But I referred to it as we are most accustomed to seeing them empty, in order to try to convey its posture while swimming.]

* * *

After another peaceful and beautiful night I went on deck to look around at the lovely setting of thick verdant jungle reaching out over the sand beach, when in the distance at the far end of this beach, I spotted a huge dug-out canoe with its bow up on the beach. It looked from here to be forty feet long! I told Peggy about it and off we went with the dinghy to investigate.

What we found was a trading canoe propelled by a lateen sail. We have never seen nor heard of such canoes in New Guinea and it may well have sailed here from Irian Jaya just to the north, or even Indonesia. It was built with a platform between two huge dug-out logs. On it, a small hut offered shelter from the rain. This was clearly a family business. In his youth, the man may well have been a child aboard his family's canoe, even as now his wife and children lived aboard this one, which may even have been where he was born as well. A cooking fire burned perpetually on the boat as they moved along the coast way down here into Papua New Guinea, trading with the local villages. It was a wonderful sight and I wished them well.

The next day a light breeze blew up and we were passing the day moving very slowly as we saw a small boat with outboard motor coming toward us from the shore. We greeted him warmly and as he pulled even with us, he said that a four-knot current would be starting in about half an hour. It was a kind warning which we heeded by making for shallow water to anchor. And just as predicted, we no sooner got the anchor set when the current slammed into us. The southeast cape was near, and that huge tide that unsettled us in Australia's Bay of Carpentaria, now came racing its way, destined toward the north shore of Australia. This happened to be one of those spots that funneled more than usual quantities of it. I was pleased to have an anchor down without effort, not that we would have been unduly exercised without the warning. But we would have missed a very pleasant evening spent as guests of our benefactors.

As required, a couple of days latter, we presented ourselves and the *Osprey*'s papers to customs at Samuri and we felt at home in familiar surroundings. In time, however, it was to become evident that Peggy did not share the comfort of my homelike feelings as warmly as I.

We sailed onward and, as when we had been here before, we filled our water tanks with that wonderful clear water that the US Army Corps of Engineers had piped from way up in the mountain down almost to the sea. Well done guys!

We have a very efficient rain catching system to replace our water supply, but we never ignore a bounty such as this.

"Peggy, we're getting close to Rabaul." Many years ago when we were in New Zealand we had heard that the volcano in Rabaul was expected to erupt at any time and was expected to cause absolute devastation. We planned to stay away from it! But since that time, it was reported to have chosen a nap instead, and was reported to be nonthreatening now as well. I took us into the harbor of Rabaul. It was a great place to anchor. The water was quiet. The volcano and another smaller mountain offered us a wind shadow. There was a valley between them, but the locals told us that the wind seldom came from there. This was a German town where settlers had come many years ago. They had a small yacht club and even had a number of moorings for visiting yachts. We were given the use of one and I put down an anchor a well. The maintenance of moorings should not be assumed to be perpetually in perfection.

What a lovely setting this is with the old houses of this town mixed with a nice little hotel at the shore which was built in the ever pleasing tropic style with its thatch-roofed open-walled bar and its music. A couple of concrete commercial wharfs jutted out from the shore and the area had a healthy "bustling" feeling about it, if one remembers that this is, after all, the tropics and that it bustles with a special pace. A shopping district actually was bustling. Lots of shops and lots of people with a surprising number of cars! But even here there seemed to me a distinct charm. Does one truly just see what one wishes to see? I liked everything about Rabaul. But perhaps paradise might be a small stretch to claim. And how do we fit Peggy's bizarre report when she came back to the boat a few days later saying, "Dan! This was amazing! I was in town and saw a woman just walk up and break two car windshields with a pipe wrench!" Are there serpents in the garden of Rabaul?

This was a mere shadow of what Rabaul was at one time when "bustling" was in all of its European best. The plantations far and wide flourished as did this center which supplied all of their requirements for import of tools and export of copra and other coconut products. Though not German, I visited the German Club which by now sadly had very few members in a rather rundown house.

Rabaul is not to be thought of as being non New Guinean. Very close at hand, and at the very base of the volcano was a village entirely of members of our church to which we walked one day choosing to walk on the beach sand as we went. However, as we were walking in bare feet we walked in the water as well, and were astonished to find the water too hot for more than a few steps. The volcano most assuredly was not dead! The village chief was pleased by the fact that his land was being considerably increased every year. He showed us that in just this last year the area of land whose beach we had been walking along had all been several feet below water.

In what now is the old area of Rabaul, Australians now very much out numbered the original German population. I asked John Mills, an Australian at the yacht club, if anyone here was able to service diesel injectors. "Oh sure! Go to the machine shop," and he told me where.

I went. And I was impressed! This machine shop had about 8 or 10 lathes of various sizes up to really huge ones lined up in a row, plus various drill presses, and band saws etc., and a proper air filtered separate and enclosed injector room. Wow, I was delighted. I talked to the owner, a local man called

George. I told him how the *Osprey*'s engine was running and asked what his fee was to service four injectors. I was ecstatic to find such a professional shop as this one right on our door step (if we had a door and if we had a step). This was miraculous! My feet were on that proverbial cloud nine as I walked back to the yacht club!

I removed the injectors; brought them to the shop; received a proper receipt for them and was told when they would be ready. Cloud nine waited for me at the shops door and brought me back to the boat. At the appointed date, I returned and was told that they weren't ready. When I returned to the boat this time, my cloud may have been marked as an eight-and-a-half, but eventually the injectors were ready to be picked up.

I installed them and bled the air out of the lines and turned the ignition switch key. The engine did not start. I lowered my head slightly and I sighed my resignation. My momentary glimpse of our future episodes with the machine shop fortunately was only dimly seen.

I returned to the machine shop where I could not prevent myself from responding in kind to George's infectiously broad smile. Our mutual enjoyment of each other's personalities lingered to the time of our departure. We became friends.

That afternoon, we were joined by folks from two other yachts for a tour to the Rabaul Museum and the military caves of the Japanese. Peggy's daily records included that the museum stated an estimation of the enormous tonnage of bombs dropped on Rabaul by the US. Rabaul was Japan's main supply harbor for this area during the Second World War. And told of how ingeniously, the Japanese hide the lighters (the small boats of about forty feet in length which unloaded the supply ships to bring cargo ashore) by pulling them out of the water onto rail-car type frames on railway tracks, and thus bring them into caves which they had dug into the hills for the purpose of hiding them. The railway tracks and cave openings were made invisible to aircraft by being covered with tree branches and camouflage nets. Many of the boats were still in these caves for us to walk directly up to and inspect, (after paying a fee to the local village representative where these caves were located). This is not an unusual type of revenue income activity throughout the islands.

Two nights later *I sprang from my bed to see what was the matter* – well, okay – it wasn't Christmas and it wasn't reindeer; the boat was hurled over on her side by a truly violent and continuous blast of wind that sent us suddenly flying in the opposite direction from where the boat had been lying at her mooring. She was moving so fast by this time, that she broke the mooring line without slowing down. Next she came to the end of our anchor line by which time she was moving even faster and jerked the anchor out of its holding and dragged this 45 pound CQR anchor plus the forty pounds of chain along the bottom by its ½ inch nylon line as though it were nothing.

All ten tons of the *Osprey* was traveling sideways across the harbor as though she were a mere feather before this screaming squall-line of wind. Absolute certainty for destruction lay down wind of us as we sped toward it! From the anchor bow-sprit I launched our second forty-five-pound CQR anchor with its forty pounds of lead chain, and this ½ inch nylon line instantly began flying over the bow and disappearing into the blackness of the water. The bitter end of this line, of course, was securely belayed. The rock protected wall of the harbor's edge loomed closer every second, but I needed to get enough line out for a really low angle of pull between the anchor on the bottom and the boat on the surface to have any chance of slowing down the inertia of this ten-ton boat plus the force of the wind against her and still leave some distance for dragging the anchor after setting it before coming up on the rocks. I looked at the distance remaining and forced myself to let more line out. Then I took one turn of the line around the aft horn of the anchor windless. As expected, the line did not slow and I could sense the heat from its friction pouring off of it. I took a second turn of the line on the horn and slowed the rush of line but immediately let a few feet out again to establish a jerking action of tension on the anchor windless to get the anchor set deeply enough for it to have any chance of stopping us. I was allowing a distance from the rocks for maybe three such dragging attempts by easing all tension on the line and restarting the setting process. If the third time failed, we would be on the rocks. After several of these anchor setting attempts of jerking on the line by feeding more line overboard in a jerking motion to farther and farther set the anchor, I threw a tie-down on the anchor windless and the boat spun around bow into the wind with such violence that her side deck was almost to the water as she heeled over in the turn! The rocks were not far away! But we were stopped! The anchor held!

We have a seventy-five pound storm anchor. It's a Herrishoff designed "fisherman" style anchor. This is what a non-yachtsman artist would draw the shape of if asked to draw an anchor. He designed this anchor to disassemble into three parts for ease of one man's ability to get it from below to a storm tossed deck which also makes it easy to store in the bilge, such as where I store ours. As I was getting it on deck and launched as security against a more severe blast, two dinghies arrived with fellow yachtsmen who immediately came aboard to help. We were all in sleep attire, which was without anything at all. None of us noticed.

In perhaps an hour or so, the squall that sent this wind which funneled between the mountains and through that valley, had mostly stopped. Our helpers gave a hand to re-anchor the *Osprey*, and the next day we all enjoyed a hardy feast of Chesapeake Chicken aboard the *Osprey*. Our anchors had been retrieved in the reverse order of their usage; and our mooring had been repaired by us.

All was well again — for about five days. A knock on our hull awakened us and we heard a voice calling out, "Hello Dan! Hello Peggy! Are you alright? We haven't seen you in three days."

We weren't alright. We had both collapsed with high fever at the same time. Our callers were Bret and Nora from the boat *"Time."* And hearing our feeble response they came aboard, asked us a couple of questions which we both immediately forgot, but very shortly they returned with some mushroom soup, as I recall. The folks on a German yacht, Sybille and her good husband, also brought food to us. Then they returned later in the day with food again and urged us to go to a doctor, which we were totally unable to do. We could hardly get into a sitting position to drink the soup. They brought another couple from another yacht the next day, both bringing light food and drink and the following day we managed to get ourselves into the dinghy; helped each other up the small incline of the shore; got to the edge of the street to hail a taxi; saw a police car and waved it down. We told him that we were very ill and asked if he knew a doctor to whom he would bring us. He knew his town and gladly took us to a doctor.

She said that in all likelihood we had malaria. She took blood samples from us, gave us medication, and told us when to return for her to tell us the result of the blood tests.

We had been taking a Malaria preventative medication since we first had come into malaria territory but the best prevention is to avoid the mosquitoes which we had religiously sought to do. But *the best laid plans of mice and men*, etc.—and here we are.

We returned a few days later feeling much improved and were relieved to hear that it was not cerebral malaria. That one has a good chance of killing you. The "bugs of malaria infection linger in one's kidneys and has the nasty habit of knocking one down with another bout, usually when least expected. It is said that taking enough Fancidar may permanently cure one, but the side effects may include permanent eye damage in the process.

Thanks to our yachting friends, and the policeman, and the doctor, we were soon on the mend and back to our engine problem.

The machine shop ordered parts from Australia which had to be reordered because they were the wrong parts. We contacted a friend in the US to send a starter motor to us. It was not the correct one. He sent us a second one which was correct. And the perpetual parts acquisition attempts never ceased.

Nor had the vigil of the Immigration Department change. We were required to leave the country so that we could ask permission of the government to visit PNG. That's just the way it is done. Peggy flew to The Solomon Islands and acquired the necessary permit to enter PNG. I flew to Australia, because my US passport was also expiring and could be renewed in Melbourne at the

US Consulate. There I applied for permission to revisit PNG. While awaiting this paper shuffling to take place, I was invited to spend the time with friends whom we had met in Carins aboard their boat.

They had a very pleasant place with a couple of horses on their grounds outside of Melbourne. And because they had a swimming pool I was surprised when it was proposed that we all go to "the swimming hole." Another couple from the area was also there this day and the four of them were insistent that I join them. I had offered to stay at the house so as not to crowd the car as much as not wishing to interlope some prior plan, but they would not hear of it.

For all I knew, the swimming hole may have been some recreation center or even restaurant and they clearly were not going to tell me. Well, when in Rome, one goes along with the activity, which in this case turned out to be a nudist camp. And indeed there was a swimming pool there as well, with the entire area *covered* with all manner of distractions. It was indeed a revealing experience for one such as me whose friends took him unawares with many afternoon chuckles at my expense. But, oh well . . when in Rome . . .

My passport was ready, my visa for PNG was in hand, and I thanked my hosts for a most unusual and entertaining four days. Broad smiles were evidenced all about!

Again the starter motor would not start the engine. Water was in the pistons. The engine now left the boat to take up residency in the machine shop. To enable the work of rebuilding our engine, I stood beside the mechanic with our shop manual for this engine which is supplied by the Ford Motor Company. I read it silently in English and would then translate it into Pidgin-English, of which I was only partially fluent.

At the conclusion of this elegant process, and with the engine bristling with all of its new parts internal as well as external, it was a thing of immense beauty. Water was hooked up to supply cooling right there in the shop for "the bench run." Battery power had been placed in readiness and connected to the starter motor. And with the shop activities all stopped for everyone's preparation of cheers, the starter motor was engaged with a flourish! We could all pre-hear in our minds the glory of the event.

But alas, the sound of its starting remained in utter silence, and only had lived but a moment in our minds, and this after *an actual calendar year* has past since I first ventured into the machine shop of Rabaul.

George smiled. "We'll look into it," he said. "Surely, there is just some small problem."

* * *

John Mills came to the yacht club that evening and it was cathartic to tell him of my day not quite fulfilling my expectations, which launched him to one of his stories of New Guinea.

John had been here for about ten years when he decided that he needed a diversion from routine and loving boats he decided to build a sailboat behind his house. He had the fun of searching for the ideal design, ordering the plans and at long last he began the building.

Untold hours and months and years of loving care and attention to even the smallest detail, do finally conclude. And here stood a boat of absolute beauty. It was the pride and joy of his many years of planning and labor. She was a small boat of twenty-eight feet. And every line and profile was a delight to the eye.

She was small enough to not be a problem to launch. Lift straps were slung under her and lifted by a simple "auto-wrecker" which is a small truck built with a small boom that extends behind it. A power winch operated a drum on the forward bed of the truck on which steel cable winds and by which cars are lifted at their front end and thusly towed.

In this case, the boat would be lifted and restrained from swinging about in transit; and then simply be lowered into the waters of the bay from the big commercial wharf where the ships now dock. The height of the wharf would not be a problem.

There, of course, were no difficulties with any of this transport, and the wrecker drove onto this strong pier; backed to the edge; and with broad grins of pleasure on all of the faces gathered, the boat started its downward travel to the bay. But the brake on the drum winch failed, and the boat had nothing to slow its very long dash toward the water!

Next, the cable on the wrecker's drum was not long enough for the boat to reach the water! And as the weight of the boat and the inertia of its speed came to a sudden stop at the end of the cable – and to the end of the boom of the wrecker which protruded outward over the water – this acted like a fulcrum by which the wrecker was flipped over by its front end passing over top of the back end – and all of it being flipped off the dock – and the wrecker landed on top of that lovely new sailboat! The boat, and the wrecker, and John's plans and dreams disappeared from view, never to be seen again.

John grinned. I could only shake my head in commiseration as I bought him another iced tea.

In a few days, George and company got our engine running on the bench. The work was declared complete and the engine was ready to return to the boat. I had use a car wrecker to get the engine out of the boat and to the machine shop, so I ordered one to pickup the engine for the short drive back to our local small wharf.

We were ready and ecstatic. The boat was secured to the wharf, and the truck is scheduled to arrive shortly.

The wrecker could now be seen coming slowly down the street and as it turned toward the wharf we could see the engine dangling from its boom. The driver had a second person with him. That looked like a plus, and the wrecker drove onto the wharf. When he got to the boat, the wrecker stopped, the driver looked around, the second man got out and came aboard. I told the driver where I wanted the engine lowered and broad smiles of confidence lightened the mood.

The driver got the truck lined up for his turn which he executed professionally, and began backing toward the boat. I watched the approaching wheels as they proceeded toward us. I stood on the side deck of the boat, just to the side view of the truck so that the driver could see my hand signals. I had lost sight of the second man. When the back wheels were about five feet from the edge of the wharf I began my hand signals by indicating to the driver the remaining distance of travel to the edge. The truck continued very slowly toward the edge, and I continued bringing my hands closer together to exactly display the remaining distance to the edge. When the tires got to the edge I raised both arm with the stop signal of open palms toward the driver with my arms fully raised. He didn't stop. Now the bottom of the back tires were half on and half off the edge of the wharf! I yelled STOP!! And the truck shot backward, off the wharf and onto the *Osprey* and struck the driver's assistant in the leg. The boat, taking the weight of half of the truck on its side deck, slammed over sideways and thus released the man who had been pinned between the back of the truck and the side of the boat's cabin top. The bone of his thigh was instantly evident as it protruded through the leg of his pants.

We had to move him to a safer place lest he go overboard, and we yelled to the people at the street who were gathered there watching, to call an ambulance. The hospital was not far away. Someone said he would go and did; only to return shortly to announce that the ambulance could not come because it had no gasoline. The phone number of the wrecker company was on the truck's door. It was given to the prior caller who ran to make the second call. He reported back that the owner was coming with his car.

In the midst of all of this, which included our caring for the injured man, yachting friends who were with us had unhooked the engine from the lift cable just where it was on the cabin top. And no sooner than that was done, then the captain of a tugboat on the other side of the wharf from where we were, had his crew attach a heavy line to the front end of the wrecker, and with his huge winch capacity, pulled it back onto the wharf.

The driver's boss arrived and his people got the man with the compound fracture off the boat and into his car and off they went to the hospital.

I chocked the engine in place, started our outboard engine on the dinghy, cast off our dock lines, and with another grateful wave and bringing together of my hands with a bow of my head, I presented my prayer of appreciation. The tugboat captain nodded and saluted in response as the dinghy moved us away, toward our mooring at the yacht club.

CHAPTER 14

A New Beginning

Back to our mooring at the Rabaul yacht club, the engine was securely on the boat. On top of the boat, that is, not in the engine room. But Harry brought his two sons; and with a *come-along* from the mainsail halyard, the engine was eased downward and three-quarters of the way into the engine room. Brute strength and prying finished the job of getting it back into position and Jussi Rytkonen from the yacht *Nimble John* also helped in the process. The next day required the alignment of the engine and transmission to the propeller shaft as it passes through the stuffing box and out of the hull to the propeller.

With all connections of fuel, water, throttle, and batteries complete, I reached for the starter key, turned it, and once again the *Osprey* heard her engine speak. Ah how sweet the sound after so long an absence! Next the damage that resulted from the collision of the wrecker ramming into the boat required solution, and in a few more days all of that was properly accomplished as well.

It had taken us quite a while to get reorganized after being in this harbor for over an entire year, but the next day, as we turned the *Osprey* toward her departure from Rabaul, I looked back over the stern and I was able to smile. Our time here had certainly been a series of unexpected experiences, and countless of them had nonetheless been filled with fondness. But dominating our thoughts was the awful tragedy of the breaking of a man's leg while aboard our boat which most surely placed anguish for him in our hearts. However, we knew that his hospital care would be completely professional in all respects, and will surely restore him accordingly.

Chapter 14 — A New Beginning

We made for Kavieng on the north of the Island of New Ireland, a distance of less than two hundred miles. The wind was too light to sail, so we had ample opportunity to test the engine. The engine failed most of these trials miserably. It ran roughly, but it at least ran.

There is a boatyard here being operated by Doctor Chris Smith, an Englishman whom we had met several years ago. It was great to see him again!

This was a government fisheries school. He was the director and only teacher of which I was aware. One of the primary subjects appeared to be boat building and maintenance. The school had a proper railway into the water on which a cradle is launched to be fitted around a boat whereby it is winched out of the water for service and repairs. The *Osprey* used this facility to come up for bottom painting where I was busily engaged with paint brush in hand and a smile on my face when with no warning of any kind I suddenly dropped down to a sitting position on a cross beam of the cradle with my head spinning! Every ounce of strength vanished in an instant. I could not manage another stroke of the brush. I could hardly hold it. But I managed to slowly drag myself up the ladder that leaned against the boat to drop onto my bunk. I was having my first recurrence of malaria!

This was the first time that Peggy had been helping me with this particular job. We were painting the bottom of the boat with anti-fouling paint, and Brother John from a Catholic trade school was there at the time. While I was literally collapsed on my bunk for two days, John helped Peggy to finish the painting of the bottom.

We had met Brother John a week or so ago. A "Singsing" was to occur on the grounds of the Kavieng

Catholic Church. We wanted to be present for the event and arrived at the appropriate time. When a Singsing is scheduled, a festival of New Guineans brings to one location people from surrounding villages, or in this case, those who are employed on surrounding plantations as well. It has nothing to do with singing. None of it occurs. Each group comes in the local equivalent of the New Guinean parade. They are attired in the manner of the tribe of their origin, arriving with others only of their tribe to the beat of various kinds of drums. It is a time of greatest joy and pride. Many hours and often days are required to create elaborate head dress with feathers of birds and sundry flowers. It is a glorious display of joy!

A couple of the groups had arrived and others were coming, when a man came to us, introduced himself as being from the church staff and said, "You are invited to come to the house of the priest."

Well we thought that this was very gracious of them, but we wanted to just watch the singsing and thanked him for the invitation. But he would have none of it! He actually was insisting that we not stay where we were. Well, perhaps he knew something that we didn't about possible "unrest," so we went with him and found the large room of the house absolutely packed with the owners and managers of the plantations plus all of the priests and brothers of the area.

Good Brother John was the first to greet us, and remembering that we were here aboard a yacht, he had said, "Oh, you must meet one of our priests. He runs a boat throughout the islands holding mass in the villages." And thus began our acquaintance with a very interesting and dedicated group of people who had come here from many varied places. Brother John had come from Florida, USA, and perhaps felt a kinship with us by virtue of our son David living in Florida as well.

Our plan was to leave as soon as possible. And as required on our list of things to do, I bought a new battery to replace the oldest one that was aboard; and when all was done we checked out of PNG bound for the Federated States of Micronesia. Even the day shone brightly with promise as we took our departure. Our New Guinea adventures had come to an end, and I raised the anchors, having taken our leave of this new group of friends.

The eastern end of the harbor was the departure point of our leaving PNG. It has a reef across it that carries northward a short distance beyond the end of the island, the land of which continues in the same direction, but an opening exists very close ashore which if carefully followed brings you to a navigable pass. The day was bright, the sun was high. With excellent water clarity the coral was easily seen as we proceeded without incident through this very narrow area. We were at long last underway! But it is not likely that this historic stay will soon fade from our memory, which may in a small way be even connected to the recent history of the country.

Papua New Guinea gained its independence not very many years before our arrival. One of its early declarations established the requirement that any business in the country must immediately change to a 51% PNG local ownership. Few locals had the capacity to buy such ownership, nor were they interested in doing so in view of the fact that the owners of business were simply abandoning them and leaving the country.

The Rabaul Machine Shop had a huge investment of super heavy equipment such as giant metal turning lathes. The cost of transporting such equipment would be greater than purchasing such lathes back home. So, as it was later told to me in this case, they simply walked away from their business and gave it to George — who had been their faithful stockroom boy.

***

Our destination was Guam, which is northward from here, but to use the changing wind systems farther north of the equator, required our sailing due westward to the southerly most of the Islands of Micronesia. It's that very small island way out by itself which is most readily noticed by its name printed across the charts. **Kapingamarangi.**

I worked harder in this passage than I had ever been called on before. For a week now the wind would oscillate from very light which needed full sails, to howlingly strong wind which needed a deep reef in the mainsail and our smallest jib; to everything in-between. This included half a dozen different sail combinations to match the wind as it increased or decreased without ceasing.

There is no self furling system for our headsail. All jibs are unbagged, hanked onto the head stay, raised by their halyards and set by the jib sheet until a change is required. At that time (which on this passage seemed perpetual) the reverse order is processed and the next size jib is gotten from below, unbagged, etc. But soon, I was keeping the sail bags on deck at the fife rail.

To match the changed jib size, the mainsail is either reduced in size by lowering it to the next smaller area of reef points, securing the required tack cringle, haling the foot tight by use of that reef's out-hale and belaying it, followed by the mid reefing lines along the new foot as required; only to shortly either increase the reef or decrease it farther to best use the changing wind strength. During a one-hour period, much to my regret there often were three sail changes.

After about ten days of this, a final light wind sequence brought us to the shore of Kapingamarangi. I had chosen to save the use of our brand new battery for starting the engine at the end of this passage to have the benefit of its full charge. I had been using the older one for the running lights and the house lights and water pumps and that battery was now virtually without any remaining charge.

One does not sail into Kapingamarangi. It is a sunken volcano, the center of which is now filled with water which has a coral reef around the edge of it and low-lying land around that as with other atolls where we have sailed. When one enters through this one pass, a 90% right turn is required into a channel of water too narrow to tack through, followed some distance farther by a left turn which brings you to the village area quite a long distance beyond and northward where there is room to anchor.

I changed the battery selector to the position of the new battery, turned the starter key, and could you possibly believe it? Nothing happened! The engine did not start! The connections were all secure. I checked the battery with a hydrometer. It was dead. I had the seller in Kavieng charge the battery before taking it aboard. The problem was that it had a bad cell. Surely this was not—

Suddenly the boat was HURLED ONTO HER SIDE!!!!

We were hit by a squall that was harder than anything had ever hit us in all of our years of sailing!!! Instantly I was at the mast clawing down the mainsail. "PEGGY, GET TO THE WHEEL! TURN HER TO PORT!"

"I can't do it! I can't. I'm scared!!" She shouted.

"YES YOU CAN!!! -- DO IT!!" I yelled to be heard over the sound of the screaming wind.

And she did and I got the main down. I got to the bow. There is a place to sit on webbing straps slung between the pulpit sides which allow both hands to be used to drag the jib down and not get dumped into the sea in the process. I got it down. I kept encouraging Peggy to her vital task. The wind actually screamed!!

Chapter 14 — A New Beginning

We were now headed westward! And with bar poles she was going at hull speed!! I took the wheel. What a great sight as she churned the water in her wake! The *Osprey* was flying!

This epic squall was stronger and lasted longer than even the blast that we took at Rabaul! Never before nor since, have we encountered such a violent squall.

We had been right at the pass into Kapingamarangi, some 600 miles eastward from Kavieng and are now on a course back to it. Well, I knew that the squall would not last much longer, but without the ability to start the engine (the older battery was too depleted to start it); Kapingamarangi was not the only problem without having an engine usage.

I refused to take us through the reef-encumbered waters between the islands of the Federated States of Micronesia because even though we could tack to windward or any other direction since there was plenty of sea room, the problem lies in the fact that, were a few days of calm to occur, the tidal currents could easily set us onto a reef due to the water being too deep for an anchor to reach bottom with our limited lengths of a few hundred feet of ground tackle. The second very real fact at issue here is that **I was given a faulty battery!**

I chose to sail a thousand eight hundred miles to acquire a battery replacement; sailing from Kavieng to Kapingamarangi-Kapingamarangi to Kavieng and back again to Kapingamarangi, 600 miles each way. The time involved would be a mere month – probably less. Peggy totally hid her frustration.

It was a black night when we got back to the pass into the Kavieng harbor. I was exhausted from the constant sail changes. I desperately longed for a quiet uninterrupted sleep. The proportions of the island and the reef where the narrow passage is, was clear in my mind.

We would need engine power to get through, and I told Peggy how we would do it by securing the dinghy to the starboard quarter of the *Osprey* with the dinghy outboard motor aft of the *Osprey* for maximum steering assistance. I would stand in the dinghy to maintain visibility of the proportions between land and water to enable my choices of course changes while going through the pass and along the hidden reef while operating the dinghy motor.

Peggy's only duty would be to turn the *Osprey*'s steering wheel when told to do so as a required aid to efficiency in accomplishing the turns.

I launched the dinghy when we were close to the pass, and secured her movement while attached to the *Osprey*. Her obvious job was to be a platform on which to have a motor for the power of entry. I knew that Peggy was apprehensive, in case of disaster she did not want to feel that her rudder steering may have caused any part of it, even though not once have I ever blamed her for anything. I did not know that there was an accumulation of stresses which she had been silently carrying.

Almost in tears she declared that she couldn't do this, but by now we were committed. My memory of the "lay of the land" and the water and its reef, served us well even in the dark. The outboard motor was run full throttle to get us through the pass and at lesser speed through the harbor to where we had anchored before.

I slept all of the rest of the night and most of the next day. People were surprised to see us, including Customs and Immigration. They did not believe that we had sailed into the territory of another country. With our history of delays, they appeared to believe that we had hidden the boat somewhere during this time period and made up the story because we yearned to stay longer in PNG. We enjoyed PNG. We had multitudes of wonderful experiences, but we really, really wanted to be somewhere else by now!

The very next place that I went to, after re-checking in with Customs, was to the seller of our battery. I may have looked sternly at him as I relayed our 1200 mile sail in adverse conditions which had brought us back here for a replacement battery. He supplied a replacement, charged it and checked its charge-holding capacity and assured me that no cells were dead. I nodded my acceptance. He returned the node and voiced his apology. Though we were in PNG, contrary to the prevailing custom, I required no payback.

Chapter 14 — A New Beginning

The shock didn't come for another day or two. But when it came, I was undone.

Peggy said, "I've got to go home to take care of my mother. She is old now, and I've got to go home."

There was a little stammer in the sound of her voice as she said it. I knew that her mother lived on the same property as Peggy's sister. Simultaneous to these thoughts other statements came rushing into my mind about what seemed to be slight frustrations like, "Are we ever going to get out of this harbor?" (Rabaul) – and her expressed fear to steer a few times that she had felt were under high stress – and now sailing a thousand two hundred miles because of a battery – and that we were now in our thirteenth year of sailing which was only supposed to take three and a half years – and *we were only half way around the world so far* gave me pause.

She had immediately begun packing after her announcement, and clearly I understood that she had decided to get off the boat. I was shaken to the core and said, "Okay, I'll go with you."

"You'd do that?"

"Yes."

"Oh thank you." I felt a little like the teenager whose girlfriend just announced that she wanted him to stop the car and let her out; who asked if he might be permitted to drive her home instead. This hardly describes all of the emotions of a man who sees his wife in the process of leaving him.

I could see the valid reasons for her frustration, even though the same events and problems and time had not had the same effect on me. I accepted her leaving the boat and therefore me, as being a decision that seemed beyond change.

I told our friend Chris Smith, and gave him a letter of authorization regarding the boat and his representation of us accordingly. Customs and Immigration were advised. We bought the plane tickets and we were off.

It seemed that the least that I could do, would be to proceed in a way that would bring the fewest probing questions to her as possible. We had been married for a very long time.

I did tell our son David and my sister Sharon and maybe one or two others of the reality, but otherwise we made the rounds of friends and relatives, even going to our school alumni weekend. Such events recall early acquaintances, and this was no exception.

* * *

While we were going through all of this traveling about, the man to whom we had sold our apartment building paid off the balance of our note and suddenly we had some actual cash in quantity. It had been the payments on that note which had sustained us these years of sailing with the *Osprey*.

Of course, my first thoughts quickly went to the *Osprey*. I could see a new engine and a full refit of the boat in Guam when we get there, and then off to Palau and the Philippines and then Indonesia, the Indian Ocean crossing to Africa and a safari or two, and then to the islands of the Caribbean and home to Florida, to complete our circumnavigation of the world. As you can see, I still was using the word we in this paragraph, because it is still in my mind and heart.

I started researching for new diesel engines for the boat that would do the job and fit our framing in the engine room to receive such an engine without undue changes. I found it in Japan via computer search.

A few months passed. Peggy and I both ignored the occasional awkwardness, when we were hit with a communiqué from PNG that announced that ten days had been granted for us to have the boat out of the country before it would be confiscated by the government.

I contacted our friend Chris Smith for confirmation, and then retained a barrister in Port Moresby to delay this event, sighting that we needed more time to

Chapter 14 — A New Beginning

get there since half the time had already expired before the word had reached our representative and then us in the US.

We were granted the time, and Peggy came back to the boat with me.

We bought a new engine from Australia, built in Japan, and delivered to the government fisheries school in New Guinea. It took six months to get here, but joy reigns supreme.

In reasonably short order our new engine took up its residency aboard the *Osprey* and upon the completion of all related matters, our final departure from this magnificent country of such stark contrasts is now ours to take. And with us we take experiences and friends whose presence shall remain always within a special and cherished memory.

Our motor sailing to Kapingamarangi with our new engine was more than wonderful. It was also interspersed with unique glimpses from below and from above. Only once before have we seen a sailfish on the surface, and on each of the following days we saw a whale which has never failed to fill us with a feeling of awe.

Most of the species of whales can be identified by the shape and manner of their gigantic exhalations that blast sea water out of their nostrils before breathing. Some are blown forward of the whale's head which makes that one easy to identify

But I have generally been so fascinated by the sight of these behemoths that I am only secondarily interested in the identification by which we happen to name them. And for a first time for us, from above we had the unusual pleasure of seeing a moon-bow. Specifically, it's a rainbow formed as a halo all the way around the moon. What an interesting sight!

We stayed only a couple of days in Kapingamarangi. A chief wanted to share his very serious concern with me about some of the garden areas where salt water was entering below ground. If this were to continue, it could force evacuation. I could not give him comfort. Judging by the rapidity of this development, the likely cause of the situation is from the settling of the island. This is not an unheard of scenario. Sea levels themselves have not risen precipitously.

This is the first place where we have found a walk-bridge from one island to another. Each has its own village and chief, even though they are only about eight feet apart.

We now are able to change our course northward toward Guam which is NNW of us, well beyond Micronesia. But the course direction seemed to bring with it an added anticipation aboard the *Osprey*.

We were sailing nicely and making good headway when I said, "Peg, look at how fast those cirrus clouds are moving!" I had been watching them ever since they had started zooming eastward.

I knew that all of the islands have radio contact abilities with their capitol for storm warnings, etc., so I decided to sail into the next atoll. The first question that I asked after the chief of the Nukukuodo Atoll met us as we entered the pass was, "Have you been warned about any storm coming this way?"

He assured me that there were no warnings, but I told him that I would like to stay anyway. We were welcomed to do so, and I put out two anchors. The next morning early, there was a knock on the hull. Three fellows were in a dugout, and they reported that a "*stormrush was coming.*" My interpretation was likely to mean that heavy squalls were expected in the manner of storms rushing past. Our barometer had not changed much, but I put out our seventy-five-pound storm anchor anyway because of my concerns over the unusual cloud movements.

The actual translation was that *Typhoon Russ* was on the way, and in a day or two it actually passed just north of us. Even so, the winds in this case could easily have been anywhere between 50 to 70 miles per hour. The only difference between a typhoon and a hurricane is its name which changes in various parts of the world.

Happily we were on the "survivable side" as it is called, and is far less severe than the other side. When at sea in the northern hemisphere, and you were unfortunate enough to have a hurricane (typhoon) coming directly toward you on the course that you are sailing, you must immediately turn 90% to starboard [to the right] from the path of the storm.

You can't expect to out run it. Your only chance of survival is on the side with the lesser wind. (A reminder: In the southern hemisphere the weather systems rotate in the opposite direction wherefore the survival side is also opposite.) We were already in the northern hemisphere here.

When the typhoon was well past us and I wanted the storm anchor up, I had to enlist the help of five local men to get the anchor out of its deeply dug-in grasp of the bottom and it was bringing part of it with him. The help was worth every cent of the fee.

Our stay at the Nukukuodo Atoll was enjoyable in every way, but we only stayed a few more days.

It was as we were approaching Satawan Island in the Nomoi Group that we had our first engine shock. With practiced dexterity, the engine off switch was engaged and silence reigned aboard the boat. I found that the engine alignment with the propeller shaft had suddenly changed due to the physical position of the engine having shifted from its bolted place. "HOW?" was the question that I asked myself as the answer just as quickly presented itself.

The engine mounts had detached from the engine!

These mounts are brackets of thick steel which are bolted to the side of the engine and have a 90 degree angled flat foot, which in turn is lag-screwed to the timber framing members of the boat's engine room.

The bolts that secured these brackets to the engine had not been checked for tightness at the boatyard and vibration had loosened them to the point that they were completely falling out of the bracket and into the bilge. Those remaining had sheared off flush with the outside of the engine. The engine therefore dropped partially downward.

I have an "easy-out" tool. This has a series of hard steel bits that have their broad screw threads made with a left hand turn, opposite from all others. When a hole is drilled into the body of a bolt that has been sheared off and this bit is screwed into it, it is tightened as it is turned leftward into the body of the bolt, which is also the direction that the bolt must turn to be removed. Therefore, the tighter that the bit is turned, the more strength is applied toward its removal. My problem was that I needed to drill a hole in the body of the bolt which remains in the engine. I do not have a twelve-volt power drill. I do have a hand drill that looks rather like an egg beater with a steel drill bit in the end. By hitting a nail punch with a hammer, a dimple is made in the center of the bolt so that the drill bit can engage its cutting threads to enable it to start cutting a hole. By a constant pressing with one hand and turning with the other, eventually a hole can be cut.

The only way into the engine room is either by crawling past the port side of the engine or by lying on top of it. In this case it was necessary for me to push my way past the engine on the port side and bend my body at a 90% angle to the left behind the engine and then reach at another 90% to the left at arms length to work a hole into one of the sheared off bolts. This was being done in this enclosed dark engine room in the heat of the tropics, while forcibly suppressing my slight tendency toward claustrophobia.

I got it done; found a metric bolt of the correct size by good fortune on this non metric boat. Another but more accessible bolt was sheared off and extracted in like manner. By wedging the engine back into possession, the bolts were re-entered and tightened. Some bolts were found in the bilge with the aid of a strong magnet on an extendable shaft, but after hours of trying all conveyable magnet movement, I still needed three bolts. I found two in our spare parts supply.

I was able to get through the coral and into the next island where wonder of wonders the local man who kept the outboard motors running had two of these bolts which he was happy to give to me realizing how important they were to our need. I only needed one. The second one was offered as a spare. Well done Samuel! We spent the night there, and Samuel and his wife had dinner with us aboard the *Osprey*.

We had a couple of really wonderful sailing days as we were approaching the Truk Lagoon. This is where at one time during the Second World War the Japanese Navy had anchored most of its fleet and was discovered by the US Army Air Force which sank them all in one attack. It is said to have been about twelve times more devastating to Japan than what the Perl Harbor attack was to the US.

With about a hundred mile to go before arriving there, the wind had continued to pipe up smartly. I had up the full main and the number three jib. We were at maximum speed with wind abeam, and there was the look of heavier weather to come — perhaps shortly.

"Peggy, I'd like to reduce sail." When she had the wheel I was almost to the mast to begin reefing when a gust hit us hard enough to dip her boom into the water as I clawed the mainsail down to her reef. It takes awhile to get a reef in the mainsail, but when I was finished and I had returned to the cockpit to take the wheel from Peggy she went below. Her notes say that she was still literally shaking when she got below to write in her journal.

It was a bright moonlit night when we were approaching the Truk Lagoon, so I slow sailed northward, well off the reef, and by morning we were close to another pass and entered there. After formalities with Customs, I slept most of the rest of the day and gloriously through the night in the now still waters of this marvelous huge lagoon.

We spent ten very pleasant days here as we leisurely restocked the boat with food and water. Yet there was a horizon that beckoned toward rewarding the *Osprey* with a major refit. The ship's papers were brought to Customs and Immigration and they were advised of our next port, as is the normal requirement when leaving. There was a different feeling to be making toward

US flag territory. So after sailing northward through the remaining waters of The Federated States of Micronesia, we laid a course for Guam over a week away. The harbor there is a few miles southward from the northwest portion of Guam, so I chose a course to pass the south of the island and then proceed northward to the harbor where Customs, as well as the yacht club, is located. Such a course will sail over the deepest water in the world, which is the Mariana Trench! If we could see the bottom, which of course we can't, we would be looking 6.8 miles downward. That in feet is a depth of three million six hundred and six thousand seven hundred seventeen feet. I can't picture such depth in my mind! Maybe this will help. Let's say that the average one story house from the ground to the ridge of its roof is twenty feet tall. If you were to place one house on top of another, you would need 180,317 houses stacked on top of each other to represent the depth of the water in the Mariana Trench at its deepest point! What may lurk in such depth? – No one knows. And we shall pass over those depths on a very, very dark and strangely clouded night.

One of the reasons that Peggy does not like to snorkel over the top of coral reefs is due to seeing the deep wide holes that sometimes are fifteen or twenty feet deep. She gets a very uncomfortable feeling in the pit of her stomach as she passes over them. I did not mention anything to her about the Mariana Trench.

Sailing is always a delight, be it gentle or with gusto! And always the sights of the sea and its creatures, the sky during the day with its birds and clouds, and at night to see the stars when no other light exists in the entire world (at least in ours) is a magnificence beyond words. And at night to contemplate the universe that blazes before us from our little neighborhood in our own galaxy is humbling, perhaps bringing us to an appropriate realization of our selves.

We sailed onward.

Maybe I shouldn't mention that the engine was not functioning as we fetched the goodly harbor of Guam. Nor perhaps that the wind was blowing right out of the harbor as we were entering which required me to tack out of the

Chapter 14   A New Beginning

way of an outbound ship at the entrance way, and that we had been unable to acquire a chart of this harbor. This was not unsettling, however, since we were comfortable in anticipating a proper buoy system to mark any shallows.

Our anticipations have in past occasionally required some adjustment, as was the case here. This tiny spot in the midst of the North Pacific Ocean with only a few square miles of harbor, rather than using the international buoy system was using the US system of "red to right returning" which is opposite from all of the rest of the world! It did not give us any trouble other than perhaps an unnecessary loss of pride.

Nothing untoward occurred as plain sailing brought us to where we awaited Customs and Immigration to process our papers. No time-limiting visas need concern us here as indeed we flew the same flag. We had arrived!

We tacked to windward through the harbor and saw a mooring float close up to the vicinity of the commercial wharf. The task of picking up a mooring float which is to windward from you in a strong blow, when it is very close to the shore, takes a little planning. You cannot be going so fast in your approach that you cannot stop before going aground in case you miss the pickup. In this case, there was not enough room to be able to tack away for another approach either. Of course, modesty prevents my direct mention of this seamanship to you, but by some good fortune, the boat was turned into the wind just far enough away so that the boat came to a stop with the mooring float at the starboard bow, permitting the skipper to stroll forward in a leisure and gentlemanly manor for its acquisition...

We awaited customs arrival. We were after all, flying the "Q" flag as protocol universally specifies. No one came, nor was our radio call answered, which did not bother our sleeping for the night. When no one came the next mid day, I launched the dinghy and went ashore asking my way to their office.

Well, there was an established procedure. "Sail over to the yacht club, and when you're assigned a mooring, call us and we'll come there. Tomorrow any time is okay."

We saw masts and started in that direction, but oops, wrong masts. That was US Navy territory mooring their personal boats. Someone from the club had spotted us and rushed over to us in their fast dinghy and before long a truly lovely relationship with the good folks at the Guam Yacht Club had begun!

And oh how fortunate for our cherished *Osprey*! Truly talented shipwrights were found and this fine wooden vessel of nearly 70 years of age took on the look of her youth. A couple of months of full-time labor of this crew of workers passed quickly.

And a few weeks later, almost all of the work had been completed, with a matched frequency of our reaching into our pockets in exchange. Even the entire below decks cabin area was re-varnished, which of course required many hours of the team just in the process of sandpaper carefully being rubbed on all surfaces in preparation of the wonderful stuff called varnish.

The boat was out of the water on the grounds of the Navy's yacht club which had the only boatyard facility to lift and move boats ashore. Peggy and I were staying aboard a yacht built in Panama, whose American people were living ashore while working here.

None of us were concerned about a typhoon that was passing well south of the island which would be continuing west of us. We knew this because the weatherman said so. What he didn't know was that it was going to turn eastward and have a direct hit on Guam with its heavy weather side.

When all of Guam heard about this, everybody ducked for shelter. We phoned the owners of the boat on which we were staying, to tell them that we would not be aboard their boat during this storm, and that if they were going to do anything for her such as to bring her to a safer spot, it needed to be done right now, and that I would gladly help them if they wished. However, they were content to leave her where she was, and as she was, so we went ashore.

Peggy had taken a job as accountant with a structural engineering firm. And this storm was so immense that we sheltered in her office and were the only ones there. During the worst of the storm we actually got under her boss' desk. It was the strongest piece of furniture there. We even managed to sleep a bit under it. We had covered all of the computers with plastic against rain damage and were mesmerized to watch one of those huge cargo ship containers being moved down the street by the wind. We later learned that it was full of cargo.

We had bought a car from an auto rental agency, and when the storm was past, I managed to carefully zigzag my way around the enormous debris of even entire trees with their root systems that littered the four-lane roadway to the boat.

Not surprisingly the boat had been hurled off her support cradle and the lovely *Osprey* lay prostrate on the ground. It had taken a truly massive tropical storm to have lain her to her rest. But ohh how she sails majestically upon the seas of our mind. Forever, she is enshrined as with full sails set and filled by the winds of many joys recalled, and never to be forgotten. While having sailed over half of the world's oceans, she has smiled at the gentle breeze and snarled at the storms, as she remained always mindful of the people in her care.

On a quiet night, and only in its stillness; perhaps you too may hear her contented sigh; for she too must know that she always did her duty well.

"Sleep on good *Osprey* -- this gentle sleep is well deserved!"

APPENDIX A

✺ A Detailed Look ✺
at the Boat Handling Arrangement

This might be a good time for you to look around the boat to see how we are arranged for ocean passages. Let's look below first. There is a crowned bridge deck between the cockpit and the companion way into the cabin. This is a good arrangement in that were the cockpit well to be filled by a wave coming aboard, this water cannot find its way into the cabin. This is more important than the inconvenience of getting our stuff wet. If the cabin is filled with the weight of the sea, the boat will sink. But even with this barrier protecting the cabin, the cockpit should drain with some dispatch so that the stern not be held down below her water line too long so that she is not refilled by subsequent waves and thereby sunk.

Before starting this venture, I had plugged the drain pipes, filled the cockpit with water from a hose, and timed how long it took to empty. The cockpit is large, and although the motion of the boat in a sea way would throw some water out, I was not satisfied with the time factor. I had the drains enlarged.

A further protection of the cabin is that water on the bridge deck does not have free access to the cabin. One steps over a portion of the structure of the aft of the cabin to place a foot on the top step of the companion way ladder. This step is level with the bridge deck, so ease of entry is maintained.

When entering the cabin, Peggy's bunk is to starboard. Mine is to port. They serve as couches and otherwise and as seats for the dining table during meals. The centerboard trunk which divides the cabin fore and aft has a hinged table leaf which can accommodate two people on each side of the trunk. There is a simple hook which secures the leaves to the trunk when they are not in use for the table, so that they not swing up due to motion in a sea way, which thereby would impede our passing.

Forward, beyond Peggy's bunk, is a lovely cabinet and bulkhead, beyond which rests our stainless steel coal stove not used in the tropics. Now, our regularly used stove is mounted atop the coal stove on its gimbals. It is a two burner kerosene cooking stove. The centerboard trunk continues forward through this area, and a bulkhead built atop it divides the galley from the other side, making a great place to mount Peggy's copper cook pans. The pans simply hang of brass hooks by their handles and are all available as needed. When at sea, the pans are held securely and noiselessly in place, by elastic bungee cords, which are attached to the bulkhead at each side of the lower portion of each pan. To ready the galley for sea, the bungee is lifted over each pan, and all else is stowed in its usual place. Even the sharp knives have a home in the same area as the pans.

On the port side, just forward of the bridge deck and cockpit, where I rest my head in sleep, a gamboling compass is mounted well above my pillow. Mounted on the bulkhead below the compass is a pull switch to light the compass card at night. It has a red lens on it to ease my reading of this compass which is made specifically to be read from the under side. So when in open waters, with no one on watch, I can check our course to see if a wind shift has appreciably put us on another heading. A windvane steering system will, of course, continue following the wind setting which has been chosen. I have used the old system of pulling a hitch in a sheet line brought to a tiller opposed by surgical tubing to maintain a reasonable course, but a good windvane is essential for short handed ocean passages. We also had an autopilot, but while sailing, it is wonderful to have a windvane system to be shipmates with you. As with everything else aboard, this device requires some occasional ingenuity to keep it functional.

There is a space forward of my bunk for currently used books and navigation tools, above which is a mirror fronted cabinet storing the glass crystal wear, none of which was ever broken underway. Beyond the foot of my bed and forward, is a door which encloses the necessary room comprised of the head (toilet) and shower and sink, closed by a door forward of it as well. Forward of this area is a hanging closet and next a built-in chest of drawers. The upper part of this opened by a drop down door in which our charts were stored. The drawers required lifting over a small barrier to be opened, thereby keeping the drawers closed during sailing in protected waters with little heeling, but for our intended voyage I drilled a hole through the framing of the cabinet and through the drawer's side at an angle downward so that a metal pin could be inserted, whereby the drawers were kept closed in severe conditions as well. The inward extension of the forward edge of the dresser enabled my choice of this solution. I formed the pins out of bronze rod with a diameter of about 3/16 of an inch and bent an eye in one end to comfortably fit my finger. The pin hangs comfortably from that finger while extracting the item needed from inside the drawer and the pin thereby was at hand to relock the drawer.

A very important matter for being underway during even modest durations of time is a comfortable sleeping arrangement.

Mine supplies a level sleeping surface regardless of the extent of the *Osprey*'s heeling degree whether on a port or starboard tack. Translated into English, this means that, to whichever side the boat is leaning and regardless of the amount of the lean, I sleep level to the horizon.

<u>Please skip this paragraph if you don't want the details of the arrangement regarding this bed</u>, because I shall go into detail describing it. I found this arrangement wonderful in the extreme. And for those who appreciate this comfort, and as I who cannot sleep on airplanes for lack of comfort, I recommend this to you with unbounded enthusiasm! Please picture a book, at which you look end on, with the binding to your left. If you place this book in your mind onto the surface of a desk, and now picture the desk toward your left leaning downward from the horizontal, if you had a hinge at the

bottom edge of the book cover as it extends along the opening edge of the book as you open it, you can readily see that by lifting the binding edge of the book, you can bring the book to the level of where the desk had been before its left surface dropped down from the horizontal. And if you have a line from the corners of the book's binding cover, and a third one from the center of the binding edge, and had a place to affix the lines, the book would stay at the level you chose.

Now picture the above desk leaning downward on the right side. If you lift the book, having a hinge at the binding position, you can see how the top cover of the book can be brought level to the horizon. Beds on most boats do not have springs. They boast a comfortable mattress on plywood. Now, for the application of the above, to that of my bunk, I shall finish the picture. On the plywood designed to receive the mattress, I have placed two additional sheets of plywood of the same size and shape. Following the description sequence used above, I placed a hinge the length of the bed at the point where the lower of my two additions meet along its inboard edge of the original plywood, which is along the right side as looking forward. This allows for the mattress to be raised from the left side when the boat heels to the left, resulting in a horizontal mattress. Now, by placing a full length hinge between the two plywoods which I added, along the left length of the plywood, upon the boat heeling to starboard the mattress can be brought to horizontal in like manner.

So let's say that we are on a starboard tack, wherefore the wind is coming over our starboard deck and the boat is heeled to port, (our left side as we face forward). Since my berth is on the port side, I could lie against the hull and sleep quite well. If on the other tack, I would be rolled out of bed unless somehow retained in it. But rather than lying against the hull, I can bring the mattress up to just below horizontal, whereby I am slightly retained in place as the boat rolls as she makes her way through the sea, and my comfort, and hence my rest, is greatly enhanced. The greatest hazard at sea is fatigue. You can readily see that the position of the bed and its mattress is likewise cared for on a port tack. Magic is not used in this accommodation. On the outboard edge of the top plywood a line is attached to each non hinged corner and one midway between them, as likewise the lower of my added plywood received such lines at its non hinged corners and mid point. I tied a knot in each line at strategic points so the knot in the lines could be placed over a retaining hook which carried the weight of the bed. With a certain private jest of my own, I enjoyed thinking of a port heel as being a three knotter or a four knot heel, etc. Mixing word usage can be fun. You can see that on a starboard tack, there are no lines obstructing my entry or leaving from my bed, whereas on a port tack, the center lift-line obstructs my way. This is an inconvenience which is not a hindrance to me in any way. But it is the reason why Peggy refused the arrangement, preferring the more traditional lee board comprised of a canvas slung to leeward when on a starboard tack. On a port tack, she sleeps against the hull. Her bunk is on the starboard side of the boat, opposite from mine.

I wish to emphasize what I said above. *Fatigue is the greatest hazard to which you can be exposed at sea.*

A reader who does not need the minutiae of the boat's seamanship could choose to omit this paragraph. For those who remain, I would like to "show you the ropes" above decks. Let's see what the boat looks like and how she is handled in straight-forward sailing as well as in heavy weather.

She has a short anchor sprit forward which carries two forty-five pound CQR anchors, one on all chain and the other with three fathoms of chain (eighteen feet), and the remainder with half-inch three-lay nylon line. These anchors are lashed in place for passages. A hand-cranking anchor windlass has an open drum to starboard and for the chain rode, there is the usual chain accepting drum to its port. The deck is teak to the topsides. The topsides continue upward beyond deck level by six inches, forming a very generous toe rail on which feet may walk safely when the lee rail is under water. The toe rail is topped by a cap which extends ¾ inch beyond the toe rail both inboard and out. The outer is for aesthetics, while the inboard extension keeps the foot from slipping overboard. The forward end of the cabin terminates about eight feet from the stem. On the deck, at the forward end of the cabin, the life raft canister is chained to the deck. The eye bolts to which the chain is attached are poured in one poring rather than welded parts or the eye being bent to form itself. The bolts are passed through the deck and through large backing plates under it to spread the force of a heavy sea's effort to wash the life raft overboard. Tension of the chains which kept the canister in place between its chocks was done by a lashing. Life rafts are generally patterned after the commercial shipping kind, which wants to try to stay where a ship has sunk in order to be located by another ship plying the same route. In my view, this does not properly serve the yachtsman who seeks to remain outside of shipping lanes when at all possible and who sails from or toward non commercial areas. But I found one made to form a rectangle with two parallel below water pontoons giving direction ability to make way with the square sail and mast which is part of the package. I added fishing gear and more solar stills which make water by condensation. I added some other sundries which you might choose differently, such as hats, some clothing, and medications including sun block and hand bailers, etc.

The *Osprey* is sloop-rigged, having one mast, therefore one mainsail and one jib. Our voyage started with twelve bags of sails. I will only mention two specifically because of my affinity for them. They were made of Egyptian cotton which was of uniquely long fibers grown only in the Aswan valley which has been forever taken away by the building of the Aswan Dam. It caused the valley to disappear below enormous waters. The storm jib would noiselessly set to perfection. It was roped all around for strength and endurance. I always dried the sail carefully before stowing it away, but as they say, nothing is forever, and she and her partner, a storm trysail, were respectfully taken ashore after they had lost their battle with age, the grim reaper. And as time passed, first the drifter disintegrated as did the genoa thereafter, leaving the boat without enough sail power forward. So I rigged a temporary inner stay whereby I could sail her as a cutter instead of as a sloop. I could not logically move the mast farther aft, so she was less efficient than before, but perfectly able nonetheless. There was no self furling system aboard, so I did a reasonable amount of sail changing underway.

The reefing of the mainsail was a one man job as well, which certainly was the requirement. Three rows of reef points crossed the main. Each reefing was set up as the others, so I will describe only one. In the usual manner, there is a clue (ring) at the luff (the edge of the mainsail at the mast) and at the leach (the trailing edge) of the mainsail. Between them are placed a row of reefing points or ties. A few feet from the mast I have placed a winch on the boom, and I made and attached a row of varnished, wooden cleats to the boom as well. I like the base of a cleat to be about 20% wider than the top width and I like this to taper in a straight line as viewed from the end, forming the horns in the same plain. The cleat should be made to fit the size of line to be worked on it and be relieved where the line takes its first full turn around the throat before it turns and lock on the horns. Before we finish our tour, let's look at the mainsail reefing procedure for a one-man operation. I sail with the three luff and three leach reef lines in place, as of course all the reef points have permanent ties on each side of the sail. To reef the mainsail, I ease the main halyard and belay it to the fife rail at the mast. I pull down the luff cringle and belay it so that it aligns with the rest of the reef so that it cannot be pulled aft. The leach line which also is half inch nylon, terminates on the port side of the boom several inches aft of where the leach cringle will be brought when tightly in position. The line from the port side of the boom passes through the leach cringle to the starboard side, and then down to a cheek block attached to the starboard side of the boom opposite the location of the point of its termination which therefore is also a few inches aft of where the leach cringle must be brought, and lead to the winch on the boom where I can bring great force to bear. The position of the cheek block and the lines point of origin, keep the cringle snug to the boom and forms a perfect sail set. If the "bag" formed along the boom by the excess sail is not threatened to be filled with sea or rain, the row of reef points need not be used. However, if wished or needed, these points can easily be tied. To do so, I step on the cabin roof top to the center point of the boom, reach down until my hand stops at the deepest point of the sail pocket, grab the sail at this point and pull it up. The wind will often slam the pocket closed bringing the rest of the loose sail pocket along the windward side of the boom. This sail fabric can now be readily rolled in a tight, neat, even roll along the length of the boom. Tying the reef point ties keeps the reefed sail efficiently and neatly in place. As weather worsens, the second and third reefs can all be taken without disturbing any of the prior ones.

The headsails, of course, are taken down and replaced by smaller sails as required. This too is a one man job, and provision is made at the bow to keep me aboard. The bow pulpit narrows as it passes around the point of the bow. It is wide enough for my hips to pass through. Wherefore, I made a seat out of strips of nylon webbing which hold my posterior about six inches below the pulpit keeping me snuggly in place. I was also able to keep one foot below a projection that kept me from being launched out of my perch. Having eased the jib halyard with the bitter end always secured, I needed only to claw down the jib being replaced, having first brought the next bagged jib and attached its tack as the first part of this action. With the old jib down but still hanked, I could hank the new one, get it up, resettle the sail balance and then get the old jib below to the forecastle Thusly, the *Osprey* lent herself very readily to single-handing, which in this case for several years was in fact single handing with company. And wonderful company it was. This paragraph would have been easier to read perhaps, had I used the normal rules for same, but you may recall that I gave those less interested in these details to identify the paragraphs which they could choose to pass over.

So you now, have had the opportunity to look about before we get underway making toward New Zealand, and after perhaps rereading the above paragraph a time or two, you are now ready to come aboard for a sail in the fabled southern South Pacific Ocean.

APPENDIX B

⚓ Peggy's Log III: Gove ⚓

- 1987 -

8/11 Dan talked to Don on ham. We had left last anchorage 8:35am. We had a lovely sail arriving at Gove 2:30pm. Anchored and waited for customs. //as we were having dinner a couple Dan knew before came over.

8/12 Dan off to see Bill? About a survey. After lunch we went to town & tried to get money at bank with visa or AMX cards (no deal) when we find out how much we need we'll have to have it wired from Riggs. Nice little town. We got a ride to town and back. We stayed at Yacht Club awhile talking to friends we knew in Cairns. Dan talked to Bill again.

8/13 Dan looked at both sinks and solved that problem. He fixed my light a shoe cabinet. We took the top of trunk and cleaned the salt off, etc. We when to shore 2:30-6:30 had showers and I washed cloths and hung out to dry. Early 7:00 Dan met Paul the welder, about windvane & engine room. Paul will come out tomorrow about 7:00.

8/14 Paul came he says engine must come out before bracing engine?? After lunch Dan Spence hours in engine room. I baked bread and typed a letter to Ambon. Dan talked to customs. We have a full moon in September.

8/15 Wrote letters, rested it was very windy. Bill Gibson came out to look at engine mounts.

8/16 Windy, read, Dan went in to club to see if Bill was there at 10:00 so he could help him (he wasn't) After lunch we walked to plant and dock where Bill's boat is Dan helped him sand 2 hours. We saw a Dugong by boat.

8/17 We went to town ordered money from Riggs. Got a few groceries. Mailed 7 letters. We got a ride back to club.

8/18 High wind. I made a new cover for outboard.

8/19 High wind. Dan checked our #2 sail. Called customs again.

8/20 Windy. Went early for bus tour of (aluminum) Bauxite mine. It is on top of ground here. Biggest trunks I had ever seen. Stop at bank again no money yet. Had lunch at Walkabout Hotel. Ok but very little of it. Got a loaf of bread in town.

8/21 Windy. Went for walk early with June, Ann, Rosie, Mal, Dan and I spend rest of day reading. Moved boat closer in.

8/22 Sabbath lovely day went for a walk early had NO WIND we showed & rested. Dan cleaned telescope on sexton had to go to town to find a small screw driver, I talked to Dave and David Allen on a tape.

8/23 Walked early with Dan No wind. Dan worked on getting some junk out of engine room and he found an oil leak. He also found bed log firm. Later in day we went to shore and talked awhile to Lucy, Ann 7 June also their husbands.

8/24 Mailed letters to Elyse, mother, Margret, tape to Dave. No wind walked with Dan. Dan glued sextant telescope prisms (here's hoping) Looks good so far.

8/25 Met new boat " Ronna" Doug, Evone, Kathy & John from Melbourne. We went to check at bank no money yet. They sent 2nd request for us. Ordered book from Sydney

8/26 Washed early, and walked also. To town about 2:00 NO MONEY AGAIN. June loan us $50.00 got a few groceries and mailed a letter. Dan cleaned white of boat.

8/27 Washed more cloths and walked

8/28 Windy. Walked early went to town 2:00 Surprise, money was there. We had dinner at club. A good T bone steak.

8/29 Roman left this am. It is windy nice folks. They are starting around the world. Dan teaching sexton classes free of course, has been over a week now.

8/30 Read, typing all day forms for sextant class.

8/31 Went for walk with June she just got back from Darwin. Went to town for Grocery, mailed letters to the Philippines and mother. Dan put new hanks on storm jib. Met Yirrkla, and mission president, Johnny

9/1 Walked early I guess I have not said this but it is very, very hot here. When waiting for bus I even try to stand in the shade of the telephone poles. Of course we wear our hats. We took a school bus to Yirrkla Aboriginal Mission. We went to craft shop, purchased a necklace of shells walked around, but president had left about time we got there so no talking to him today. Rosie got us gas (fuel) for our outboard. We relieved a letter at Yacht club from Trevor & Evelyn. They have purchased another Yacht.

9/2 Walked early check out storm main.

9/3 Walked early to town with June, and back by the bus.

9/4 Walked early I have not said what all we have seen on some of the walks, snake, kite, large ants something 4 times their size, small kangaroos, large lizard, 2in wide 12 to 14 in long grayish white and greenish, and water buffalo.

9/5	Walk early Saw bush turkeys flying and in trees large green, black & red parrots also a stork and other birds, dinner at June & Harold's lovely time,
9/6	Made most of Philippine flag awaiting white material. Dan working on winch switch
9/7	Mailed letter to AMX in Philippines to hold mail. Washed went to town got a few groceries
9/8	Windy. Stayed in Yacht — wind warm — Met June & Roy of Penrod. Read
9/9	Windy, Did not haul. Too much wind to bounces on grid land. Went to town read
9/10	Windy Went to town, June & Harold had dinner with us and he looked in the engine room. Maybe that job will get started now. Dan charged batteries and sea water pump started leaking read
9/11	Dan worked on sea pump (not fixed yet) I didn't feel good.
9/12	Went to Harold and June for rest of a day and night. Navigation was the thing. Harold had done 1st part of metal for engine room. Good food also. Dan called Trevor about the pump parts $19.00 for call. That's awful Book came from Sydney.
9/13	Home about 7:00a m to club about 5:00pm Navigation most of day
9/14	Windy. Fog in morning. I went to town to mail letters. Dan worked on metal pieces for engine mounts. He had to change hot water pipe to a hose.

Dan talked to Trevor and Evelyn about more parts. |
| 9/15 | Read. Windy after 10:am. Dan talked again to Trevor about parts. Harold did more welding. I worked more on Philippine flag. |

9/16 Worked more on Philippine flag. Dan worked on metal on bolts in engine room. I got some jugs of water.

9/17 I finished the flag and got more water. Read.

9/18 I went to town. Dan put old pump back together again and charged batteries. He worked on Metal place a bit. I got my water and we ate at club,

9/19 Rested. We went to see a boat that came in yesterday. They had been to Ambon.

9/20 Dan worked with metal in engine room. We spend night with Harold & June again. I made pizza and Dan talked navigation.

9/21 Trevor sent telegram. Dan talked navigation till 11 am. I walked to Library and exchanged 14 books on ours for 14 of Libraries'. Trevor called again. We went home(meaning back to boat) about 2:00 pm.

9/22 To town at 10.00 and home & read. Harold made another part for Dan in engine room. We went to a barbeque with a couple boats from Addailla. Don &Claudia and Noel and crew of Moonraker again. I made a cake for Noel's birthday and it turned out he is a baker by trade, Ha!

9/23 We are going out with a school teacher and her husband tonight.

9/24 Washed. Dan worked on sink in bathroom. I read and we got 6 letters. Wow.

9/25 I got grocery in town, wrote mother and John. We treated June & Harold at club.

9/26 Read. At 3:00 went to June's. Dan still teaching Harold Navigation.

9/27 Dan & Harold Navigation home about 4:00 pm

9/28 Tou –Che is name of Trevor new Yacht. Went to town and read

9/29 Washed & read Dan wrote Arnold and I typed the letter for him. Boat from Denmark came in this pm.

9/30 Typing Arnold's letter all afternoon

10/1 Finished typing Arnold's letter. June said metal sand blast today. I spent all morning in town. Afternoon met folks flying from McKay. They came out to Yacht finally got passports back from Sydney tonight Trevor said hell mail things tomorrow.

10/2 Count down on my visa here////Grass on boat port side 7 feet long. Wrote 3 letters. Dan got metal from Harold and we ate at club.

10/3 Up earlier 11:10 bus. Joy and Ron Sharman & we got lunch for them. She told us a lot about the Aboriginal here. We whet to June and Harold for Dan to teach more to Harold.

10/4 Dan worked with Harold on navigation. We went to church with Joyce & Ron. Lunch at June's. Home by 2:00. 3:15 An electronics man is here to look at auto Pilot.

10/5 Dan off early for package from Trevor. Part was missing from Kit. Dan off again to find log blots & drill bit.

10/6 Dan got steel under engine. Went to town to look at clocks. Yacht Segel came in from Darwin.

10/7 To town early for nut for switch didn't find. Electric man came.

10/8 Washed. Dan worked on bolt all day and didn't get it in. I got 4 jugs of water.

10/9 I went to town for package & groceries. Package was there & had screws & seal hurray! Dan charged batteries all day so they would be high for auto pilot test. Bob came and after he got wires back on correctly it worked. It was a

CIC's whatever that is. Susie & Bruce had lunch with us and when Dan came back after 8:30pm from taking Bob to shore we had more company. We had our dinner at 10:30pm that's the latest we have ever had dinner on boat.

10/10 Porpoise right by boat in AM. BQ on beach with friends. Saw 2 crocodiles at a long distance away back to June's for the night.

10/11 Spend day with June & Harold

10/12 Dan worked on pump and found he needs another seal. We sent pump to Cairns. We had letters from mother & Dave.

10/13 Dan worked on getting a bolt in and finally did it . I typed Dave a letter for Dan. Trevor got package ok

10/14 Dan got 3 lag screws in today. I went to town to return some bolts & plug & books. Friends from the church BQ came at 3:45 to 7:00. Bob D came to look at auto pilot again at 4:45 Trevor called at 7:00 pm He got pump fixed.

10/15 Got Gasoline today. I washed, Dan worked on putting shaft back together. We got more water. Dan went to town to look for more washers.

10/16 More work on auto pilot. Windvane and rudder fixed. Pump came back and Dan installed it. Dan went to hospital for hand but its ok I went to town. Crocodile in trap 11 ft long. Today, 12 foot one we saw on way to shore floating with eyes on top of water.

10/17 Dan worked on clutch of auto Pilot. We were invited out to dinner by Mycheek & wife. Lovely dinner. 7:00pm to 1:00am

10/18 I washed early. Dan was doing something with auto pilot. Putting the motor back together. Afterward, Dewberry came to us for a fast ride in their run about. We went to Granites and swam. We both had lots of fun and ate at club. Saw Mycheek & wife and ate with them.

10/19 Up at 6:30. Dan scrubbed anchor chain. We beached boat by 7:15 am. Dan scrubbed the bottom of the boat while I was in dinghy watching for crocodiles. Boat when over more than we did whet we went aground. Water came in galley sink and got everything on my bunk wet. Off before high tide. June & Howard came to say good bye.

10/20 Two more crocodiles seen today. 1 taken. 8:30 going to get fuel. To town, got money from Trevor & bought fresh groceries.

10/21 Up anchor 12:05 left Gove

APPENDIX C

⚙ In His Own Words ⚙

These are the exact words of the chief. He wanted someone ashore to write his exact words for him, that we might have the entire story in fullest accuracy. His doing so was a personal gift showing great honor to us, undeserved though it is. He had no concept that others might someday read his words. Nor was it my expectation to actually find myself recording these events for you. But here are his words verbatim:

> Away back in olden days the people from the Western Province were head hunters and cannibals. They left Western Province and went so far as Choiseul, Sta Ysabel and Guadalcanal by their big war canoe and kill those people and bring back their beard skull and put them in to their houses or sometimes in their tambu places. And when they returned they make a big devil feasts and gathered many people to celebrate the feasts and killed many pigs up to ten or twenty pigs. Sometimes they bought a very young child age two or three years old and offer sacrifice to the devils and eat there be the dead bodies. We have some fish tambu fish such as Bonitors: that fish is very tambu they did not drop it or let it falling on the ground if you allowed it to falling on the ground the devils will angry with you. We have snakes for some tambu birds such as Eagles or other birds. We have also Shark, or Crocodilla. We have tambu for nuli nuts. The first fruit & give to Devils after two or three weeks letup then the devil priest give to the women who is leader and she eat it first

and all the women could eat it. We have a big devil spirit we called it (Mabeama) that is to say very tambu spirit. Our people in those gone by years are look like naked. And the women also. They have a little peace of rag around there waist. We have some small house where we could put the head skull for the chiefs when they die and the build a small house where they could put the heads for the chiefs.

We call that small house (oru) that house is very tambu for common people to go there except the priest who always could go and carry those heads. We have some ground where the could not go there but the men only because tambu for women those heads. We have some ground where the could not go there but the men only because tambu for women to go on that spot. Where they could grow Ginger and other bitter plants like Ginger those Ginger is for the devils. Those war canoes are tambu for the women could not so touch them. In older days if the big chiefs make a big feast they took some women to be like juicy they give the custom money to the chief before they could go and sex intercourse. This is the big Provinet chief could do, but the common chief they could not do it. They build the big houses for the chiefs about 80 feet length by 30 feet wide. We are men for fishing for Bonitor and others fish we have our nets so catch fish some times we caught thousand fish, we have net for Turtles that net is diffent to the fishing net. We caught Bonitor for bamboo. We made fish hooks from the shells not fish hooks for the Europeans but we made it by to go on that spot. And put a fishing line for bamboos and went to the ocean by our canoes to hunting bonitors. We are growing our own foods in our gardens. We cooking copra and sell them to the Europeans or the Chinois. We have our own money which made from the shells those our own money we could buy a girl for wife and also buy canoes and pigs in our old custom we buy a girls so be wife to our sons or for other men is wish to be married.

www.ingramcontent.com/pod-product-compliance
Lightning Source LLC
Chambersburg PA
CBHW050528300426
44113CB00012B/1995